WITCH

A MAGICKAL JOURNEY

WITCH

A MAGICKAL JOURNEY

A Hip Guide to Modern Witchcraft

FIONA HORNE

Thorsons

Thorsons
An Imprint of HarperCollins*Publishers*
77–85 Fulham Palace Road,
Hammersmith, London W6 8JB

The Thorsons website address is:
www.thorsons.com

First published as
Witch: A Personal Journey
& Witch: A Magickal Year
Random House, Australia 1998, 1999
This combined edition published by Thorsons 2000

1 3 5 7 9 10 8 6 4 2

© Fiona Horne 1998, 1999, 2000

Fiona Horne asserts the moral right to
be identified as the author of this work

A catalogue record for this book
is available from the British Library

ISBN 0 0071399 9

Printed and bound in Great Britain by Scotprint

CONTENTS

✦ CONTENTS ✦

BLESSED BE

My heartfelt thanks goes to:

My special friend Liam Cyfrin. I couldn't have written this book without his advice and Witchy insights.

The brilliant girls, Tracey Shaw and Lauren O'Keefe, who not only do a magnificent job of running my website (www.fionahorne.com) but are also good friends!

All the wonderful Witches who shared their stories with me.

All the generous people who took the time to write in to my website and who sent me letters offering their comments and support.

My gorgeous friends and family who supported me during the writing of this book.

My awesome management team in London – Terry Blamey and Alli Macgregor, and in Australia – Melissa LeGear, Justin McNeany and Rochelle Nolan.

And, last but not least, the spunky team at Thorsons, especially Louise, Joanna, Jo, Jessica, Karen, Paul and Meg.

SPELLING
IT OUT

READ THIS FIRST!

Some say that you have to be born a Witch – a Witch cannot be 'made'.
I disagree. In our society, where the majority of alternative
spirituality is hushed or treated with derision and
scepticism, it can be hard to hear your
inner calling.

I spent most of my teenage years as a practising Catholic, going to Mass every Sunday with my parents and attending a Catholic girls-only high school. At times I found comfort in the rituals that many people of all faiths reduce their religion to. It was pleasant to think that all I had to do was be good and I would go to heaven, and that the only spiritual responsibility I had in my life was to obey the Ten Commandments.

When I was thirteen I had a favourite nun, Sister Geraldine, who taught at my high school – she was tough and cool and didn't take crap from the school heavies. She told me one lunchtime that she'd never had a boyfriend in her life, that she's always loved God and He'd always loved her back, and she always felt happy and good about herself. I was in High School Hell at the time, no girlfriends, no boyfriend, constant fighting at home, and in her words I saw freedom from the depressing nightmare my life had become. So, I decided to become a nun.

I started to read the Bible and educational books about the Catholic faith but I found so many contradictions and disempowering female stereotypes, that instead of my usual attitude of blind acceptance – of having faith – I started to question everything spiritual I'd been brought up to believe. The deeper I delved into the religion the stranger it seemed to me, being made mostly of legends and unexplained laws, yet demanding absolute faith in these stories and rigid adherence to the rules. I listened to the sermons preached from the pulpit and became more and more convinced that the Catholic faith was not for me.

I started to look for alternatives. The most obvious one to an angry, rebellious thirteen-year-old who didn't want to be Catholic any more was Satanism. So I went to the library and discovered the tacky fiction writer, Dennis Wheatley. All his books featured demons and evil witches, Satanic sabbats, sex and death. This all seemed quite thrilling at the time and I happily lit black candles in my bedroom, said the Lord's Prayer backwards and read the *Malleus Maleficarum* under my sheets at night by the light of a torch. However, rather than becoming seduced by black magic, I became depressed with its banal, cruel and perverse obsessions and my interest waned. About the same time my attractiveness to boys increased and not long after discovering Satanism I discovered boys, and they were to occupy my every waking thought for the next few years of high school.

Later in my teens, having established my independence by leaving home and getting a job, I started thinking about my spirituality again. It was now the 1980s and the New Age movement was exploding. Lots of books on alternative spirituality started to appear and I got swept up by the 'positive thinking' brigade. I bought books on affirmations and personal healing by Louise Hay and books on manifesting pleasing things in my life – like Shakti Gawain's *Creative Visualisation*. If anything bad happened in my life I would focus on the positive and attempt to think only happy and constructive thoughts. Consequently I felt frustrated and let down when I wasn't always able to avoid unpleasant experiences and it became quite a struggle to stay positive all the time. My wholesome interest in the New Age mutated into scepticism.

Some of the New Age books I read over my late teens mentioned the word 'paganism' and I strongly identified with its concept of living close to the land, being environmentally responsible and finding divinity in Nature. So I became a vegan, avoiding all animal products in my life, including

3

leather and honey, and recycling everything that I could. As I read more books I started feeling drawn to those that had that mysterious and exotic word 'witchcraft' in them. At first I thought I was going to be inundated with Satanic scare stories again, but instead I was excited to find a documented nature-worshipping religion that placed great emphasis on the sacredness of the individual and the land.

For a while I browsed through these books finding all the terminology and rigmarole a bit off-putting – but then one day I saw Ly Warren-Clarke's *The Way of the Goddess* (now published as *Witchcraft – in Theory and Practice*) and my life changed. Here was a book about Witchcraft, or more specifically, Wicca, that was both easy and thrilling to read, and I realized that all along I had been a Witch, even since those early naïve days of Satanism. Here was a religion that made sense: it was dynamic and logical, loving and responsible, sensuous and holy.

I felt very attracted to the fact that **Wicca acknowledges many different Goddesses and Gods, but most importantly, recognizes that they can exist within the individual, not in the sky out of our reach.** In fact, the Craft doesn't provide answers as to what the Goddesses and Gods actually are, but emphasizes that whichever way the individual relates to them is the right way for her/him. I have always felt that the Gods and Goddesses do not exist in their own right but are projections of our consciousness.

Over the ages humans have created deities to teach us about ourselves. In Witchcraft ritual I treat the Goddesses and Gods as if they are real and I do feel I commune with some kind of presence, but I consider that I'm tapping into a deeper level of personal consciousness. There is, however, something called the 'egregor' in which most Wiccans believe. This term involves the concept that Goddesses and Gods and other metaphysical entities actually gain 'astral substance' as more and more people think about and relate to them, and through this they come into a kind of sentient existence.

Anyway, back to the story! I was twenty-one when I bought Ly's book and within a year my bookshelf was crammed with over fifty books on Wicca, and using *The Way of the Goddess* as a guide, on the Summer Solstice of my twenty-first year I declared my love of the many faces of the Goddess and God to the Universe and initiated myself as a first degree Witch. Over the next few years I practised as a solitary Witch, keeping it pretty quiet, often not really sure if what I was doing was 'right', but persevering anyway. I started studying naturopathy to learn how to heal, because from my reading I ascertained that my Witchy ancestors were primarily healers and I felt it appropriate that I respect the fact by becoming a healer myself. So I worked in a health food store by day, studied naturopathy at night and played guitar and sang in a punk band on the weekend.

When I was twenty-four I received a phone call from a guy who asked me if I wanted to sing in a band that played a techno-metal fusion style of music. It sounded cool to me and I said yes. This band eventually became Def FX, and it was ultimately through the lyrics that I wrote and some interviews that I did in various publications and television shows a few years into the life of the band, that I 'came out of the broom closet' and let people know that I am a Witch.

Originally, I would never have wanted to be a spokesperson for the Craft, being wary of having my beliefs treated with the usual lack of respect most Witches who come out in the media

5

receive. But, as more and more people kept asking questions I sensed a genuine and respectful interest – so here I am writing a book about Witchcraft.

Hubble bubble too much trouble

The above heading is the title of a newspaper article in which the journalist said that after attending a seminar on Witchcraft that Witches 'ain't what they used to be'; that in the search for acceptance we have become whitewashed and there's nothing wicked or titillating about it anymore. The journalist said 'These days, your self-proclaimed Witch looks like a suburban mother of three, more used to Tupperware parties ... These "white" Witches are just about as scary as lady bowlers and about a tenth as interesting.' She obviously got a dose of the lighter side – but what else could she have expected in the first meeting? If you meet someone at a party, you don't usually begin telling them your darkest sexual fantasies or your worst fears – you just show them your lighter side. Only when someone's earned your trust do you let them into your darker side. Anyway, she certainly wasn't going to get an in-depth education in a complex subject in an afternoon.

However, in some ways I agree with her sentiment; for instance, I avoid the term 'White Witch'. It's so New Agey I believe that a lot of the New Age is like a big, happy band-aid. I always emphasize that Witchcraft is about embracing polarities – the Light and the Dark – respecting the darker emotions of anger and hatred as much as the lighter of love and empathy. Bear in mind, of course, that light and dark are by no means the same as good and evil (the latter being terms which most Witches would see as completely relative; after all, if you're human, a little purring cat might be the epitome of goodness but if you're a mouse it might be the personification of cold-hearted, rodent-torturing terror and dismay).

Even though that journalist didn't get her stereotypes fulfilled at the seminar she attended, in our patriarchally-dominated society there is unfortunately something scary about a woman who is in control of her mind, soul and body. And there's something confronting about a male who values a woman and the role they have in society and in the heavens, the role of the feminine within him, and who's in touch with a type of power completely removed from conventional male brute force. I'm talking about Witches (well, most of them anyway). The kind of Witchcraft I and a lot of my Witch friends practise means we don't shy away from pain and fear, and we agree with Hungarian Witch, Z Budapest, who states, 'A Witch who cannot hex cannot heal.'

Having said that, we certainly don't go around hexing at random and roasting small children or sacrificing furry animals (actually, I do feed mice to my hungry snake familiar, Lulu, but snakes have to eat). And our lives don't revolve around goodness and niceness either, but we certainly aren't the sworn enemies of these qualities. We're into finding our own balance between sun and moon, day and night, light and darkness.

In fact it's the dark, difficult and avoided parts of life that are often the most fertile of human experiences that give rise to our most enlightened achievements. **Being a Witch is about having your eyes *wide open* and experiencing the whole onslaught of existence** – and that can be pretty

7

scary. A Witch's view of the world in a time when much seems uncertain is sometimes frightening because we accept change and death as much as we welcome stability and life. It's chaotic, somewhat anarchic and it runs on Goddess time: all things happening at all times. The human body is sacred and the individual is Goddess/God. We lead ourselves without too much trouble, are powerful, but don't shove it down anyone's throats (and if you know someone who does, they're a Wanker not a Witch).

About This Book

This book is pretty much my vision, the way I do things. It's different from a lot of other Witches' traditions, but similar in that all Witches tailor their own form of the Craft. Witchcraft is reliant on the individual to give it meaning and power. Witches are not sheep or lemmings who like playing follow the leader. We lead ourselves in the knowledge that the Universe is big and beautiful enough for everyone. We don't demand converts but we are interested in letting people know we are not screwed-up Satan worshippers. Most Witches find the idea of a God who'd create a demigod of evil with whom to play cosmic war-games a little mystifying.

In this book I've included some essential Witchcraft information, i.e. altar implements, Circle casting and Sabbat details. There are also lots of spells to try, but as I emphasize throughout the book, **the most powerful and effective spells will be the ones you create yourself, specifically tuned to your requirements and charged with your creative passion.**

Right now I'm going to mention a few things worthy of getting a good grip on.

All the Magick You'll Ever Need is Already Inside You

Where Witchcraft comes in is to help you tap into and unleash that power, and harness the forces of nature to help you create change at will.

For a Spell to Work, it Has to be Fuelled with Your Magickal Intent

It's not enough to buy a ready-made boxed spell, or to follow a spell suggested in this book to the letter and then 'do it' passively and politely. You're not in church being told what to say and when to stand, sit and kneel! You're doing Witchcraft! Making Magick! Get excited about it! Get passionate, dirty and downright messy! Well, not necessarily to those extremes, but what I mean is: get involved. A spell is only fuelled by your intent, otherwise it just sits there like a blob glued to this world not going anywhere, not doing anything. Don't be afraid of making mistakes or doing things 'a bit wrong'. In *Quotable Women* the divine Italian actress/Goddess, Sophia Loren, has been quoted as saying, 'Mistakes are part of the dues one pays for a full life.' In living a full, empowered life mistakes are inevitable and fantastic learning tools. So don't be afraid to experiment, just keep in mind:

The Laws of Witchcraft

1. Do what you will as long as it harms none;
2. Do what you will as long as you don't interfere with anyone else's free will;
3. That which you send out returns to you threefold.

As long as you are clear on the above, you are on your way to becoming a formidable Witchy presence on the planet – and beyond!

WHICH WITCH IS WHICH?

THE HERSTORY OF WITCHCRAFT

There are many versions of the herstory of Witchcraft. Some idealists believe it can be traced through an unbroken lineage – handed down from mother to daughter, grandmother to granddaughter, generation after generation, existing in various levels of exposure and secrecy since the dawn of humankind. Witches who believe this consider Wicca to be the original religion of humankind, rooted in an ancient utopian time when women held the deciding vote, and the ability to give life was worshipped more than the ability to kill, as is honoured now in this time of patriarchal dominance.

Before the role men played in procreation was understood, Woman was revered as Goddess because of her ability to give and nurture life.

For prehistoric humans, a woman's stomach mysteriously swelling, then nine moon cycles later, a baby emerging from between her legs was one of the most awe-inspiring spectacles they could witness. That she could also produce food – the life sustaining milk that squirted from her breasts – made her representative of the nurturing and providing elements of Nature. The oldest work of art discovered from prehistoric times, the Venus of Willendorf, is a small clay statue of a fertile woman with a rotund stomach and huge pendulous breasts. It is a representation of the Fertility Goddess worshipped in those times, and has evolved into the multi-faceted Goddess all Witches love and worship today.

In ancient times the ability to hunt for food, rather than kill for sport as in the present-day, was also worshipped. Cave paintings from pre-historic times show that (most likely male) humans would throw on animal skins and antlered masks and

in a kind of 'sympathetic' magickal ritual, play out a successful hunt for food, hoping to ensure a successful real hunt outside the cave on the plains the next day. The humans enacting these rituals were 'shamans' who were considered to have magickal relationships with the animals, able to communicate with and woo their spirits, so that they would be prepared to give their lives in order that the human tribe could continue. From this the concept of a God of Hunting developed which went on to evolve to the present day Witches' God of Nature and Animals, the Horned God.

Most Wiccans now relate to the concept of Witchcraft existing as an unbroken mythic tradition. **The Craft today is really built on the sense of our culture having lost, buried or corrupted the old traditions and Witches are attempting to rediscover them and make them relevant to this brave new world.** Some do this through historical research and re-enactment, but most work more on tapping into the intuition and the collective unconscious to recreate a Witchcraft in which the voices of the lost past are reawoken in fresh, new chants, rites and spells.

As the mythic and objective herstory of the Craft has been discussed at great length in many books, rather than attempt to restate it at length here, I'll recommend some of the better works on the subject. For more detailed publishing information see 'The Library' chapter at the back.

Starhawk's *Spiral Dance* has an excellent first chapter 'Witchcraft as Goddess Religion'. Laurie Cabot and Tom Cowan's *Power of the Witch* has an inspiring chapter called 'The Old Religion'. Margaret A. Murray's *The Witchcraft in Western Europe* is considered a classic on the herstory of ancient Witchcraft, but some dispute its accuracy. Murray was an English Egyptologist who claimed Witchcraft originated in Palaeolithic times 25,000 years ago long before Christianity. After persecution by the Church in the Middle Ages, Murray claims it continued as a secret tradition until its re-emergence around the time she was writing in the 1920s. Scholars and historians have refuted her work saying that she largely contrived the whole thing, but it still makes for thought-provoking reading.

Anthony Kemp's *Witchcraft and Paganism Today* has an easy to read and comprehensive examination of the historical background of Witchcraft and Paganism, starting in primitive times and then moving on to cover the Egyptians and then the Celts – specifically the Druids whose teachings and lore have greatly influenced contemporary Wicca. He then discusses the Middle Ages, specifically the persecution of Witches during the Inquisition, and continues to move through herstory until the present day.

I also recommend Diane Purkiss's *The Witch in History*. It is interesting in that she has thoroughly researched the presence of Witch figures throughout modern history yet ultimately construes that the Witch is only a fantasy figure. If you want to know everything that Witchcraft never was nor will be, track down a copy of Montague Summers' *The History of Witchcraft*. Written in 1925 by a Catholic priest, it celebrates the atrocities committed during the seventeenth and eighteenth centuries by the Church in its attempts to wipe out 'witchcraft' and heresy – otherwise known as 'The Burning Times' – where many people in Europe were burned at the stake or hung after being forced to admit they were Witches and in league with the Devil. It is alternately horrifying and laughable.

Modern Witchcraft, specifically Wicca, probably owes much of its origins to an Englishman named Gerald Gardner. In 1939 he claimed that he was initiated into a traditional Witchcraft coven in England and from his teachings and writings, especially his book *Witchcraft Today* written in 1954, the Gardnerian tradition established itself. Before discovering Wicca, Gardner was involved in Co-Masonry, Rosicrucianism and travelled for many years in the Far East observing the lives of indigenous people and spiritual beliefs.

The Wiccan tradition reflects a lot of the teachings and experiences Gardner himself was exposed to in the first half of his life and many wonder if he truly was initiated into an established tradition or if he just made it up himself. But as the Craft isn't into gurus and most religions are initiated in one form by individuals (from Moses to Manson, and Hubbard to Koresh) before morphing drastically into something else altogether, most Witches aren't too concerned about the issue of who invented the Craft. In fact the Craft is often described by Witches as a 'non-prophet disorganization'!

Anti-witchcraft laws were only repealed in England in 1951 and suburban covens sprang up everywhere. Gardner died in 1964 and subsequently the worldwide Witchcraft movement divided somewhat as other individuals made their presence noticed. One in particular was Alex Sanders, founder of the Alexandrian Tradition, a prominent Wiccan tradition today. He based his rituals on Gardner's work, but introduced more material from other Western magickal practices when he established his own tradition.

Sanders claimed to be a hereditary Witch initiated by his grandmother, but who knows? He was a bit of an attention-seeker, claiming to have been crowned 'King of the Witches' in 1965, presumably nominated by over 2,000 English Witches. This is debatable because Wiccans are really way too independent to ever accept a 'King' or 'Queen'. He also recorded an album and appeared on lots of TV and radio shows and ... sounds a bit like me, eh? I'm kidding! He continued to popularize the Craft in the Western World until his death in 1988. Many Wiccan covens now will have their open coven meetings in the Alexandrian tradition, reserving the Gardnerian work for their initiated and more experienced members.

A lot of other traditions established themselves in the late 1960s and early 1970s. One which has had a big influence on me is the Dianic Tradition, popularized by the charismatic Hungarian, Zsuzsanna Budapest, who now lives in America. Her mother was an artist and Witch who initiated Zsuzsanna into Witchcraft when she was very young. In the 1970s when Zsuzsanna became a feminist, she realized her Witchcraft background was an appropriate expression of feminist spirituality and wrote *The Holy Book of Women's Mysteries*, which is an excellent and thorough guide book for anyone wanting to practise Witchcraft with an emphasis on feminism and women's mysteries.

Zsuzsanna is a colourful and controversial public figure in America. In 1975 she was arrested reading Tarot for an undercover policewoman, tried, and found guilty of 'predicting the future'(!) leading her to fight against anti-prophecy laws for nine years before the laws were repealed. She now has her own Cable TV show in America on women's spirituality, broadcasts on radio and regularly releases books and articles on feminist Wicca.

Overall, I have a pretty ambivalent attitude towards the herstory of Wicca. While I value the wisdom gained from trial and error, tradition and experience, I like to focus on the present. That the herstory is as nebulous as it is makes the present-day Craft no less valid for me than if it did have a seamlessly documented record of existence back to prehistoric times.

I sometimes think herstory is given too much importance in

the present day scheme of things. To have an elitist attitude because your tradition has the longest documented herstory; or because your mother initiated you, her mother initiated her, her mother's mother initiated her, (i.e. you're a Hereditary), etc, etc, seems a bit narrow-minded. It goes against one of the few things I actually *believe* in, which is everyone has the right to their own opinion and there's plenty of room in the Universe for everyone's opinion. Herstory is so subjective – what we often perceive as indisputable fact is, in most cases, just one person's opinion, and the events viewed through the veil of that person's scrutiny are often incomplete. It's obvious that the only person that can preach on a pedestal and say, 'This is what *really* happened' would have to have actually been there, which, in the case of ancient magickal practices, is impossible.

What I like about Witchcraft is that it creates its own herstory as it goes. There's very little documentation from before the last hundred years or so and most of what is available is dubious in accuracy. Lots of present day individuals will make up an ancient history that fits their current view of the Craft. I like this: the stories people fabricate of the past are fascinating insights into the structure of the present. I also like the fact that the present-day Craft draws from so many different cultures' spiritual traditions from all over the world. It truly is a holistic religion that acknowledges and respects all manifestations of spirit in humans on the planet, even the ones it doesn't necessarily relate to or agree with.

For example, throughout this book there are many references to my frustration and disillusionment with Christianity; however I dig Jesus and so do many other Witches. It's not his fault that Christianity is so confused today, and as a person he was a very special guy, wise and generous, selfless and loving.

17

I think he'd be horrified to see what his teachings have come to today. In fact, I'd go so far as to say that if he was around today, with his values of tolerance, acceptance, respect for Nature and fellow people, he'd be a Witch!

One more thing before finishing up this chapter – why the word *'Witch'?* There is an old Germanic root word *wit* meaning 'to know', which some consider to be the origin, but there are many other possible origins. The one that seems most likely is that it is evolved from the Anglo-Saxon root word *wicce* meaning 'to bend or shape'. Witches relate to this from the premise that we *bend* the energies of nature to promote healing and growth and we *shape* our lives and environments to be harmonious with Nature. I like the word 'Witch'. For so long, because of fear and ignorance, it has been considered a negative term. I enjoy being a part of reinstating its rightful meaning. In a nutshell, the word Witch describes a person who sees divinity in nature, worships Goddesses always, and Gods most of the time, practises the healing arts, is in touch with their psychic abilities, practises magick and experiences their lives as an ever-evolving miracle.

WITCHES' BRITCHES

WITCHY STYLE AND WHEN TO TAKE YOUR CLOTHES OFF!

Going to a coven meeting wearing dramatic robes and ceremonial jewellery can be fun and stimulating but for me, being a Witch is about being relaxed and happy with yourself. Wearing dramatic Witchy clothing all the time reminds me too much of when I was a teenager screaming out for people to look at me and notice me. The same goes for making a big deal about my beliefs in public, i.e. waving my arms around in public and casting spells on all and sundry.

Running Around in the Nude

... or 'going skyclad' is the more dignified way of putting it. All jokes aside (and indeed, why should there be any?), it is appropriate for Witches to perform their rituals and spell-castings without clothing, though by no means is it essential. The body is sacred to Witches and nudity is considered a blessed and whole state, not debauched or vulgar. When a Witch is naked nothing comes between her/him and the Universe – after all, everyone is born naked. In group gatherings, depending on people's preferences, ritual robes and other clothing are most often worn, but personally, in any solo rituals or gatherings with trusted kinfolk, I am comfortable working naked. It is a personal choice, and no-one should ever feel pressured to perhaps drop their guard and reveal themselves as they truly are, unless they are ready to. Going skyclad should have you feeling blessed, perfect and magickal just the way you are, never uncomfortable or exposed. If you do feel the latter, put something on straight away!

Some Witches I know enjoy the drama and shock value of elaborate clothing, jewellery, hair colours and the unleashing of grandiose eccentric behaviour on the average suburban community. However, two of the most powerful and knowledgeable Wiccan High Priestesses I know are very low key. They are both uniquely beautiful middle-aged women who work in corporate environments, and the only concessions they make to traditional Witchy gear are predominantly black wardrobes. Of course, the majority of office working women have wardrobes with a high black content anyway. A lot of male Witches I know tend to grow the pointy goatee beard, like Pan, and wear black clothing and pointy-toed shoes but then, a lot don't, too. The general consensus amongst most Witches is that if someone walks around advertising their spiritual path in a self-aggrandising way then they're a bit of a loser and probably more of a talker than a doer.

It can be a pretty spectacular sight, however, when you attend a coven meeting or festival gathering and everyone is out in full Witchy clobber. A lot of people go for a medieval theme; woman bedecking themselves in sumptuous, swishy velvet skirts, lace-up bodices and wide belts with athames, amulet pouches and purses hanging off them; while the men have big shirts tucked into tight pants and boots, long hair and medallion necklaces. Others are into looks like the esoteric street-urchin fairy look with dreads, hand-dyed tattered threads, glitter everywhere and leather thonging cluttered with crystals tied around their necks.

People following specific traditions such as those based on Nordic teachings, may dress in animal fur and leathers with elaborate headgear – like a hat I saw made from the head and body of a skinned feral cat, and at one gathering, one of the members was in a full chain mail suit! Celtic groups have the men dress in authentic bardic costume with woven wool tunics over leggings and swirling capes secured at the shoulder with a decorative metal pin.

So, what do I wear at these gatherings? Well, seeing as I'm a bit of a rebel, I rarely wear black. For daytime I've been known to stomp around in lurid red boots, a t-shirt or jumper and flared fluorescent coloured patchwork pants with a big brown

21

belt, on which I hitch my athame in its sheath and from which I also hang a couple of amulet pouches, their contents being part of spells in progress. I always wear my pentacle tight at my throat, and maybe a big chunk of citrine quartz crystal hanging on leather suspended over my solar plexus chakra to facilitate mental awareness and communication – handy qualities to amplify when you're mixing with lots of strangers.

For one of the first coven meetings I attended I was told to wear a cape, but for many years as a solitary Witch I didn't own one, practising my rituals in the privacy of my own home and usually skyclad. Then one day I was visiting my Aunt Magda and she was getting rid of a whole lot of old clothes and she invited me to go through a bag and see if there was anything I wanted. I pulled out a full-length black satin cape lined in white which fastened at the throat with three little diamante buttons – a perfect Witch's cape! Aunt Magda used to wear it to parties in the 1960s but she was more than happy to give it to me to wear to coven meetings.

The black cape has a lot of symbolic meanings, beyond being just a fashion trend for 'gothic' Witches. **Wearing any kind of ceremonial garb is a technique for helping you to leave the mundane, everyday world and enter into the special, magickal realm of ritual.** If you're working with a group, like a coven meeting, wearing a kind of occult uniform helps to visually demonstrate unity and encourage everyone to work with a singular focus. For me, having the black cape draped over my shoulders prepares me for the inward journey into the subconscious required for all magickal work. The white lining symbolizes the enlightenment and power waiting there between the worlds for me to tap into.

Usually when it is time for ritual at coven meetings and

gatherings, everyone removes their capes – ritual work nearly always requires working with fire and you don't want capes lighting up as people dance around flaming cauldrons or lean over burning candles on altars! Witches are also usually careful not to wear garments with big, draping sleeves that could knock over altar tools and drag in bowls of water. Long, simple robes, usually black, are often worn by both sexes and sometimes specifically coloured robes are made for different events; for instance, white is worn for full moon rituals and often red is popular for Sabbats.

As I mentioned earlier, unless it's cold, I work skyclad at home. This means naked and it has nothing to do with debauchery and sex! To a Witch the naked body represents the dropping of illusions and social masks; to us the human body is sacred and needs no tricks or props to make it Divine and empowered. Clothes can also sometimes present a barrier to raising power, and in groups they can be a barrier to unity as they can indicate potentially divisive situations like lower income and differing social status. The theory is: when everyone is naked, everyone is equal. Witches aim not to be intimidated by cultural stereotypes, and in ritual would not consider older bodies to be less attractive than younger ones, nor slimmer bodies to be more appealing than fatter ones – in Circle all bodies are beautiful, sacred and honoured.

The only group gatherings that I've attended skyclad have been exclusively for women – like the Wemoon weekend discussed in the *'Witches Are All Rite'* chapter. It is very rare for a large mixed group of strangers to gather naked, usually out of respect for individual preferences – though many smaller initiated covens work skyclad 99% of the time. Within these groups members are well-known to each other and committed

23

to the coven, and have the tolerance and support to deal with situations that occasionally arise when working skyclad. For example, some guys when attending their first few skyclad group Circles (especially if they're young) will get a hard-on – from nerves. No true Wiccan would think anything negative about it and inexperienced female Witches don't need to feel threatened sexually if this happens. Nakedness is sacred and sexual, procreative energy is honoured as Divine by Wiccans and so no-one needs to feel embarrassed.

Most Witches have a special piece of jewellery that they always wear for ritual work. Traditionally, women wear a necklace of amber and jet, or a large silver bracelet that is inscribed with meaningful symbols; and men wear a silver ring which can be also inscribed. Personally, I change my ritual jewellery periodically as I don't like to become too attached to a singular piece and run the risk of becoming dependent upon it. For example, if I decided that my silver moon ring was my 'power object' and I *had* to have it for any bona fide ritual work or spellcasting, then I would be externalizing my power which is ultimately destructive. If I lost the ring it would also be tempting to consider that a 'bad omen' – which is succumbing to the consumerist notion that the accumulation of material goods will bring success and happiness. I like to change my ritual jewellery according to the sort of work I'm doing and the mood I'm in. I have a wonderful, enormous amber sphere set in a silver pendant that I often wear for rituals that require a lot of meditation, since amber can be used to assist grounding and centring. I also love my Celtic pewter and amethyst pentacle necklace which I wear when I want to announce to the world that I am a Witch!

✦ ✦ ✦

Many Western Witches mark themselves with tattoos much like the shamans and witchdoctors of indigenous peoples. Symbolic designs and talismans have been painted on the skin to enhance and commemorate spiritual practices since the time of our earliest ancestors. A lot of Witches have pentagrams tattooed somewhere on their bodies or perhaps Egyptian symbols like the ankh and Eye of Horus – whatever visually expresses their particular paths and experiences.

I have four tattoos, each one representing a major Witchy turning point in my life. Above my left ankle is my first tattoo. It is the symbol '69' representing my star sign, Cancer, and above is the noonday sun and below the waxing moon, both being symbols that I equated with positive, forward moving energy. At the time I was twenty-three and feeling good about myself and my life. I wanted a tattoo that, when I looked at it, would remind me not to take life for granted and to celebrate every day that I am alive.

The next tattoo I had done a couple of years later is on the right-hand side of my lower back and is a shark backed by a spray of water. My first scuba dive involved a private, intro- ductory dive in the waters just off Manly Beach in Sydney, Australia. The instructor and I had only descended a few metres and I was just getting used to breathing underwater (definitely a bit of a claustro- phobic experience at first!) when a five-foot bronze whaler shark glided by about two metres in front of me. I was stunned: the biggest fear you can have as a fledgling diver is

of sharks and here was a *big one* (everything looks magnified underwater) with a reputation as a bit of a 'snapper' (i.e. known to bite humans)! But after a reassuring squeeze of my hand by my instructor, I relaxed and just watched this magnificent creature swim. Watery sunbeams glanced off its tawny brown skin as its long, thick body weaved effortlessly through the water, circling us. I felt that it was communicating telepathically to me saying, 'Just watch me; you're in my territory now but I am happy to share it with you.' I was in awe and even more thrilled when a second shark suddenly appeared out of the murky depths. It was a sleek grey nurse, and together they swam around us in graceful arcs for another five minutes before moving away out of sight.

Later, back on shore, I stared at the ocean for an hour, its calm blue surface belying the existence of a busy, thriving alien world below that I could now visit every day if I wished. Diving is really like going to another planet and when I had the shark tattooed on my back I thought about how nothing is necessarily what it first appears to be, or ever completely predictable. The Universe and my place in it is in a constant state of enriching, surprising and stimulating flux, where dangers can be safe, safety can be suffocating and the key to physical and spiritual evolution is to be prepared to explore and love the unknown and the unfamiliar.

Another tattoo I have is a Knot of Eternity on my left inner wrist. It is a design of two short loops and one long loop of rope weaving in and out of each other into a square shape, consisting of nine inner and eight outer spaces. It is a mandala of contemplation and Buddhists consider it the pattern of their Enlightened One's entrails as they are arranged while he is sitting in meditation. I got this done in early 1993 after a particularly traumatic experience overseas when touring with my band. I thought I would never get through this experience but I did and the Knot of Eternity will always remind me that what doesn't kill you, can make you stronger and the more sorrow carves out of you, the more joy you can ultimately pour in.

Finally I have a large tattoo of the skull of a water dragon crowning an interlaced band around my upper left arm. This I had done in late 1995 and it celebrates a profound period of personal growth involving the magickal exploration of the inner, darker realms of my psyche. In mythologies from many different cultures the dragon has traditionally represented the underworld, the subconscious, as well as the astral realm. Essentially a serpent with wings, it can 'burrow deep' and 'fly high'. Water is the element most associated with emotions and the period represented by this tattoo was a time in which I learnt how to harness my emotions with the strength of a dragon, and how to use them as fuel for magickal workings and personal growth. The head of the dragon is decorated with 'URUZ', a Viking rune symbolizing endings, new beginnings and strength. Positive growth often requires a trip into the darker realms as part of the cycle of renewal and this was the lesson I learnt through a series of losses and hardships that ultimately led to new, better opportunities and experiences.

Another work of Witchy body modification I undertook around the same time as my dragon tattoo is my labret piercing. This is a ten-gauge steel stud inserted about one centimetre below the centre of my bottom lip. To mark myself so drastically in such a visible position required quite a serious reason. My labret represents one of the most unnerving spiritual challenges I have ever experienced – a ten-day Buddhist meditation retreat called Vipassana in July, 1995. During this time I learnt a very difficult technique of meditation: it requires complete dedication, as you have to agree at the orientation lecture that under no circumstances will you shoot through and abandon the course. The teachers of Vipassana ask for this reassurance from you because they know how hard the course is. For ten days, although you are surrounded by others, you must neither speak, look nor make gestures at anyone, and you concentrate solely on Vipassana meditation. For two hours in the middle of the day you are able to speak to the teachers but other than that you are guided by a morning and afternoon teaching session. Your day consists of rising at 4am and focusing only on your breathing and the subtle sensations in your body for no less than fourteen hours of sitting meditation. In addition, your food intake is very strict with a light vegetarian meal for breakfast and lunch, and only herbal tea and fruit for dinner – and of course there is no coffee, smoking or alcohol.

You become paranoid, depressed, frustrated, and occasionally ecstatic over the ten days, but on completion the peace of mind you have achieved is better than sex! Vipassana was one of the most difficult yet rewarding things I have ever done, and I'm sure my teachers would be horrified to know that the experience inspired me to pierce my body with steel. However, during the course you are encouraged to contemplate the notion of the impermanence of the flesh and the permanence of the spirit, and the transitory nature of pleasure and suffering. Essentially, the ritual of my labret piercing

was a permanent piece of steel inserted into the imperma-
nent, organic medium of flesh. The pain of the piercing was so
intense that transcending it became blissful and as such it
summed up what I learnt at Vipassana.

Another form of body modification is makeup – when applied
with intent it can be a magickal expression. Colour affects our
emotions and others' emotions around us, and enhancing or
exaggerating our facial features can be a magickal act. Usually
Witches wear no makeup when attending coven meetings, but
for open group gatherings everyone dresses up, and on these
occasions I outline my eyes with black and smear silver glitter
onto my eyelids. Doing this, I am announcing to others that I
am ready to enter into a realm of mystery and enchantment.

I have a headband that sits low across my forehead set with
a quartz crystal over the third eye area which I often wear
when doing intense meditation, as the crystal placed here can
amplify psychic powers. It was a tradition among the ancient
Druids to wear crowns with open-set jewels in the centre of
the forehead for similar reasons.

As a Witch **I believe everything can be imbued with a
sense of magickal purpose – even the most routine of
chores like getting dressed every morning.** As a Catholic
I was brought up to think that an overt interest in personal
appearance was vain and to be frowned upon. As a Witch I
think vanity is a good thing, though by this I am subverting
the generally accepted meaning of vanity. To me, vanity
means having an ever-evolving interest in your appearance for
completely personal reasons, not because you want to appeal
to, impress, manipulate or dominate others. Vanity can be a

29

form of self-expression that involves being aware of, and in touch with, the inner self and expressing that externally.

After my teen years of dressing radically, I went through a stage in my early twenties where I downplayed my personal appearance and convinced myself I was ugly and undeserving of any special enhancement. I would throw on any old thing or just buy an item of clothing that thousands of other people were wearing, I didn't experiment with makeup and I stuck to a few basic, familiar things.

But as I continued developing my Witchcraft over the next few years, I saw my inner world reflecting more and more on my outer world, and so I got in touch with enjoying and play-ing with my appearance again, but with a more evolved sense of purpose. The creative process of dressing up and wearing elaborate makeup is an empowering Witchy act and as I con-tinue to grow, I continue to take decorating myself seriously as an outward expression of my ever-evolving spiritual psyche. Of course there are days when nothing beats a neat little black dress and smoothed back hair and discreetly applied makeup (or a pair of crappy trackies!), but that's my point – Witchy style is about being in touch with your needs and desires. It is an expression of self-interest and self-love, and that is very empowering.

THIS GOES WITH THIS AND THAT GOES WITH THAT

ALL YOU NEED TO MAKE YOUR OWN SPELLS

The most powerful magickal experiences will always be the ones that you have had a major hand in creating.

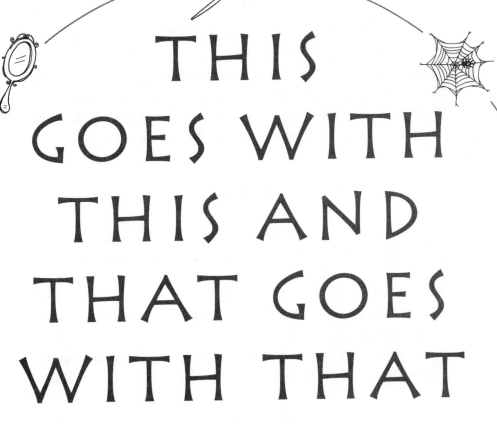

Here you can tailor-make your own spells by following all or some of the steps below and utilizing the magickal correspondences which follow in the rest of this chapter. Don't be afraid to try anything, and remember – it doesn't have to go like clockwork! Be prepared to get confused, make mistakes and learn. The more spells you cast, the better you get!

Steps

1 Decide what you want to do, e.g.: A spell for courage;
2 Go to 'Days' on p. 34 for the best day on which to perform the spell;
3 Go to 'Moon Phases' on p. 35 for the best time in the lunar cycle;
4 Go to 'Colours' on p. 37 for colour advice regarding candles, paper, cloth and thread, etc;
5 Go to 'Numbers' on p. 40 for advice on how many candles should be used, how many pentagrams should be carved into candles, etc;
6 Go to 'Crystals' on p. 44 to find which stones should be used to focus energy or should be included in amulets and charms;
7 Go to 'Herbs and Oils' on p. 52 to find which herbs and oils to mix into incense to use for anointing, and to include in charms;
8 Go to 'Goddesses and Gods' on p. 66 to find the appropriate Deities to ask for assistance and blessings;
9 Go to 'Elementals, Angels and Mythical Animals' on p. 72 for extra magickal help.

A Suggested Spell-Plan Using the Above

On your chosen day, and your chosen time, set up your altar with the appropriate candles, incense, crystals and other items, and brew some tea (see *Seven Days to a Magickal New You!* for more information on tea-brewing) using herbs appropriate for your intent.

Cast Circle, invoking the Deities and any other beings, e.g. Elementals, Angels, etc (see the *Spell Boundaries* chapter for details). Burn some of the incense and place the rest in the centre of the cloth with a small piece of crystal. Anoint yourself with the Pentagram (see p. 107), using some of your chosen oil and take a few sips of the tea you have prepared,

(see p. 107)

O p e n   Y o u r   M i n d ...

Sometimes to access the 'world between the worlds' doesn't require elaborate ritual, dedicated meditation, or initiation into occult secrets. Often all that is needed is a silencing of the 'censor' that is in the hearts and minds of so many of us. The censor is the voice that says, 'This is stupid, this is make-believe, you're imagining things, what would everyone think?' I find that a warm, relaxed, intuitive headspace is the key to worlds beyond, and the lock that bars those worlds is only self-doubt.

The most magickal thought you can achieve is the unshakeable, unconditional faith in your own infinite abilities.

33

being aware that you are stimulating your magickal powers and aligning all the energies within Circle to work your spell. Write your desire on a piece of paper, fold it seven times and place in the centre of the cloth (in this instance, you are sealing all the gathered items into the cloth to create a charm). Place your hands over the charm and call on the powers of any Elementals, Angels or animal spirits that you have invited into Circle to channel their energies through you to strengthen the charm. Now, tie up the edges of the cloth with thread or ribbon, sealing the contents inside. Take another few sips of your herb tea to ground yourself and the spell is complete. Thank and bid farewell to the attending beings, and close Circle in the usual way.

Days

Monday

❈ Ruled by the Moon;
❈ Divination and female health issues.

Tuesday

❈ Ruled by Mars;
❈ Courage, confrontations and strength.

Wednesday

❈ Ruled by Mercury;
❈ Travel, money, academic success.

Thursday

❃ Ruled by Jupiter;
❃ Jobs, careers, friendships, wealth (not just of money, but of spirit, confidence, etc).

Friday

❃ Ruled by Venus;
❃ Love, sex partnerships.

Saturday

❃ Ruled by Saturn;
❃ Knowledge, especially esoteric/occult knowledge, banishing of limitations, exorcisms, legal issues.

Sunday

❃ Ruled by the Sun;
❃ Growth, healing, male health issues.

Moon Phases

If it's been overcast for days and you're not sure which phase the moon is in, you can buy a moon calendar from a New Age occult supply store (see *Crafty Contacts* at the back of this book). Also, most newspapers report the phase of the moon every day on the weather page.

Full Moon

A great time to do any magick as the lunar energies are ripe and potent.

New Moon

New plans and new beginnings; a time to sow the seeds of future success.

Dark Moon

The three days of the dark moon are not the best for spell-casting, but are particularly good for divination.

Waxing Moon

Building, growth, strengthening, encouragement, a time to set things in motion and put impetus behind them.

Waning Moon

Retreat, reversal, banishing, protection, cleansing – a time of reflection on what occurred during the waxing moon.

✦ Note: be resourceful when you are working with lunar energies. For example, if you want to do a spell for personal empowerment, but it is the time of the waning moon, concoct a spell to banish fear, loneliness and insecurity. If you want to do a spell for prosperity, but it is the dark moon, do a Tarot or rune reading for information on what actions will best suit your goals in the coming weeks. ✦

Magickal Music

Music is the voice of the soul and playing music during certain ritual work can enhance the proceedings. Often Witches, in being attached to the old Western European roots of their tradition, will play pan pipes or folky, bardic music, but personally I find these really put me off. I have been known to play hard metal at home rituals when I have needed to conjure up a lot of adrenalin, and really trippy, ambient trance techno, as well as recordings of Tibetan throat singers for deep introspective, meditation work. You can sometimes get really interesting results by using fairly unusual music in magickal ritual. At other times, however, music can be distracting, especially if there are lots of lyrics, so it is really up to you as to whether you include it. At group gatherings and coven meetings I have attended, music is often used at key points in the ritual, whether it is spontaneous drumming, hymns to the Goddess, or songs performed by coven members with lyrics pertaining to the work at hand.

Colours

Colours permeate every moment of our lives, each having its own unique vibration and psychological, therapeutical and magickal effect. At the core of everything is light (an interaction of electrical energy and magnetism) and colours are the various wavelengths that form light. Occult scholars believe that the seven colours of the light spectrum (red, orange, yellow, green, blue, indigo, violet) represent the evolution of the Universe and that we have already passed through three: red, orange and yellow, and are now midway through the green period, moving beyond primitive development and into higher periods of spiritual development. Human auras are electrical emanations from our bodies which manifest as colours and scientists have determined that our brains emit thoughts measurable as colours, as well as infra-red and ultra-violet waves and beyond! Using colour in magickal work empowers spells in a huge way as they can be used to manip-ulate the potential of events and objects, so put some thought into the colour of the candles, paper, cloth and ink you use; the colour of the clothing or jewellery you wear when doing ritual, as well as the colour of flowers or other objects you may have on your altar. Following are the magickal properties of colours for use in rituals and spells:

White

Cleansing, protection and spirituality. White is not considered a true colour, as it contains all seven of the spectrum. It can take the place of any colour. For example, if you need to do a spell for healing in a hurry and you can't get any blue candles, you can use white instead.

Purple

Power, success and commitment, psychic matters.

Red

Lust, passion, courage, willpower, vigour, endurance and ambition.

Blue

Healing, happiness, guidance, truth and religious inspiration.

Green

Prosperity, fertility, employment, good luck and beauty.

Yellow

Concentration, action, wisdom, intellect and learning.

Orange

Legal matters, confidence, pride and empathy.

Pink

Love, friendship, leisure, gentleness, reconciliation.

Black

Used for accessing the subconscious, banishing and binding and for invoking periods of rest; it can also be used in legal spells. Not considered a true colour, black is actually the absence of colour.

Silver

Representative of the Goddess and the Moon, silver can be used to stimulate visions and intuition.

Gold

Representative of the God and the Sun, gold can be used to stimulate the Life Force and the longevity of things.

Brown

Can be used to assist things of a practical nature which need to be grounded in solid application of effort; can also eliminate indecisiveness.

Grey

Legal matters and other formal issues.

Numbers

Pythagoras, the famous 6th-century BC Greek philosopher and mathematician, believed that all things could be defined by numbers and their values; and Carl Jung, the (fairly esoteric) Swiss psychologist, considered numbers to be pre-existent to consciousness, that is, they were not invented by humans but are the original form of order in the Universe. Ancient peoples like the Egyptians, Babylonians, Sumerians, the Hindu Vedas and Celts all considered numbers to have mystical and sacred properties.

When working spells, incorporate number energy by, for example, carving a certain number of notches or pentagrams into a candle to represent an outcome or quality you desire. Tie a certain number of knots into a cord or ribbon to attract specific energies. Use a certain number of drops of oil or pinches of incense or herbs to focus magickal results. Following are the various magickal properties of numbers:

1

✽ Colour: white
✽ Planet: the Sun
✽ Beginnings; agreements; God energy; success, fame and money; and male fertility.

2

✽ Colour: blue
✽ Planet: the Moon
✽ Duality; symmetry; balance; protection; spells to do with health, vitality and women's fertility; visions and intuition.

3

✽ Colour: green
✽ Planet: Jupiter
✽ Life's journey, birth/life/death; the Triple Goddess, Maiden/ Mother/Crone; goals; objectives; expansion in endeavours; education and financial prosperity (especially involving dealings with banks or financial advisors).

4

❋ Colour: brown
❋ Planet: Uranus
❋ Relates to the four elements (air/earth/fire/water), so it can work for spells to do with manifesting things on the physical plane. The influence of Uranus can work to shatter preconceptions of the self leading to new growth, so it also relates to spells to do with necessary changes and triumphs over adversity, and also removing the veils of misconception, and perhaps ego.

5

❋ Colour: red
❋ Planet: Mercury
❋ Considered a lucky number, it relates to the five points of the pentagram, as well as the four elements, plus the fifth, being spirit. It also represents a human's place in the scheme of life's evolution and so can be used for spells involving perception; psychic endeavours; communication; flexibility to change and virtuous quality of thoughts; as well as teaching and travel with a view to gaining and sharing knowledge.

6

❋ Colour: yellow
❋ Planet: Venus
❋ Devotion; completion of tasks (according to the Bible, the world was created in six days); love and passion; family and

children concerns; the seeking of pleasure and contentment; and anything to do with supporting and enhancing the arts – music, literature, acting, etc.

7

❋ Colour: purple
❋ Planet: Neptune
❋ This is a very mystical number and is connected to the seeking of wisdom (as opposed to information and knowledge), visions and prophecy. It can assist spells to do with initiation into mysteries and also reconciling the past with present.

8

❋ Colour: orange
❋ Planet: Saturn
❋ Relates to justice and legal matters; fate; redemption; and personal transformation, power and career matters. Also for communicating with the dead, and it can assist in lifting the veils between the worlds (as at Samhain).

9

❋ Colour: silver
❋ Planet: Mars
❋ Nine is an amazing number as it can be multiplied by any number and the result, when added together, will always add to nine. It is the number of perfection, Universal law and the ultimate truth of life which is 'energy cannot be destroyed –

it only changes form'. Use this number when the going is particularly hard to guarantee a successful outcome. The Mars energy ensures valour and triumph over obstacles.

Double digit numbers

The number 13 is often associated with Hollywood Witchcraft and is considered bad luck. Magickally though, double digit numbers are generally added together to be reduced to a single digit (there are a few exceptions like 10, 11 and 22) so 13 actually becomes 4 which relates to positive change, but also conflict through change.

Crystals

Crystals sometimes get ridiculed for being overused New Age crutches, but ancient cultures have always held them sacred and used them in meditation and healing. Today, crystals are used in watches, computers and laser technology and this can be considered magickal.

Crystals are created by geological processes when super-heated steam carrying minerals is released from the Earth's magma under the crust. The minerals crystallize on the walls of the fissures in the Earth's crust through which the steam passes. All crystals form in beautifully intricate and geometrically precise patterns. Quartz is a spiral of silicon and oxygen atoms held in place by shared electrons, so the electrical properties of a tiny piece of crystal in a watch make it accurate.

In magickal work, a wand is often topped with a crystal, which amplifies its conjuring and manifestation abilities;

crystals can be placed on objects (including human bodies!) to clear blockages; they can be used in communicating with the dead (since they are considered to be capable of channelling spirits into the physical world), as well as divination. They always look beautiful, so they are featured in a lot of Witches' ceremonial jewellery and on top of a lot of altars for their allure and energy-enhancing and attracting properties.

Crystals are very important as they are used in healing to pass energy (often channelled from the Universal source) through the healer to the person, animal or thing requiring treatment. Crystals can also work to clear and clarify human auras and release suppressed fears and other destructive emotions.

You don't have to be a New Age hippie to benefit from crystals – just have an open mind. Every object, living or inanimate, has its own energy aura that extends about three feet around it, so keep an appropriate crystal on your desk, in your handbag, backpack, briefcase, purse, around your neck or wrist as jewellery, or in a charm bag tucked into your pocket, to receive its benefits. Below, I have listed a selection of often-used crystals in magickal work.

✹ *Note: when buying crystals try to get them in as natural a form as possible. If they're all smooth and round usually they have been treated with chemicals and tumbled in a violent way (supposedly to enhance their colours and uniformity).* ✹

Quartz

Amethyst: The ultimate New Age crystal! Amethyst is fantastic to use when meditating (lie down and place a piece over the third eye) as it initiates wisdom, understanding and humility, helping you to let go of what is blocking you and allowing your true destiny to emerge. It's great for work in eradicating addictions, moodiness, stress and sadness. Folklore has it that it can cure drunkenness!

Clear Quartz: This is the most common crystal and can be used in almost limitless ways. It contains the full spectrum of light and can enhance creativity and inspiration, increase confidence and often works particularly well when used by males. Use this to amplify the intent of any spell, to screen out bad vibes and to bestow blessings and protection.

Rose Quartz: Known as the Love stone, Rose Quartz works to release the pain of a broken heart and to bring new love and friendship into your life. It promotes harmony in established relationships, as well as fertility. It can also work in any healing spells when the impulse to heal comes from unconditional love.

Smoky Quartz: Relates to strength, physical stamina and the material plane. It can transform negativity into positivity and, as it stimulates primal energy, is good for spells involving sex magick.

Agate

There are many types of agate and they all work towards enhancing communication and sometimes healing (Blue Lace Agate is good for this). Have agate around if you are having problems with getting on with people at work or school; and also to assist in job finding and fulfilment at work.

Other Crystals

Black Obsidian: Polished slices of this are great for scrying (see the chapter *Divine Dealings* for more about this). Its energy is aligned with the planet Pluto and as such can be used to encourage deeper journeys into the self. Use it in talismans where you are working to enhance your ability to reach an ego-less state (the right space to be in when doing divinatory work).

Bloodstone: Aids in power for all spells, protects against hexing and gives wisdom and courage.

Citrine: This is one of my favourites – it's great for stimulating intellect (wear some around your neck when studying or doing mentally taxing work). Wear a large chunk dangling over your solar plexus chakra to enhance personal power and have it around for spells involving material gain and career success. It can also protect from harm (as Angels are supposedly attracted to it!).

Diamond: Protects from evil, clears out psychic dangers, assures the owner of love and comfort.

Fluorite: Another of my favourites, especially when it is cut into pyramid form. I know I explained earlier how to get nice raw rocks, and I'm breaking my own rule here – but rules are made to be broken! The pyramid cut really does enhance this particular crystal's qualities. It's extremely good for thinking processes, helping to clear out the dross and get focused, as well as stimulating original creative ideas. It can also stimulate prophetic dreams and aid in magickal power.

Hematite: Good for relieving RSI (repetitive strain injury). I discovered this whilst writing this book! One day my hands were hurting so much I couldn't pick up a pencil, but I handled a piece of this stone and after a few minutes the pain was gone. Quite a miracle! It's a great healing stone and good for spells to do with growth and prowess.

Jasper: Ensures success in business and courage.

Lapis Lazuli: The ancient Egyptians used lapis lazuli to stimulate psychic abilities and to represent royal status, especially if the stone had lots of gold flecks – which is actually iron pyrite. They would grind the stones down and make blue dyes for the robes of their exulted ones. Today it can be used as a mental and spiritual cleanser, as well as a way to connect with the Goddess and God (within!) or in any spell where you need to really rise above anything that's holding you back and do something spectacular! It can also encourage fidelity in love, peace, happiness and beauty.

Malachite: Use this in any empowerment spells where you really want to let go of past memories and fears and move on … but beware! Malachite amplifies your current mood and mirrors externally what is within, so, while it can be a powerful aid for transformation, you should use it only when you *really* know it's time to change. Because it can effectively hold negativity and malice, it can be used in hexing and binding spells.

Moonstone: Good for spells involving 'female issues', e.g. menstruation, lactation, ovulation – anything to do with a woman's body's ability to breed. Also, hold a piece in each hand when you are trying to see auras – it can help. It enhances any spells to do with invoking Lunar essence.

Onyx: Carry to banish woes and bring self-control to the emotions.

Sodalite: Dispels guilt and fear and gives divine inspiration.

Tiger's Eye: Great for spells involving courage, legal battles and luck.

Tourmaline: As I mention in my chapter *Cyber-Sorcery*, it's great to have Tourmaline around your computer not only to enhance the effectiveness of your Internet surfing, but also to ward off problems with electrical equipment (like a computer crash).

Notes on Caring for Crystals

Rinse them periodically in salty water (the ocean is best) and put them under the light of the full moon or the morning sun to charge them up again. You can also bury them in earth for seven days or place them on a large, cleansed amethyst cluster to clear any stored vibrations. Use your intuition as to how often you clean your crystals.

Other (Non-Crystals)

Amber: This is a fossilised resin that can sometimes have insects and other things embedded in it (remember *Jurassic Park*?!). It is used for healing, luck and protection when working with spirits and other Beings. It can aid in childbirth (wear a necklace of amber), and it is also used in the traditional Witch's necklace of amber and jet.

Cats Claws: Carry to protect from slander, arguments and harassment from enemies.

Coral: This is the skeletal matter of sea creatures – it has magickal properties of protection and healing.

Cowrie Shells: These look a bit like female genitalia and represent Goddess energy on my altar. Whenever I find one I consider it a sign of good fortune.

Dried Lizards: If you find a little one in the countryside or by the road, keep it on your altar when doing spells to increase success and for luck.

Jade: Protects from psychic attack and nightmares, and gives health and long life.

Pig's Tusk: I found one of these on a beach on Tanna, the southernmost Pacific island of Vanuatu (it has a live volcano which you can climb). In Vanuatu, a pig's tusk worn around the necks of male chiefs is a symbol of prosperity and fertility. I have it on my altar to represent male energy.

Opal: Great for use in beauty (self-appreciation) spells, and it can protect from curses.

Pearl: Confers beauty and grace, and is great for love spells working for long-lasting, deep relationships.

Petrified Wood: Protects against illness and injury and gives security in relationships. Can also help to ensure a safe journey.

Ruby: The greatest stone for ensuring good health; it also protects against financial ruin.

Shark's Tooth: Keep one in your wallet to ensure plenty of money.

Snail Shell: Gives stability in money and business, brings patience and aids in meditations.

Snake's Skin: Rumour has it that if you carry one with you in a yellow bag when you go to the casino you can win lots of money! Personally I think snake skins bestow wisdom and a sense of moving beyond time, so they can assist in rituals to do with rebirthing of the spirit.

Topaz: Aids in clairvoyance and protects from accidents. Also heals anger and hurt.

Turquoise: Brings health and optimism and has a calming effect.

51

Gold and Silver: A lot of Witchy books suggest that male Witches' ceremonial jewellery should be gold, and female Witches' silver, as gold is ruled by the Sun and silver by the Moon. But everyone has male and female in them and just as many men are drawn to silver as women are to gold. Both substances are powerful to use in magickal work. Flecks of gold, when added to any spell-working, whether it be in charms, amulets, or, for example, sprinkled over a sick person, will give it an added boost. When worn, silver amplifies magickal powers and assists with accurate intuition. Silver and gold jewellery set with crystals becomes powerful magickal accessories, but make sure that the settings are open – for example, in a ring, make sure the base of the stone where it is closest to the skin is not covered by metal – it has to be suspended in the setting for it to work as an energy amplifier.

Herbs and Oils

There are many thorough and comprehensive books on herbs and oils and their magickal uses and I won't try to list them all here. What I have done is listed everything that is in my magickal pantry right now to give you an idea of what is handy to keep on hand. It's worth noting that herbs used in magickal work are kept just for that – don't use them for cooking (unless you're doing a food spell) – and it's best to grow them yourself when possible.

A Tip On Making Magickal Incense

Take one teaspoon each of three different dried plant herbs, one teaspoon of resin, and one of wood or woody substance all relating to your magickal intent, grind them together in a mortar and pestle (or coffee grinder if you can't be bothered doing it by hand), then add a specific number of drops of various oils depending on your intent and the scent (try not to add more than nine drops to this proportion of ingredients).

Don't add too much resin or oil or else when you burn it on charcoal discs it will get all gummy and put itself out. The above proportions are suggestions only, though, and can be increased proportionally for larger quantities. Don't be afraid to experiment, just make sure when you hit on a great smelling and magickally powerful combination you jot down the exact combination in your Book of Shadows.

Herbs, Gums and Resins

Belladonna: Poisonous herb which produces out-of-body states when ingested. I never take it internally – instead I have a flying ointment which includes a little of this and a couple of other things in a base of coconut oil with a few drops of wintergreen, which, when applied to the pulse points, is good for achieving the frame of mind required for divination.

Benzoin Gum: Has purification qualities and is a good base for any incenses.

Chamomile: Prepares the mind and body for magick work by opening the inner psychic doors. Drink it and float a muslin sachet filled with the flowers in your purification bath before ritual. If you wash your hands in cool chamomile tea it can help ensure dexterity and success with manual tasks.

Comfrey: Ensures safety during travel and protects against your money being stolen. An external poultice of the leaves will help knit broken bones and heal burns, swelling, broken skin and bruises, and the root can be boiled in wine or water to make a tea to help with coughs, lung infections and diarrhoea.

Copal: Another resin that makes a good base for incenses and works well in love spells.

Damiana: Used in lust and love spells and to induce visions of future lovers. Drunk before bed, it can relax one for lovemaking and promote pleasant dreams.

Dittany of Crete: When burnt it is thought that spirits will appear in the smoke. When included in incense it's good for astral projections.

Dragon's Blood Powder: This dramatically named substance is actually resin from a palm tree. I use a pinch in nearly all spell workings as it binds good fortune to any outcome and protects against spells misfiring in any way.

Elderflower: I mainly use this to make a mild tea as it is a blood purifier. I also a make a light infusion, cool it in the fridge and splash my eyes with it after working on the computer for too long as it eases eye strain.

Frankincense: A magickal substance! Can be used in any spell and is extremely potent as a base for any incenses with its protection and opulence qualities. If you're feeling really spooked about anything, burn some frankincense as it increases your safety straight away. Baby Jesus was thrilled when three wise men gave him some – it's precious stuff!

Galangal: I have dried pieces of this root – it's used in Indian and Thai cooking, but is very effective for lust spells, and at the other end of the spectrum, it can help win the favour of a jury!

Gardenia: This is my favourite flower and I dried the petals from my own plant. They can be used in healing and love spells and are a good offering to the Goddess during Full Moon rituals.

Hemlock: A classic Witches' herb. I make a small brew of this and dip my athame into it every now and again to keep it charged and aligned with the 'worlds between the worlds' (so that I can slice through astral veils more effectively to access those worlds).

High John the Conqueror Root: I keep a piece of this root soaking in jojoba oil with three drops of peppermint oil, and one of lemon, in a sealed glass container out of the sun. I use this as an anointing oil any time I'm doing a spell where I'm concerned I'm not focused enough but I really need to do the spell. It helps ensure success at endeavours.

Hops: I make sleep charms with these to help deal with my insomnia (which I often have because I worry too much!). I stuff a pale blue cloth bag with hops, vervain and lavender and hang it from the bed post.

Lavender: Lavender is one of those herbs that can be used in any spell to enhance its effect. Good for spells for love, peace, youthful vigour and also for dealing constructively with grief over any kind of loss.

Mandrake Root: An infamous Witches' herb. Myth has it that the plant is so powerful and inherently evil that it kills or sends mad anyone who tries to pull it up. Apparently the only safe way to acquire it is to tie a dog firmly to the plant and then entice the dog away so that it pulls up the plant by the root. It has narcotic properties and can be used as an aphrodisiac. It is prized by Witches for use as a poppet, as the root resembles the body of a human. The root is hard to come by and generally will be dried. To reactivate the mandrake root for magickal use, place in a glass or crystal bowl filled with spring water and a quartz crystal and leave out under the moon – it will be charged according to which moon you leave it under, waxing (for building), waning (for banishing), dark (divination) or full (just about anything).

Mugwort: Use to enhance psychic powers (burn in incense) and prophetic dreams (drink a cup of tea before bed and place some under the pillow). Purify any items you use for

55

A Few Essentials

It's a good idea to have a basic supply of a few commonly used herbs and oils. If you are doing a spell from a book it will often have a lengthy list of ingredients and, especially if the book was written overseas, some of these may be very hard to come by. From experience I have found that there are a few staples that will get you through any ritual, because it's OK to substitute if you really can't get hold of something.

One essential is **frankincense gum**. It can be used in any spell and its purification and protective powers always come in handy. Another good thing to have is some **sandalwood**, either the chips or the powder. It also has protective and purification powers and can be substituted for any missing ingredient in healing spells.

Dragon's Blood Powder is another staple. It can be used as a purification and protection agent and is an important ingredient for spells focusing on love energy. The above three substances might seem bizarre and exotic but they are easily available at New Age and Witchcraft supply stores.

I always have a jar of **rosemary** on hand too as it has purification qualities and can be added to any healing and love sachets, or incense mixes. **Mugwort** is another essential. It is often called 'the Witches' herb' as it pops up in heaps of spells, mainly for the role it plays in increasing psychic powers.

Lavender oil is an important staple. It's not too expensive and can be used in spells of protection, purification, healing and love. **Bergamot oil** is another I always have on hand now. It has qualities of protection and is good for attracting prosperity in all areas of life. I also always have **basil oil** on hand as it is great for spells that focus on promoting harmony and open communication.

When you are substituting one ingredient for another it's a good idea to enchant the substituted item to align its vibrations with the requirements of the spell. For example, specific protection spells may require St John's Wort for the protective charm but you can substitute frankincense. Before adding the frankincense to the mix place it in a separate bowl and rest both hands over it. Close your eyes and visualize white light entering through your crown chakra and flowing into your hands. See the light form a glowing orb around the bowl and say, 'Frankincense, I call on your protectiveness' repeatedly until you sense that it is indeed emanating its most protective vibrations. I usually feel this as a heat that builds up under my palms until they are tingling and I get an instinctive feeling that the substituted item is ready to be added to a spell.

57

divination and prophecy (such as a crystal ball) by placing them in an infusion of the herb and also store some of it dried with your Tarot cards and runes, etc. It can also be used in protection spells, and spells to do with physical endurance (Roman soldiers used to place it in their shoes before commencing long marches) and libido.

Myrrh: A beauty! Remember what the Three Wise Men gave to baby Jesus? Perhaps he would have preferred a small stuffed bear or something, but maybe babies had different tastes back then. Myrrh works much the same as frankincense and the two burned together are very good to exorcise negativity.

Nettle: Best for use in reversing hexes. If someone sends you a poppet or effigy that's meant to be you, cut it open, stuff it with nettle and send it back, or throw it into the sea, and it nullifies the spell. Also sprinkle nettle around the outside of your house, or over the doormat if you live in a flat, to prevent people you don't like from entering.

Orris Root (powdered): Used in love spells. Sprinkle a little onto the sheets for passionate love-making, as opposed to sexual gymnastics!

Patchouli: Use in love and desire spells as well as money and prosperity spells.

Rosemary: Use for spells to do with mental ability (drink a light brew of rosemary tea during ritual). Also, its strong smell and voluminous smoke when burnt means that it's great for cleansing and purifying areas. It's also reputed to strengthen the memory and can be used in spells to keep a lover faithful, as well as enhancing commitment and loyalty in other endeavours. Sprigs under the pillow can prevent bad dreams and if you make a box from the wood of the plant and keep it where you sleep, it will preserve your youth!

Rose Petals: I dry these myself from roses given to me as gifts. I use them in any spell where I want to promote purity of intent and an unconditional appreciation of the outcome. They can obviously be used in love spells.

Rue: Can be used to exorcise negativity as well as enhancing mental powers and the ability to apply oneself to a task. Mix nine drops of morning dew into half a cup of cool, brewed rue tea and sprinkle it around the circumference when casting Circle for help in manifesting a protected and sacred space. Add it to salads as it enhances eyesight.

Sage: Used in money spells, as well as wisdom and longevity spells.

Sandalwood Chips and Powder: Protection, exorcism, healing – sprinkle the dust around a place to clear negative energy. This burns really well and is good to add to incense to encourage combustion.

St John's Wort: Used for health, happiness, strength and protection. It's now used medicinally to treat depression and even out mood swings.

Vervain: Use to promote peace, harmonious interactions, love and protection. If you have a pot of the plant where you earn money it will ensure prosperous endeavours. Placing some in a bowl of spring water will protect from unpleasant spirits when doing divination. It's also considered a charm against snake bite. The Ancient Romans would place it on altars (especially when they were sacrificing young virgins!). Supposedly it was originally discovered on the Mount of Calvary and used to staunch the blood flow from Christ's wounds.

Yarrow: Good for spells where you need courage, and also for love spells. It can be good to incorporate this into a charm for a newly-married couple as it will ensure seven years of happiness and fidelity!

Gosh! Having documented the contents of my magickal pantry makes me realize there's quite a lot of stuff there! I have been practising Witchcraft for many years and certainly have acquired a selection of fairly exotic stuff. But don't feel pressured to go out and get everything at once – a few basic staples are a good idea. Let your collection grow gradually.

Witchdoctor

When I first started exploring Witchcraft, the main impression I got from all the books was that Witches were primarily benevolent healers, constantly thinking about the welfare of others and looking out for someone to heal. So I enrolled in a naturopathy college and for two years studied herbal medicine, nutrition and massage. I found all this enormously interesting and after classes during the day I would go home and pore over my Witchy books and be excited to find corresponding medicinal and metaphysical properties in the herbs and foods I used in ritual. At college we also studied anatomy, physiology, symptomatology, diagnosis and basic medical science, and I found what I learnt there augmented my rituals at home when I was making healing potions and charms for friends and myself. For example, knowing exactly where the liver was in the body and what the surrounding tissues and blood vessels looked like really enhanced my visualizations when I made a healing charm for a friend who had a long history of alcohol and drug abuse and had been diagnosed with Hepatitis B.

I work differently at healing now. For a start, since I left college nine years ago and did not keep up my study, a lot of what I learned has become a dim memory, but this hasn't necessarily diminished my healing abilities. As I reinforce throughout this book, **I've increasingly discovered that it is the intent and the passion of the subconcious, not the props of the logical mind and physical tools, that magick mostly works with.** These days, if I feel I am getting sick or run down, I say a few firm words to myself and maybe a couple of affirmations and perform a brief visualization. Now on the rare occasions I do get ill it's usually when I have a few days off and my body says, 'Ahh … cool! Some time to rest and detoxify!'

The one part of my body that can be vulnerable is my throat. As soon as I sense a tickle, I imagine a 'neck cuff' of azure blue light that not only encircles my throat but penetrates right through to my red, sore, swollen vocal cords. I immediately sense a calming and defusing coolness and then I say a few words to myself like, 'Get well, body, we don't have time to be sick!' These words might sound a bit harsh, but magick works best when you are completely honest and don't try to pull the wool over your own or anyone else's eyes.

When I suffer from period cramps, I visualize a cool, blue, fluffy light gently nursing my womb and a white diamond egg-like sphere of light surrounding my body to shield me from the draining, masculine energies to which women can be more susceptible when bleeding. Injuries don't stop me either. Once, I sprained my ankle and was

61

on crutches. Again I used cooling blue light, but this time I saw it as a weightless, inflated, ice-bubble that clung to my ankle like a child's swimming float, supporting it and metaphysically taking the weight off it.

Visualizing a healing light only takes a split second. If you try to spend ten minutes doggedly seeing a blue light around your neck, often your mind will wander or you might even fight the image, get stressed, feel inadequate and then be much more likely to feel worse. Some Witches I know insist on very disciplined visualization and in the early days I would spend a lot of time training my 'mind's eye' – but often I would get frustrated at not being able to hold an unwavering mental image for over ten seconds. It was a big breakthrough for me the day that I realized magick works *between* the worlds of the physical and supernatural and, as such, linear time means little when it comes to effective magickal workings. That's not to say that certain times of the day, month and year aren't more effective for certain magick, but when you need a quick fix you should let go of patriarchal notions of past, present and future.

The Goddess's concept of time is that every potential of every reality that ever was, is and will be is all happening at once in a big stupendous sphere. All you have to do is see the reality that you want and be it – just *know* that you are well, and when you feel that deep shift of reality go 'clunk' in your gut, let go of it and get on with your day. Of course you can tap into the image of healing light for reassurance any time you need to after that, but don't feel you have to be a vigilante against illness. A few seconds of calm, confident *knowing* is better than a day full of 'trying to know'. Obviously, when you're ill it's a good idea to take some action on the physical plane too, like rest, vitamins, and whatever natural remedies are suitable. If you're just not together enough to heal yourself, see a naturopath and/or a doctor. Of course, if you know a competent Witch definitely ask her or him to do a healing spell for you.

Oils

I have a lot of essential oils. Always try to get pure essential oils and not perfumed ones (mine are all pure except for the carnation one which is slightly perfumed). I use them in amulets and charms, as anointing oils (usually a combination of nine different drops in two teaspoons of jojoba), and in traditional aromatherapy ways (oil burning, in the bath, etc). Below are the oils I have on hand with a brief description of their qualities.

Basil: Promotes harmony and helps stop fighting between loved ones.

Bergamot: Prosperity.

Black Pepper: Energy and enthusiasm.

Camphor: Purification.

Carnation: Uplifting, good for luck spells.

Cinnamon: Good for sex magick.

63

Clary Sage: Euphoric, great for PMT blues, protective (especially for women). Contraindicated during pregnancy as it can bring on contractions.

Cypress: Masculine energy (especially when combined with patchouli), good for assisting in letting go.

Eucalyptus: Healing and protection.

Frankincense: A wonderful all rounder, very purifying and protective.

Geranium: Love, happiness and protection.

Ginger: Courage, strength (mental and physical).

Jasmine: Sacred to the Moon Goddess and enhances feminine qualities.

Jojoba: As a base for anointing oils.

Lavender: Healing, love, anti-depression.

Lemon: Moon energy, for nurturing, cleansing and strengthening.

Lemongrass: Purification, enhances psychic abilities.

Mandarin: Happiness.

Marjoram: A spring cleaner (especially when combined with thyme).

Myrrh: Purification.

Neroli: Young love, enhances sensuality, and can also be calming when feeling confused.

Nutmeg: To help with divination.

Orange: Sun energy, growth and development.

Palmarosa: Healing and love.

Patchouli: Love and to invoke the Goddess Hecate.

Pennyroyal: Strength and protection (contraindicated during pregnancy).

Peppermint: Transformative properties. Rub a little on your temples and the soles of your feet to help you unwind!

Petitgrain: Protection.

Pine: Exorcism and purification.

Sandalwood: Substitutes for just about anything – healing, love, protection, purification.

Thyme: For 'spring cleaning' of the mind and body.

Ylang Ylang: An aphrodisiac and can encourage a sense of interconnectedness with all things.

Obviously a lot of the properties of extracted oils correspond with the originating substance from which they were extracted. Generally, when you use oils for anointing or as additions to amulets and charms you are connecting with earth and water elemental qualities, whereas burning herbs and oils brings in the air and fire elements, so sometimes it can be worth doubling up with an original substance and its extracted oil to give a full-on magickal punch!

Goddesses and Gods

Having been brought up in a monotheistic religion I was over-
whelmed when I discovered the plethora of Pagan and Wiccan
Goddesses and Gods – let alone those of other cultures and
religions that as a Witch I was free to respect, explore and
identify with. When I started practising Witchcraft I was drawn
to recognizing and acknowledging only the Goddess under
many guises (e.g. Kali, Diana, Cerridwen). I guess this was a
reaction to being brought up Catholic and forced to recognise
only a male God. After a couple of years as a Witch I could no
longer ignore the *animus* in me and I started to invoke the God
during ritual, primarily in the form of Pan, Lord of the Forests,
and then generally as a constant force connected to the
Goddess as her consort, lover and son. I relate to the Jungian
concept of every soul being composed of *anima* (female polarity) and *animus* (male polarity) to be equally explored by both
sexes. I now relate to Goddess energy as being omnipresent –
existing constantly in all things in equal intensity; and the
God is more dynamic in that he comes and goes and sparks
change and movement in the state of things.

I see the Goddess and God having a light and dark side. Both
are capable of creation and destruction which I see as essential and positive. Destruction is necessary and ultimately
clears the way for future growth. Similarly, the dark side isn't
always ominous and scary, it's challenging and often there's
more to learn there than in the light.

I do strongly relate to the concept of Gaia, i.e. that planet
Earth is a cohesive living entity and we are a part of it as an
organism, and our consciousness and our physicality are

directly evolved from it (which isn't to say humans won't inhabit other planets one day). The closest experience I have had of seeing the Goddess or God was looking down into the mouth of a volcano I climbed in Vanuatu, seeing the molten lava spitting out and knowing that, as a life form, I originated from something like that. I believe that the Life Force itself is sacred and I relate to it in a reverential way as an infinite and impersonal phenomenon. Everything with Life Force is divine, which is how I relate to Elementals, Nature spirits, etc – they represent ways in which humans can understand and interact with the existence of these elements, plants, flowers, etc, beyond the physical plane.

Below are some of my favourite Goddesses and Gods. It's really up to you to decide which ones you are particularly inspired by and take the time to research why you feel drawn to specific ones – they help you to understand yourself.

Goddesses

The Great Goddess or Great Lady: Maiden/Mother/Crone, reflecting the cycle of life and the seasons, and the waxing/full/waning moon.

❀ Maiden: Generally considered innocent; not ignorant but inexperienced. She is bound to no-one and can be Virgin but does not have to be celibate. She is associated with Spring, it is a time of exploring potentials, being resourceful and open to everything without fear.

❀ Mother: As much as it is often denigrated in patriarchal times, a woman's ability to produce a child is one of the most profound and powerful symbols of femininity. Symbolically the Mother is the provider and carer of Life itself. She is associated with Summer.

❋ Crone: The Wise Old Woman is exalted as the ultimate symbol of power and feminine authority. Having been Maiden and Mother and integrated these, she is now completely devoted to her own Mystery and able to dispense that wisdom to others, as well as assisting in healing of the body and spirit, child-rearing and insight into the world beyond life.

Cerridwen (Celtic): The Triple Goddess and mainly worshipped as the Death Sow (symbolized by a large white or black pig) and represented by the moon. Thought to possess a sacred Cauldron of Wisdom.

Morrigan (Celtic): The Great Queen of Battle and Death, she is often represented by a large black crow and she holds the secrets of life and death.

Morgan Le Fay (Celtic): The Great Witch and strongest female force in Arthurian mythology and (perhaps not entirely coincidentally) depicted as one of the major 'baddies' in most versions of the story.

Brigit (Celtic): Goddess of Fire, Hearth, Virginity and Fertility, the Sabbat of Candlemas (Imbolc) is held in her honour.

Diana/Artemis (Roman/Greek): Goddess of the Hunt and the Moon. She is the self-reliant Maiden, needing no other, and favoured by feminist Wiccans as their ultimate role model.

Persephone (Greek): Demeter's daughter and Queen of the Underworld. She lives with Hades in the Winter as the Earth sleeps and waits her return in Spring when everything blossoms with joy.

Demeter (Greek): Earth Goddess who presides over grains and harvests, she is Persephone's mother.

Rhea (Greek): Queen of the Universe and mother of Zeus.

Selene (Greek): Goddess of the Moon.

Aphrodite/Venus (Greek/Roman): Goddess of Love and Fertility.

Hestia (Greek): Goddess of the Home and Hearth, a Fire Goddess.

Hecate (Greek): The ultimate Crone, Goddess of Magick and Patroness of Witchcraft.

Medusa (Greek): Serpent Goddess. Prior to being deified by the Greeks Medusa was known and sacred to the Amazons of Libya. She represents the wisdom that comes with staring Death in the face.

Lilith (Hebrew): Wife of Adam and original inhabitor of Eden. She cursed Adam and went to live by the Red Sea, where she gave birth to 100 children a day. Her myth demonstrates her to be the Great Mother and keeper of the Secrets of Femininity – she is feared by Christians and was erased from the Bible but she is a source of inspiration to Witches.

Kali (Hindu): The Triple Goddess of creation, preservation and destruction, she is most often related to as the Destroyer. She is keeper of the blessings of Life and Death, birth-giver and killer all at once. She is fantastic to invoke when you want to clear out the dross of your life (and one of my favourite Goddess images).

Ishtar (Babylonian): The Great Goddess. All acts of love and voluptuous passion are sacred to her.

Maat (Egyptian): Goddess of Law and Justice – after death she weighs souls in her scales and decides whether they go to Heaven or Hell.

Isis: (Egyptian) Great Goddess and Mother of All – her dark aspect is Nephthys. She is the mother of Horus from her union with Osiris.

Sekhmet (Egyptian): Lioness Goddess, her name means 'powerful' and she will protect, guard and bring you success in home life as well as career.

G o d s

The Great God/Lord: The Great God/Lord unifies everything as he is the Son/Consort/Lover of the Goddess. Witches and Pagans mostly relate to him as the Horned God, ruler of the Forests and Animals – he is the link between all living things as they manifest in the physical world and the glue that binds the Goddess/Lady's creations. He provides by hunting and balances the life/death interaction of all life forms.

Lugh (Celtic): Sun God and God of the Arts, his festival is Lammas (Lughnasadh) – the harvest.

Cu Chulainn (Celtic): The Dying God – one that has lived as son, lover and father of the Goddess. He had a dramatic death, being bound to a post so he could keep on fighting when utterly knackered (like Odin and Christ, another God sacrificed on a tree) and so also has an aspect as a warrior God.

Merlyn (Celtic): The Great Magician, Prophet and Enchanter, Merlyn is friend and consort of Morgan Le Fay.

Cernunnos (Celtic): The Horned God – one of the oldest representations of God form. Since prehistoric times there have been images of men wearing animal horns to embody godliness. Cernunnos is Lord of the Untamed, the Primal Forces and Ruler of Animals and Forests.

Bacchus/Dionysus (Roman/Greek): God of Life and Fertility. He is honoured by feasting on food, wine and physical pleasure. His Greek form, as Dionysus, is seriously potent, being *the* God of divine intoxication and immortality. Bacchus could be seen as a kind of Dean Martin, but Dionysus rocks as a kind of Jim Morrison!

Hades (Greek): Lord of the Underworld who rules alongside Hecate (not in a consort role though). He abducted (but I prefer to think invited) Persephone to live with him in Winter.

Mercury/Hermes (Roman/Greek): The winged Messenger God, he is the guide to the Underworld and represents intelligence, magick, medicine, travel and communication.

Pan (Greek): The hoofed and horned God of the Forest and Earth. Highly sexed (hence the term 'horny'!) and honours fertility.

Jupiter/Zeus (Roman/Greek): Father of the Sky, he controls lightning and thunder and is also known as the Rain God.

71

Neptune/Poseidon (Roman/Greek): God of the Sea, Neptune/Poseidon can be invoked to ask for safe journey, and to calm disputes and arguments in relationships.

Ra (Egyptian): God of the Sun and Day, who brings harmony, peace and joy, whilst removing blockages and obstacles.

Osiris (Egyptian): Great God and Isis's partner, father of Horus. He sacrificed himself so that life could regenerate.

Horus (Egyptian): Child of Light and God of Battle. He seeks to avenge his father's death.

Set (Egyptian): God of Night and the Seeker of Knowledge beyond what is immediately apparent.

Troth (Egyptian): God of Medicine, science and higher studies. Excellent to contact if you need help with studies or you need to retain knowledge quickly.

Elementals, Angels and Mythical Animals

Elementals

Witches recognize four basic elements – Air, Earth, Fire and Water – and consider them essential in the working of magick, since balancing these elements harmonizes us with nature and our place on this planet. The four elements permeate all: the Four Quarters of our Sacred Circle; the four groupings of astrological signs and our ritual tools – the chalice (water); athame (air); pentacle (earth); wand (fire), as well as the four groups of the Minor Arcana of the Tarot – Cups (water), Pentacles (earth), Swords (air), Wands (fire).

The way the Elementals appear to you usually depends on your own proclivities and magickal tastes, and I relate to them in much the same way as Gods and Goddesses – that is, they are a way a human can relate to a form that is other than itself.

The four elements also have corresponding animal presences that can be utilized in magickal work.

Air: Bird. Seen as intermediaries between Earth and the Heavens, birds carry dreams to the planes where they come true and are believed to understand the mysteries of life and death as they can travel between both realms.

Earth: Cow. The domestication of cattle allowed humans to till the soil and plant crops, stay in one place and build settlements. The cow represents the application of physical work and manifestation on the earth plane – it is a symbol of physical nourishment and sustenance.

Fire: Cat. Famed as the symbol of the Egyptian Goddess, Bast – Goddess of the Sun. Revered as magickal animals and in many ways the ultimate Witch companion, cats are fiercely independent and yet love being with humans. Their nature is assertive and self-reliant and they, therefore, inspire effective action.

Water: Serpent/Snake. Symbolizes life, death and rebirth and is an ancient symbol of Universal Wisdom. It is one of the most recognized religious symbols in the world. The symbol of infinity is the snake looped with its tail in its mouth.

73

Angels

Angels are generally Judeo/Christian forces but I like recognizing and acknowledging them as they represent the noble qualities of those religions. They can be called on to represent and guard the Quarters when casting Circle.

Raphael: Angel of Air who frees trapped energy.

Uriel: Angel of Earth who grounds and secures all.

Michael: Angel of Fire who wields a mighty sword and encourages swift action.

Gabriel: Angel of Water who nurtures emotional harmony.

Mythical Animals

Mythical animals are usually created by combining the attributes of different animals into one creature and as such their power and magickal reputation is enhanced.

Dragon: One of my favourites! I have one tattooed on my left arm. Dragons are seen to embody the four elements: Air, with its wings; Earth, with its serpent body; Fire, with its fire-breathing lungs; and Water, with its ability to swim and breathe underwater. Dragons in various forms appear in all cultures' mythologies and have been feared and worshipped – the image of a Dragon guarding hordes of precious stones and treasures is a symbol of great wisdom.

Unicorn: A favourite of the New Agers, unicorns are seen as benevolent creatures. With their long, phallic horns they are a symbol of male virility. The horn also represents spiritual enlightenment and purity. Unicorns are sometimes represented with wings and linked to the mythical stallion, Pegasus, who is seen as manifestation of the artistic and divinely-inspired nature of humans. He is considered a Lunar animal, white and moving across the sky (the constellation of Pegasus), and when he stamps his hoofs on the earth fountains of water appear, so he also embodies the emotional element of water.

Phoenix: The myth of this amazing bird originated in Arabia. It would live for hundreds of years and then smear its wings with myrrh and dive into fire, only to rise from the ashes rejuvenated and empowered. It is an inspiring symbol of survival and the cycles of life, death and rebirth.

75

Witchy Tip

One of the best tips I can give for spellcasting is to keep your mouth shut! When a spell is done it is really important not to talk about it to anyone and also not to go over and over it in your own head. Just do the spell and forget about it – let the magick do its thing. The old proverb, 'A watched pot never boils' also applies here: the magick will manifest much faster if it is left alone. Only when your spell has come to fruition is it fine to talk about it with kindred folk if you so desire. Also, avoid worrying about whether a spell is working or not – it's like letting a seed you planted grow by itself, rather than digging it up every day or two to see how it's going.

IS IT A BIRD? IS IT A SNAKE? NO, IT'S MY FAMILIAR!

MAGICKAL ANIMAL PARTNERS

*One of the most enduring (and endearing) images in magickal
lore is the Witch in the company of their familiar: their
animal magickal partner, whether it be a cat, a dog,
a crow, frog, toad or, in my case, a snake.*

Animals can bring something to ritual that can be lacking in the Witch alone, a different perspective, a different way of experiencing the energies conjured.

Unfortunately, during times of anti-Witchcraft hysteria there were probably a lot of ordinary women hanged or burnt at the stake as Witches simply because they enjoyed the company of cats, not because they worked magick with them. During the Burning Times there were dozens of bizarre stories conjured up by sexually repressed clergymen such as Witches having an extra nipple or 'teat' that they used to suckle their familiars; or that they fed them milk from their breasts as a reward for evil work done. Familiars were also supposedly fed blood by their Witch owners to encourage the demons and imps that 'inhabited' these animals to do naughty things. It sounds almost funny but it was no joke at the time.

Animals as symbols are firmly entrenched in occult philosophy. The signs of the zodiac are represented by animals, and the qualities of these animals are attributed to human experience; for example, a person born under the sun sign of Cancer is represented by the Crab, and a common description of Cancerians is that they hide their soft, vulnerable nature under a hard exterior like the crab and its shell. Animals are also very closely connected to the elemental energies of Earth, Air, Fire and Water and can help strengthen these in magickal work.

In ritual an animal can be also be used to facilitate the forging of links to supernatural forces. Cats in particular are thought to be able to detect the presence of ghosts and spirits and it is their recognition of these entities that can help them manifest more discernibly for the Witch in ritual or spellcasting.

Part of the correlation between Witches and their familiars can be traced back to early primitive myths which still endure

My Third Nipple

OK, there were some rumours perpetrated in the Dark Ages that Witches, i.e. strong-willed, powerful and slightly scary females, were so perverted as to have a third nipple. Two wasn't enough for the fantasizing and self-flagellating clergymen! I actually do – and a few other Witches I know do as well. Occasionally magazines like *Cosmopolitan* run a story about the interesting 'deformity' of a third nipple, usually for freak value, but there is something empowering about women having three nips. Mine isn't pink and fleshy, it's a large, dark mole that sits under my right breast and in the last five years it has reshaped itself clearly to resemble a nipple (funnily enough as my Witchy powers have started to peak).

in many societies to this day. Certain South American Witchdoctors, for example, are thought to have jaguar familiars and are able to transform themselves into the big cats as well. When I travelled in the Pacific island of Vanuatu there were stories of powerful Witchdoctors from the island of Ambrym who could turn themselves into sharks and swim to other islands. As part of being a Witch involves being connected to and able to commune with nature, it makes sense that a kinship with animals would be part of magickal practice and that a Witch would find it empowering to explore elements of animal consciousness in ritual. This can be done by mimicking animal movements and sounds, by the Witch decorating themselves to resemble an animal, and by meditations. All these methods can help to isolate and absorb animal magickal qualities.

My decision to have a snake as my familiar took some time to come to fruition. Throughout my late teen and adult years I have been drawn towards animals that, for one reason or another, as a child, I was encouraged to fear. Hence my attraction to sharks, which I will search out to dive with at any opportunity (my first diving experience prompted me to have a shark tattooed on my back), and more recently, my attraction to snakes. I grew up in the Australian bush for the first fourteen years of my life and snake sightings were a regular occurrence. I still remember screaming in terror one morning when I walked to the edge of the cliff that bordered our property and saw a huge, coiled, red-bellied black snake sunning itself on the rocks. I was an impressionable child who enjoyed watching a lot of old 1940s style movies with dramatic, over-the-top acting techniques and so I put both my hands to my temples, threw my head back like a histrionic heroine and screamed a long, keening wail as I ran towards the house. The snake didn't budge until Dad crept up on it with a huge, sharp, shovel in his hand and in one violent movement lopped its head off.

I stood back, watching from a distance and feeling alternately awed at Dad's bravery and incredibly guilty that I had played a role in the ugly death of this creature.

In my early twenties a magazine interviewed me about my interest in Witchcraft and the editor suggested I might like to be photographed with a snake – snakes being symbols of the ancient matriarchal force and very relevant to Witchcraft. I arrived at the shoot as a guy on a motorbike pulled up with a large canvas bag over his shoulder. We walked up the stairs together and I didn't realize what he was there for until after my hair and make-up was done and I was seated in position

79

for the shot. He put his hand inside the bag and pulled out a four-foot long carpet python and casually plopped it over my shoulder.

This was my first encounter handling a snake and I was struck by how smooth and silky its body was – it wasn't slimy at all. I loved the way its body undulated over mine, I felt like I was getting a massage as it eased its way across the back of my neck. **After a little while our movements became quite synchronous and I felt I was dancing with it in some ancient, primal way** as I extended my arms for it to coil around.

The shoot ended a success with me wanting to handle the snake longer but I had an important appointment to go to. All day I couldn't get the experience out of my mind.

The next time I handled a snake wasn't for another three years or so. When I decided to do a photo-shoot for *Playboy*, I seized the opportunity to work with a snake again. In conceptualizing the shoot I wanted to celebrate the life of a well-known Australian cult figure, Rosaleen Norton, the 'Witch of Kings Cross'. Part of her magickal practice was to explore the ancient teachings of tantric sex and work towards releasing the serpentine energy of 'kundalini'. This potential lies coiled at the base of the spine to be released in orgasmic and enlightening pulses during tantric ritual work. I wanted to be photographed with a large snake wrapped around me to symbolize the release of that power.

Eventually I realized my dream and was lying skyclad on the grass with a six foot long python coiled around my ankle with its body resting between my legs, up my stomach and its head sitting between my breasts, over my heart. The camera was clicking away, but I was in another world – I felt dreamy as the slow heavy snort of the snake's breath flowed up to my face every fifteen seconds or so. I felt so calm and earthed, oblivious to the obvious spectacle of me lying naked with a snake and television cameras filming and the *Playboy* photographer capturing the moment. The snorts of breath from the snake were like dragon fire from its large head and reminded me of all the mythological dragons I have fantasized about and what they represent to me: the ability to merge with the elements – to fly, to swim, to burrow under the ground, to breathe fire, to inspire and create, to terrify and destroy.

A week after arriving home from the shoot I applied for a licence to own a wild animal and I visited a large aquarium shop recommended to me for their selection of reptiles. When I arrived I immediately got excited about a six-foot long, dynamically patterned carpet python, but eventually it was to a smaller and less colourful snake to which I was ultimately drawn. The three-foot long, brownish spotted python with the tiny head slid happily up my arm as the pet shop owner placed her there. He told me that she was about two years old and had come from an owner in Cairns in the tropical Northern Australia.

That night I went to sleep and had a strange dream. The little brown snake was coiled up on her log and I could hear a voice in my head saying, 'I'm waiting here for you, my name is Lulu.' When I woke I couldn't get the name Lulu out of my head. Now, I don't know anyone named Lulu, nor have I ever used the name in any of my writing, but it stuck and later that day I went back to the aquarium and put a deposit on Lulu pending the approval of my licence application. I handled her again and she seemed a little jumpy, so I held her close to my heart and tried to exert a calming influence over her – I let all my breath out and tried to emanate a deep, heavy energy from

81

my heart chakra. Lulu immediately stilled and lay coiled in my two hands. We stayed together like this for about five minutes.

Two weeks later she was home with me and she has been my constant companion since then – in fact she's sitting on my lap as I write this! She's sweet and elegant and a sight to behold when she lashes out at the mice I feed her before constricting them and dislodging her jaw to unbelievable proportions to swallow them whole. She has grown quite a lot and is now easily four foot long, healthy and sheds her skin every couple of months or so. I have kept all her skins, though I have given parts away to Witchy friends to use in spells or as fertility and good luck charms.

In ritual, Lulu's presence helps me to centre and focus my mind and I never find her distracting. Some animals can be a distraction and it's worth noting that untrained animals will often barge into a Circle during ritual and drain or disturb the power. Sometimes if you are meditating in Circle and go very still or 'trancelike', an animal can become confused, and attempt to 'bring you back' by jumping on you or licking you.

I recently welcomed another snake into my life – Sebastian. He is an eight foot long coastal carpet python from the North coast of Australia. The difference between Sebastian and Lulu is that Sebastian is definitely a playmate. I tried sharing a ritual with him and he just knocked everything over and slid out of the Circle as quickly as he could! Maybe I'll try training him further down the track but for now Sebastian and I enjoy sitting out on my balcony together while I have my morning coffee and he likes curling up under the blankets at the foot of my bed (Lulu is much happier in her basket!)

Training animals to work with you in ritual requires differ-ent approaches for different creatures. For example, a dog needs to be generally well-trained and behaved as they exude vibrant energy which can be marvellous for building power but it is also unfocused. Cats, snakes and birds are generally calmer and more psychic. My biological mother, Erika, is a bird charmer and can easily encourage wild magpies to eat out of her hand. It's hilarious to watch – sometimes a family of them will follow her from the park into her shop after she's finished her lunch! She has a very soothing manner, but also very 'chirpy', and I think the birds relate to this. My friend Liam Cyfrin told me of a little cat who used to love slipping into Circle while a wordless chant was going on, whereupon he'd settle down and purr along loudly to be part of the team. The cat also impressed the Coven one night when, as Liam was setting up the altar, he invited everyone to put any of their special, magickal objects on the altar. When people came back with athames, crystals and whatever else, they found a certain cat had deposited his stuffed catnip mouse at the foot of the altar!

When training your familiar it's important to be calm and patient, but friendly and spontaneous. Be prepared for silly mistakes, like when your dog gets over-excited and knocks over the bowl of herbs, or when your cat gets spooked and leaps onto the altar knocking everything over. However, also be prepared for your animal to teach you – keep your mind open. Also it's worth noting that, just because you are a Witch and you have a pet, it doesn't automatically mean that pet has to be a familiar. Some people take to magick and some don't, and animals are exactly the same.

But if your particular companion has all the magickal potential of an old candy wrapper, it doesn't mean you should love it any the less!

> ### Witchy Tip for Helping Communication
>
> One thing I like to do with Lulu is to breathe her breath. She puts her head just under my nose and we breathe together; she in little snorts that tickle my upper lip, and mine in a smooth steady stream that feels nice and warm to her. I think this is a really intimate way of bonding with your familar's life force and vice versa.

Basic Procedure for Training a Familiar

If you don't already have an animal that you feel could be your familiar it is best to wait until one comes to you rather than going out searching. I knew Lulu was my familiar when I dreamt about her. Let your intuition guide you to your magickal animal partner.

Once you are ready to train your familiar, mutual meditation is very good for starters. This is where you attempt to fuse your energy emanations so that you can not only influence your familiar but they can influence you. Physical proximity is important as they are close to the physical elemental energies and these can bond you both. So hold your familiar in your lap or hands, breathe deeply and, if necessary, stroke your animal in a calming way and concentrate on sending serene energy through your hands.

Now, still your mind and focus on the random images that come into your head, especially on any that seem to relate to shared experiences that you are having with your familiar. For example, when I do this with Lulu I often see dense darkness, I have a sense of undulating time and I get prickles across the back of my head. I have felt a sense of time eating and regurgitating itself, over and over in infinite repetition – life, death, rebirth, the afterlife – all collapsing inward and exploding outward.

When your animal is comfortable try burning some herbs or incenses to encourage deeper meditative states. Good combinations are white sage and rosemary or pine needles and lemon rind. Five drops of each oil can be substituted for small handfuls of the dried herbs, dripped over a handful of sandalwood chips. Burn the mixture in a cauldron or on a fireplace. If you can't do this use stick incense, one stick of each burnt at the same time.

How you experience the meditation will be unique. The main thing is to encourage stillness and comfort in your animal as you tap into the magickal spaces between the worlds. If it wants to move around or leave, let it go and try again later. It will eventually get used to the subtle energies that abound in magickal work and its involvement in ritual will become spontaneous and surprise you. For example, a friend's cat has been known to point out Tarot cards when she spreads them out and another's dog always takes the food left for libations to the Goddess outside and buries it rather than eats it.

Somehow, however, no matter how much you persevere, your familiar can still be disturbing in ritual. If this is so, keep your animal out when working magick and enjoy its presence in your life in an everyday way. Remember that every moment in every day is magickal to a Witch and having a familiar to share this with is the icing on the cake!

THIS IS THE PLACE TO BE AND I'M IN IT!

MAGICKAL HOTSPOTS

I grew up in a remote Sydney suburb called Illawong (which is the local Aboriginal name for 'land between two waters'), with the Georges River on one side and the Woronora River on the other.

Our house was surrounded by bushland, and our driveway, which was a one-kilometre dirt track, led up to a badly tarred, narrow road that snaked through the peninsula of land, servicing scattered houses and families and linking us to a small public school, tiny fire station and minuscule church hall.

Nowadays Illawong is a bustling, exclusive suburb, with large homes, wealthy families and a giant shopping centre. The original single building of the public school has expanded to become a six-building compound, and the church hall has been replaced with a modern mini-cathedral. Nearly all the bushland is gone, the suburb having been redivided to maximize the sale of property developments. My parents have moved away and sold the family home; I will never go there again, it's too sad. All that is left of my childhood magickal bush playground and animal companions are memories.

Mum always encouraged us kids 'to go and play outside'. I think she just wanted some peace and quiet to do the housework, but making me find my fun outside in nature and not watching the television all the time the way my friends did was the biggest favour she's done for me. Admittedly though, at the time I often resented her for it.

I would go wandering through the bush, often alone, sometimes with my brother Greg and, later, my sister, Samantha. I felt like an explorer and as I was a huge fan of Enid Blyton novels like *The Magic Faraway Tree* and *The Enchanted Forest* I set out to find the magickal places in the bush where fairies and elves lived. **I would go down to the river really early in the morning trying to catch mermaids sunning themselves in the first rays of dawn light,** I would look on the rocks for strands of their hair that might have fallen from their oyster shell combs. The Georges River had oyster farms all up and

87

down it, and I loved knocking the shells off the rocks, cracking them open and fingering the creamy smooth inner surface.

As I wandered through the bush I let my intuition guide me to the 'magick spots' – caves, rocky overhangs and climbable trees with thick dark canopies to hide in. I was endlessly enthralled as I discovered new special places in the bush. I would peel thick, dark green moss off granity rocks after a heavy rain to make carpet for fairy homes that I would create under bushes, with different pebbles for chairs and tables, and twigs and leaves for beds and walls. I made these homes in the evening and I would hurry back the next morning to find signs of fairies enjoying my efforts. I always found something, whether it was a flower petal or a sign of disturbance – I grew up convinced that I was not alone when I wandered through the bush.

As I grew older and continued to frequent my special spots I found that certain ones were conducive for certain frames of mind. The water hole, which was fed by an underground stream, was where I would sit in reverie for hours in a kind of daze as I watched little water flies trailing patterns through the clear water and the hazy patterns of clouds reflected on the water's surface as they blew across the sky. Here I would think about the events of my (then) short life and daydream about my long future.

I would make wishes and throw different coloured pebbles in the water for each wish. I used my intuition to match a stone to each wish and, after throwing them in the water, I would look around for signs indicating my wish had been heard – a bird flying by would let me know that my wish was travelling to the stars where it would come true, or a leaf falling from a tree was a sign that my wish had been heard by my tall, silent companions whose roots spread deep into the earth and who had the power to draw things up from the dark underground into the light.

I used to think I could control the wind. Often I would stand looking into the sky and say authoritatively, 'Blow, wind, blow! Make my feet and fingers glow!' I would look expectantly at the tree tops to see them move in response to my request and I would wait to hear the loud rustle of leaves as the wind whipped up the branches causing them to churn against each other. My memories are that every time I said my little incantation the wind would indeed arise and when I was ready for it to cease I would say, 'Stop, wind, stop! The time has come for you to stop!' In a childish way I was tapping into my Witchiness. I was convinced I could control the wind and more often than not it seemed that I was right.

There was a cave by the river that I used to climb up a steep rock-face to get into. The last couple of metres would have me suspended on sinewy tree roots clinging to the rocks as I clambered in. There were two small Aboriginal paintings in there and I always felt it was quite magickal. I ended up making a cubby house, clearing out the dirt and leaves inside and finding junk washed up along the river to furnish it. I did a lot of thinking about my life there until some local 'heavies' discovered it. One day I arrived early in the morning to find my decorations trashed, the bush flowers I'd placed there stomped on, cigarette butts and beer bottles everywhere. The paintings were scraped over with 'Shane woz ere'.

After that, I made sure my sacred spaces were more remote. Often I would get lost trying to find my way there and back, so I made little signs – arrows scraped into bark and left at the bottom of trees with a brightly coloured rock to draw my

89

attention to them but not that of trespassers. **The more remote the places, the more I would be visited by blue-tongue lizards, green tree snakes, frogs and other animals.** I always took it as a sign of good luck if they stayed near me as I talked to the nature spirits and fairies and asked them for favours.

As a young child, the natural word was magickal to me and endlessly interesting and exciting, but as puberty kicked in, although I hung around with friends at the beach, I was more interested in checking out boys than bothering to notice the magnificence of the ocean, let alone hear its call. My child-hood wonder had diminished and the only time I wandered through the bush was to meet my girlfriend to smoke ciga-rettes and drink the cooking sherry that we'd pinched from our mum's food pantries.

Later, in my early twenties when my interest in Witchcraft blossomed, I felt my childhood eyes re-open and I again was in awe of the magick in nature around me. I was once more drawn to sacred spaces. One amazing place that I visited was the eerie granite monolith of Hanging Rock in Victoria, immortalized in Joan Lindsay's book, *Picnic at Hanging Rock*, as the place where three schoolgirls disappeared. (I have to

add at this point that I highly recom-mend reading this book and espe-cially the edition with the 'missing' last chapter, *The Secret of Hanging Rock*). The story is a mystery about a group of schoolgirls who are taken on an excursion to the Rock in the year 1900. Four of them climb the rock in the afternoon and disappear. One is found four days later but the other three never return. The writer requested that the final chapter that solves the mystery be withheld until her death. Lady Joan died in 1984 and the missing chapter was published in 1987. I won't tell you what happens (I don't want to ruin it for you!) except to say that Lady Joan was quite obviously an occultist and lateral thinker – the final chapter is truly spell-binding and expounds advanced concepts relating to quantum physics and multi-dimensional worlds.

When I visited Hanging Rock, I was struck by a feeling that I was being watched: every leaf, branch and bush was noting my movements and in the crevices of the looming rocks were glittering dark eyes. I wandered away from my friends hoping, in a way, to be sucked through a vortex into another world that somehow blended with the aura of these ancient stones. Something strange happened while we were up there. At the very top are many standing and lying stones and wandering through them it's quite easy to get lost – you round a corner thinking you are back where you started from and you're not. I had been wandering around for a while, only getting my bearings vaguely from glimpses of the picnic grounds far below, when I rounded a stone and there were my friends Sean and Dave. They said, 'We've been calling out to you for ages. Didn't you hear us?' I said I hadn't and we all commented on how strange it was that we were only a few metres away from each other, albeit with rocks between us, and yet we couldn't hear each other.

For Witches, it's very important to have a strong earth con-nection so locating a safe and magickally potent place for workings is very necessary. Indoor working areas are great but very few Witches can do without the direct connection to places where the Earth's energy flows upward like spring water.

91

A lot of people acknowledge their gardens as sacred spaces where natural magickal energy is concentrated. **Having your own sacred earth space tuned to your magickal needs can enhance your Witchcraft and even act as an outdoor altar space for magickal ritual.** In urban, built-up areas a lot of nature's energy has been diluted or debased so you need to re-establish it.

Creating Your Own Sacred Earth Space

Find a corner of your garden that you feel drawn to and which won't be disturbed by others. It may be bare earth, or already populated with many plants. If you live in an apartment and have a balcony, you can create a sacred earth space using planter boxes and pots. Group them together and have some with plants, and some with just earth, perhaps gathered from an established sacred spot that you have visited; or even beach sand with shells pressed into it. I will address sacred spaces in more detail in the next chapter *Spell Boundaries*)

Press crystals and chips of precious stones into the earth, as this will saturate your plants with pure vibrations and the whole area will resonate with heightened energy.

Have the four elements represented (see page 72) – if there is no water already, have a bowl that you can fill with spring water (or even make an artificial pond), sticks of incense for air and a well-protected candle lantern for fire. If left burning at night the incense and lantern will welcome nature spirits (but be very careful not to cause a fire hazard).

Imbue the area with your personal energy by taking nine

leaves of a plant already growing in the area (or one you have placed there in a pot) and, if you have long hair, take a winding of it from your brush, enough to pass around your hand twice. If your hair is short, gather enough of it to roughly fill the palm of your hand. On the night of either a new or full moon, dig a small hole in the centre of your garden or one of the pots. Thread the leaves together with dark green thread so that they form a garland. Weave your hair into the garland and place this in the hole (if your hair is short, place it into the hole in the centre of the leaves). As you do this say something like: *'Goddess of the Moon, Selene, shine upon this charm I weave. Bind my soul in nature's light so that this earth and I bond tight.'*

Cover the charm with earth and then bow to the moon three times.

You may also like to invite the Horned God, Lord of the Forests, to acknowledge your space. Burn some cedar, pine and patchouli incense and make a garland of vines (perhaps ivy). Place it on your head and sit in a cross-legged position with your eyes closed. Inhale the heady scent deeply and focus on the God's fertile and lusty presence. Intone:

'Great Lord, Cernunnos, the Horned God, acknowledge and bless this space that is bound to me. May it always be fertile and fecund, reflective of your essence. In your presence may a link be forged here from the Earth plane to the Eternal.'

Now, whenever you are physically near your sacred space or even if you just think of it, you should be able to feel an immediate sense of calm and earthing and perhaps an euphoric sensation as your subtle energies align with universal constants of the Life Force.

You might want to dedicate your sacred space to a particular Goddess or God, in which case you could place a statue or some kind of representation there. Check out the section on Goddesses and Gods in the *This Goes With This ...* chapter for ideas. You might like to hang sea shells from branches to represent the Goddess and stand animal bones around to represent the God – be inventive! Alternatively, you might like to dedicate your space to the God/Goddess within you, in which case place a mirror there that will reflect your face when you enter the space and cover the mirror with a black cloth or waterproof casing when you are not there.

If you dedicate the space to an animal totem, like a bird, you could gather some feathers and bind them to a carved stick pressed into the earth and place a birdbath there. The more symbolism and power objects (meaningful to you) incorporated into your space – alongside the plants and other growing things – the more of a magickal place it becomes.

Growing different magickal herbs and plants will enhance a sacred space (some suggested ones and their properties are listed in the *This Goes With This ...* chapter). One thing to remember is to be reverential when taking cuttings of herbs or any other kind of harvesting. Always give thanks to the plant and always leave something in return, whether it is some of the food and wine you may be enjoying, or part of your body and life force – perhaps menstrual blood or semen. You can also offer a blessing (trace a pentagram over the plant with your forefinger, willing health and comfort on it).

Remember, all the magick you will ever need is within you. A Witch's greatest power is her/his ability to unleash that magick and the best way to do this is to be creative, intuitive and uninhibited with your ideas. The above notes are guidelines to creating a sacred space and I encourage you to come up with your own ways of connecting with your special spot of nature.

✦ ✦ ✦

Out of the Darkness ... Comes Light

Witchcraft isn't something we use just to make life easy. It can be difficult to learn the craft and many Initiates go though a tough time in the process of self-discovery. It's not a case of learn a few spells and everything will be hunky-dory (or hocus-pocus!). Magick helps us deal with our problems, to help ourselves and others, not bury our heads in the sand or obliterate life's challenges. Magick makes us stronger, and to do this we need to address our own personal Nemesis, not take the express life to Cloud Nine.

Lots of spells actually seem to make things worse at first because if there's no way around an obstacle and your spell is to take you to whatever's beyond, its first effect will be to confront you with the challenge. Wiccan adept Ly Warren Clarke points out that initiation will usually throw a stack of new challenges at you rather than just the reward itself.

So many Witches I know seem to go through very hard personal trials, especially when first stepping onto the path of the Craft. Warren Clarke speaks about what happens during the period in which she initiates other Witches:

Initiation is a journey and a process ... There is an external power or a power other than the limitation of self that makes itself known to an Initiate and it usually gives three years of hell! It's like the

95

*dance of Persephone with Lord Hades in the Underworld – it's
tough! The Initiates go through the really tough times, exploring
and confronting their deepest fears and desires. Talk about waking
up to yourself! The ones that see it through ... who understand that
for light to exist there has to be dark. They're the ones I can point
my sword at and say, 'I hand this to you.'*

I went through a very traumatic time several years ago when
my band, Def FX, broke up. The band was everything I lived
for – something I had helped give birth to and nurture – and
when the co-founder rang me and said, 'I don't want to do it
anymore' it was like my child had been murdered, the sense of
loss was so great. I was left with virtually nothing to show for
all those years: no income, no solo deal was offered to me. I
felt victimized. I had made many personal sacrifices for the
band, accepting the lot of a struggling rock star who had
enough success to be popular, but not enough to be comfortably off, and especially not able to put anything away for a
rainy day. So the band ended and I was on the dole queue a
month later – it was very humiliating. I felt stripped bare emotionally but, true to the Craft, I was aware that there was
strength in that state, not just vulnerability. I might have felt
like an unhappy little girl at times after the split but there was
also a Witchy sense of the warrior self giving out strength. And
step-by-step I clawed my way back out of the abyss.

The point of this big sob story is hopefully to inspire
anyone who feels like giving up sometimes, not to. I often get
letters from people saying they wished they were me. They
say, 'You're so beautiful and successful and magickal, you're
so together – I wish I was like you.' I suppose that from certain
angles my life could look all-powerful and crystal clean. A part

of being a rock performer can be to generally create a larger-than-life character for example, people like David Bowie and Marilyn Manson. I certainly embraced a bit of role playing in my years in Def FX and the public magickal persona is sometimes something like that, too. This might sound a bit obvious but to some impressionable youngsters I want to say, remember I brush my teeth and go to the loo, too! I know in some ways I have become a bright, shiny role model to lots of young Witches, but the most important thing I can say in regards to all that is remember that your true guide is yourself. Discover the alternative versions of yourself deep inside and let them be your role models, not someone you've seen on telly, at a rock concert, or whose books you've read – like me.

For what it's worth, I'm often plagued by self-doubt and fears, but the one redeeming quality I'll grant myself is that I never give up – I refuse to. As a Witch, I try to treat the hard times, not as the enemy, but as a worthy opponent. So the worse things get, the stronger I know I'm capable of being.

I know lots of readers will have had fiercer challenges than me, however an individual's capacity for grief shouldn't be rated according to severity – to a tiny child, the absence of the mother's breast for five minutes might feel as tragic as the loss of a relative in later life.

I'm not saying all this because I want you to think, 'Oh, poor Fiona', or 'But she has it so good, what right does she have to feel down?' My point is we're all human and everyone hurts (as REM also said!). Witchcraft helps – often a lot, but it demands you acknowledge the dark. Witchcraft encourages you to accept total responsibility for your life: you can't hide from yourself, you can't cop out. You have to go into the abyss willingly and know that you'll be all the more enriched as a human

97

when you emerge. **The myths, legends, stories, rituals and spellcasting of Witchcraft have helped me make sense of my depression and my fears, as well as my ecstasy and my goals.** I don't believe that I'm paying off bad karma or atoning for any sins when I have a hard time. I'm just learning, and I really think what doesn't kill you makes you stronger and ultimately happier.

This happened to me recently when the apartment I was renting unexpectedly came up for sale and I decided I wanted to buy it. I went about madly organizing meetings with bank managers and scrounging up every spare dollar I had – it was hard work. I did a spell to help me 'buy my perfect home' – which I thought was my apartment. Rather than my spell smoothing out the proceedings, within a week I suddenly lost two major sources of income – this was incredibly traumatic and obviously made it impossible for me to continue with my plan for purchasing the apartment. However, one week later an offer to work overseas came through and boy was I glad I wasn't shackled to a hefty home-buying commitment! I know my spell is working and my perfect home is out there – maybe it's a villa in Tuscany instead of a little apartment in Melbourne!

One of the major aspects of the Craft that's not often discussed is that magick is something to share with each other. Lots of books on the Craft are more or less self-help guides: spells to make you feel happy, wealthy, loved, powerful and so on. It is an inherent part of Wicca that each Witch is ultimately responsible for fixing up all her or his problems – but helping each other *is* allowed! Fact: spells for healing, love and prosperity often work best if we do them on someone else's behalf. When we do them for ourselves we can hit all sorts of neuroses regarding whether we feel worthy of all these good things, but if we're doing them for a friend or relative whom we love very much – Kapow! – that resistance just isn't there. We work best when we're helping each other along, not when we're looking out for numero uno.

We do need to direct some of our magic inwards to keep us going. A Red Cross nurse in a starving country isn't going to be much help if she gives all her food to hungry kids and starves herself to the point where she can no longer work. But while the Craft is sometimes a solitary path, synergy works and nothing gets us out of our own little quagmires better than directing our energy to those in equal or greater need. And, actually, this is the most traditional aspect of Witchcraft imaginable.

We can't cure all the world's evils from our little sacred space but we should certainly give our energy freely to those around us when we see them struggling under the weight of their problems. The adage 'Act locally, think globally' applies perfectly when it comes to magick!

Remember too that even when working solitary magick, you don't have to be alone. You don't have to be able to conjure up the power to prevail against all odds purely from your own soul. However we conceptualize the Old Magick – as the Goddess and the God, elemental energy or, an all-pervasive force like the Tao – much of our effectiveness in the Craft can be based on our ability to draw on its aid. Sometimes when we're run down it can help a lot to plug into the mains. The only way we can truly run out of power is if we forget to make that connection.

As you get more and more used to drawing on that energy, you'll probably make the same discovery that Shamans and Mystics have made for thousands of years: the source of the power seems to like us. That's why so many religions fall back on parental images to describe it – it very often reveals itself as something much bigger than us which wants to nurture us and bring out the best in us. So, there you go, one of the inner secrets of Witchcraft isn't all that much different from one central to nearly all religions: the Old Magick never gives us more to carry than we can manage *with its help.*

So, however rough your own life gets, hold on to the knowledge that you're always able to stretch your wings and rise like a phoenix from the flames, letting your personal hang-ups blow away like ashes as you direct your energies to bigger, more holistic concerns and to being of service to those you love.

SPELL BOUNDARIES

CASTING CIRCLES AND MAKING YOUR OWN SACRED SPACE

Before you can do any magickal work – ritual, healing, spellcasting – you need first to create a sacred space. To do this Witches cast a Circle between the worlds in which to formally worship our deities and conduct magickal workings. Circle casting is one of the most fundamental rituals a new Witch can learn as a sacred Circle plays a major role in containing and intensifying magickal energies, as well as keeping out potential unwanted 'nasties' like hostile psychic entities and negative energies (unless you invite them in of course!).

As a Catholic I would go to church, but as a Witch I carry my church in my heart. Using the powers of visualization and perhaps the appropriate tools and incantations, Witches can build a church anywhere – in a living room, on a beach, even in a car park!

Following is a step-by-step process for making your own sacred space, including self-preparation, casting Circle, raising power and closing Circle.

General Preparation

Make sure you've got all the goodies – candles, incenses, herbs, oils, body bits (!), crystals, or whatever you need for your ritual or spell. You don't want to have to wander in and out of your sacred space, disturbing your concentration because you've forgotten something. Also, make sure the phone's off the hook, or that the answering machine's volume is way down, and that no-one's going to interrupt you. If you choose to work out doors, suss out a good quiet place so you won't have hikers walking by while you're working – especially if you work skyclad (naked)! You may want to write out a basic plan for your ritual, in note form that you can refer to as you go along. If you are inside and the room is dusty give it a sweep or a vacuum and the altar top a wipe down. If you're outside you might need to set up an altar on a tree stump or flat rock. If you don't have a lot of time and want to do a quick ritual don't worry too much about housework, just make sure that the space feels like somewhere you can do a ritual.

On your altar you will have your athame, pentacle, incense, candle, Goddess and God symbols, bowl of water and bowl of salt, your chalice with some wine (or juice, etc) and a plate of biscuits or the like. Add any other special items, like, perhaps, your wand and Tarot cards, depending on what you are planning to do. (For a more detailed description of an altar's contents, please refer to the chapter *Alter-ed States*.) If I am setting up an altar outside of my bedroom (where my altar is in the East), I usually position my altar in roughly the middle of the Circle; some Witches prefer to set it in the dark of the North Quarter, others in the light of the South it's your choice.

Self-Preparation

You might want to have a purification bath, so add two cups of rosemary tea infusion to the bath water with half a handful of sea salt. If a shower is all you have, rub yourself down with a muslin sachet of mixed herbs (rosemary and lavender are

103

Deosil/Widdershins

The big confusing issue! It really is *so simple*! Deosil means 'with the sun', which in the Northern Hemisphere is clockwise (in the Southern Hemisphere it's anti-clockwise). Watch the sun move across the sky and it is very clear. In the Northern Hemisphere, as the sun travels from East to West, it veers to the South so its passage through the sky goes East-South-West, which describes a clockwise arc. The reverse applies in the Southern Hemisphere. Widdershins means 'against the sun' or, in the Northern Hemisphere, anti-clockwise, (in the Southern Hemisphere it is clockwise).

good). If you don't have time for a bath, wash your hands in the sink, adding a few drops of rosemary oil and a clear quartz crystal to the water to absorb negativity. Don't rule out a dip in the ocean or a river as a good way to cleanse yourself. Decide whether you want to be skyclad or robed and remove your jewellery, except for any special Witchy items. It is usually considered appropriate not to wear any make-up and to be as pure as possible. I think, however, that some dramatic make-up or outfit can enhance a magickal mood, so make your own mind up about it. I have often cast Circle at public gatherings looking more like a rock star than a Witch and the magick is still just as powerful.

Cleansing the Area

Before casting Circle it's good to prepare the space by presenting the elements. First light the candles and incense, then purify the water by dipping in the blade of your athame and saying, *'I cast out from you, Water, all that is impure so that you may aid me in my rite.'* Now consecrate the salt by tracing a pentagram in it with the tip of your athame saying, *'Blessed are you, Crystal of the sea, may you aid me in my rite.'* Now, add three big pinches of salt into the water and stir with your athame, deosil (with the sun, i.e. in the Northern Hemisphere clockwise). Carry the bowl around the planned perimeter of the Circle, sprinkling the salt/water with your fingers. When you have done that, carry the incense around the edge, fanning the smoke outwards as you go and then carry the candle around. You have now made the four elements known and the space cleansed. You are ready to cast Circle.

The Four Quarters

The qualities of the Four Quarters and the elements attributed to them are different in the Northern Hemisphere and Southern Hemisphere; although some Witches down under reverse the Sabbats, Deosil and Widdershins from the Northern way still keep the Northern Quarters. I take a practical approach and use my instincts.

NORTH

In the Northern Hemisphere, the North Quarter is the element of Earth. That is because we look North to the contemplative Pole, away from the hottest part of the planet. In the Southern Hemisphere, they look to the darkness of the South Pole.

SOUTH

In the Northern Hemisphere, the South Quarter is the element of Fire. That is because we are looking towards the light of the Equator away from the dark cold of the North Pole. In the Southern Hemisphere, they look North to the equator.

EAST

Now this will probably confuse you! I keep this Quarter the same whether I'm in the Northern or Southern Hemisphere. East is the Quarter of Air. That is because the Sun rises there, and it is a place of new beginnings and suits the qualities of Air. However, some Witches attribute water to either West or East depending on which direction is closer to the nearest large body of water.

WEST
Same again, I treat this Quarter as the same whether I'm in the Northern or Southern Hemisphere. West is the Quarter of Water and the fact that the Sun sets in the West indicates to me the flowing nature of cycles of completion and as such suits the qualities of Water.

When it comes to determining which elements correspond with which directions the most important thing to remember is that you are focusing on being aware. Aware of your connection with the earth and with all that surrounds you. You can draw on the energies of the elements no matter where you are. For example, if you were doing a ritual on a tropical island smack bang in the middle of the equator it would be silly to have a dilemma over whether to attribute the North or South with Fire or Earth. You need to understand what the qualities of the elements are and why they can correspond to the points of a compass, but you don't need to be hung up on it.

Casting Circle

As you get more experienced, you can embellish this ritual to your requirements, perhaps by more elaborate invocations of the Quarters. I have kept this version simple because you don't want to have to keep referring to a book to remember everything. Casting Circle properly requires a lot of concentration and good powers of visualization, so keep it simple at first until you are experienced. Remember, you are aiming to create a space that exists between the worlds, a place in which to do magick and worship, and a place to contain and intensify magickal vibrations and keep out unwanted ones.

Hold your athame in your outstretched right hand and begin to walk slowly around the circumference, deosil (clockwise). As you do this, say: *'I conjure you, Circle, so that you may be a sacred boundary between the realm of the everyday and eternal planes.'*

As you do this see light streaming from your athame blade, forming a large sphere. Perhaps visualize it as something like the 'force fields' you get in old science fiction films – a layer of energy around the Circle area, much like there are layers of atmosphere around the planet. How thick the layers are, i.e. how far the field extends, depends on how forcefully you cast Circle around you, above you and under your feet. When you get back to the start say: *'The Circle is bound and blessed, so mote it be.'*

Now you need to call in the Guardians of the Quarters (for more information, also check out the section on Elementals in the chapter, *'This Goes With This ...'*). The Guardians work to guard the Circle and witness any rites or magick, enhancing and balancing the proceedings and assisting in the manifestation of magickal goals.

First, stand facing South and, holding your athame high in the air, trace the Fire invoking pentagram and say firmly: *'Come! Guardians of the South, home of Fire and Salamander. I bid you to guard this Circle set outside of time and give your aid to my rite.'*

See the Guardians manifest through the portal of the pentagram that you have cut into the fabric between the worlds. I sometimes see the lizard-like shapes of salamanders, and other times a fiery red glow from which slanting yellow eyes seem to float.

Now stand facing the West and trace the invoking pentagram for Water. Say: *'Come! Guardians of the West, home of Water and Undine. I bid you to guard this Circle set outside of time and give your aid to my rite.'*

See shimmering mermaid forms manifest.

To the North trace the invoking pentagram for Earth and say: *'Come! Guardians of the North, home of Earth and Gnome. I bid you to guard this Circle set outside of time and give your aid to my rite.'*

See the figures of the little people manifest if you like; however, I usually see indeterminate dark shapes with wet, glistening eyes.

Finally, to the East, trace the invoking pentagram for Air and say: *'Come! Guardians of the East, home of Air and Sylph. I bid you to guard this Circle set outside of time and give your aid to my rite.'*

See the floating androgynous fairy-like figures of the Sylphs appear.

A point I'd like to make here is that using only the Earth pentagram for invoking or banishing each Quarter works fine. Some traditions feel it's better to do each different element's pentagram, so in the interests of being thorough I have included them all. Honestly, though, I've never found it to make any difference, so if learning all the elemental pentagrams for invoking/banishing freaks you out just use the Earth ones for each.

★ *Note: some Witches prefer to call in Angelic forces to the Quarters (check the section on Angels in the This Goes With This ... chapter, page 74). This can be done by striking a small bell or gong in each Quarter and saying, for example, to open the South Quarter, 'Michael! Angel of the South, join me in this rite and avail me of your fiery presence!'* ✴

and so on for each Quarter, substituting the appropriate direction, name and element.

With the Guardians in place, it is time to welcome the Goddess and God by standing at the altar, raising both arms and declaring: *'Welcome, Lady and Lord of All (or specific names of deities you wish to invite into Circle)! I bid you to witness and bless my rite, held in the realms of your eternal magick.'*

If you have chosen specific deities, perhaps you could take the time, prior to ritual, to write a special invocation of each, focusing on their qualities and what you would like them to bring to Circle and the role you would like them to play. For example: *'Welcome, Demeter, Great Goddess of the Grain and Harvest. I respectfully ask you to bring to this Circle the bounty of your abundance and fortitude to assist me in my rite.'*

Now the Circle is ready for you to do magickal work – a healing, spellcasting, ritual work, divination or anything else you choose.

Raising Power

A ritual of raising power is the best way to propel a spell along. There are various ways to do this: chanting, humming, or saying a simple mantra over and over of either words or sounds. What you are aiming to do is unleash your inner fire and passion and have it churn around, contained inside your

Circle until it is peaking and bursting at the seams, and then either blast it through a portal that you cut into the Circle to send it where it's required or, depending on the spell, channel it into an object, person, or even your familiar (my familiar is my snake, Lulu).

When I held a workshop on Witchcraft for the 1999 Sydney Women's Festival, I used a simple way of encouraging the hundred or so people attending the workshop to raise power. I passed around about ten pale green candles to the people in the front row and encouraged each as they held the candle to think of something they wanted, or wanted to let go of, in their life. When they had finished, they had to pass the candle on and start humming or doing any other constant chanting sound they chose. Everyone was a bit shy but as more and more people held the candles and the voices grew louder there was a tangible shift of atmosphere in the space.

As I stood on the podium, I started to weave the energy into a spiral, circling my athame above my head with one hand and 'conducting' everyone's efforts with my left. Soon everyone had a candle and the voices had become a roar. The hair was standing up on the back of my neck and arms, and obviously everyone in the room was feeling the same way. My eyes had gone out of focus and everything in the room seemed to look holographic and blurry. I felt the peak of energy approaching and I thrust my athame straight into the sky and screamed 'So mote it be!' The crowd repeated the words as one voice and the spell was done. I closed Circle and everyone clapped. At this point I said to them they were clapping for themselves – not for me – and for the magick they had created.

Another way of raising power is to physically run around in a circle, or spin on the spot (like the whirling Sufis), chanting a mantra; for example, in a healing spell you could say something as simple as *'Heal ____ (name of person)'* over and over. Rhythmic breathing or drumming also work well – you can use anything you want as long as it is repetitive, rhythmic and continued with increasing intensity until you feel a 'shift'.

After you have finished the spell or ritual, it's important to 'earth' any residual energy. After raising power you can feel lightheaded and tingly, 'a bit out there', and this can cause you to feel unsettled long after the Circle is closed if you don't ground it. The simplest way is to place your hands on the ground and visualize any excess streaming away into the Earth.

Cakes and Ale

An important part of a formal ceremony is this salute to the union of the Goddess and God. It celebrates that the fusing of these polarities is the spark of Life, and, despite the imagery, it is not a celebration solely of heterosexual union – it is about unconditional love and the human experience of that, and the sacredness of the body and procreation. Take the chalice (female) of mead, wine or juice and into it plunge the blade of your athame (male) intoning, something like: *'Chalice, you are now that which is Female; and, athame, you are now that which is Male. Conjoined you are equally empowered and the source of Life.'*

Now, place the tip of your athame on the food saying:

Great Mother, bless this food so that all that
partake may know joy and abundance.

As you do this, feel the Goddess energy within you (whether you're female or male) stream through your athame. Once you have done this drink the wine and eat the food, leaving some of both for libations – if you are outside, pour some of the wine onto the ground and crumble some of the biscuits; if indoors, save it and do it after closing Circle, or even offer your libations to a pot plant since all life can benefit from this magickally charged food.

Closing Circle

Thank and bid the Goddess and God farewell by standing at the altar with your arms in the air and saying: *'Gracious Lady and Lord (or specific Deity names), thank you for blessing and assisting my rite. Farewell.'*

Then dismiss the Guardians of the Quarters by cutting the banishing pentagram for South (see diagram on p. 000), saying: 'Thank you, Guardians of the South, for attending and aiding my rite. Farewell.'

See the creatures move away through the portal you have created and move to the East, repeating the process and substituting the appropriate pentagram and direction as you move around the Circle. When this is done, hold your athame out in front of you with both hands and slowly walk widdershins (anti-clockwise) around the perimeter, opening the Circle. See the sphere of light loosen up and dissipate. As you do this say: *'The Circle is open but unbroken'.*

At this point I'd like to emphasize that, although the above lengthy ritual of casting Circle is an important part of a Witch's knowledge and a very rewarding and magickally satisfying procedure, it is by no means always necessary for spell-casting. The last thing you would want to do is avoid a spell or magickal session because you didn't have time to do the 'whole thing properly'. A sacred space can be created just by visualizing with your mind's eye a sphere of bluish-white light around you as you say to yourself, *'This space is safe and blessed.'* For example, you're standing at the kitchen bench mixing up some herbs for a charm you're quickly putting together for a friend who's popping over any minute. Visualize the sacred space and, as you mix the herbs, visualize in your mind's eye the energies of earth, air, fire and water in all their various forms around you and channel that through your hands into the mixture. The sensation will be different to that of the lengthy ritual described above, but it will still be magickal and effective.

Witchcraft is about using your initiative and being resourceful, so learn from traditional ways of going about things but be ready to expand on that too and create the traditions of tomorrow.

ALTAR-ED STATES

SETTING UP YOUR OWN ALTAR

When I was first starting out I found all the new information about how to practise Witchcraft daunting sometimes and I was so eager to do things 'properly' that I would often postpone a ritual because I didn't have some 'important' ingredient. Likewise with my altar which I didn't set up for a long time because I couldn't afford a 'silver chalice', a brass pentacle, God and Goddess statues and other elaborate props that were suggested in various texts and photographs.

I was put off by the fact that I didn't own a compass and so couldn't know exactly which direction was East, West, North or South. I had read that this was essential to determine before setting up an altar and casting Circle. When I finally got a compass I realized that the exact directions lay at very odd angles in my room so I put off setting up an altar again. On and on it went for over a year, me reading books, being so attracted to it all yet never really doing anything concrete because I was afraid of doing something 'wrong'.

Finally I sat down and had a big think about what I really wanted my altar to be and how its presence would affect my life and burgeoning magickal practices – and I realized the most important element in all of this was ME. So, I put down my books and went out, letting my intuition and the general magickal knowledge I had gained guide me to the things I needed. Over the years some new elements have arrived and some older ones have disappeared, so my altar is as much a creative workbench as a sacred place of worship, ritual and spell working.

I have an altar permanently set up in my bedroom. It faces an Easterly direction so that when I sit at it I can look out the window to the sky. Many magickal paths place their altars in the East, relating to the idea that as the sun rises in the East, then East is where all things originate from. However, if the only space you have in your room for an altar faces South-West or something don't let this stop you setting one up there.

Magickal Tools

My altar and tools are very personal and not bought straight out of a new age gift store. The whole purpose of an altar is to

115

act not only as a place of worship but a place to focus, channel, attract and project magickal energies. So, the more pieces you have on it that are unique and relevant to you, the more powerful and profound your workings and meditations are going to be. All the magick you'll ever need is inside you, and your altar and its implements are your tools for accessing and enjoying that magick.

I have accumulated quite a variety of magickal and sentimental things over the years but for someone starting out there are a few appropriate basics. Though it's not essential to have magickal tools, when you know how to use them they really can enhance magickal work. Plus they're fun, often very beautiful and quite dramatic.

Note: you can charge an object with magickal power, but that power is only transitory and will gradually fade unless you keep topping it up.

Because a Witch works with the forces of nature, qualities of a Witch's tools align with the elements Air, Earth, Fire and Water. Here are some basic items for a Witch's altar:

Athame

ALIGNED WITH AIR

(or Fire in some traditions)

An athame is the notorious Witch's dagger. Every time I do a photo shoot for a magazine they ask, 'Can you bring your knife with you?' Traditionally it is a black-handled knife with an approximately twelve-inch double-sided blade. Upon a Witch's initiation, the athame's handle is usually carved with the initiate's Witch name in runes and other meaningful symbols. My athame, however, is a double-bladed dagger with the handle representing the full body of a mermaid cast in brass, with breasts, scales on her fat curling tail, and a wise, benevolent face looking out from thick strands of hair. Her body fits snugly in my hand and I feel my athame is very much an extension of me when I am casting Circle or working in ritual. The athame is probably the one tool every Witch feels called to have and whatever suits your personal taste best will be the right choice. The athame is never used for cutting anything solid, unless you drop it on your foot! It is used to 'cut' through the ether, to create portals and openings; for example, when calling in the Quarters during Circle casting, you 'cut' the appropriate pentagram through which the Guardians of the Quarters can manifest. It is also used as an important channelling and focusing tool when casting Circle and empowering objects, you channel energy through it. In the symbolic enactment of the Great Rite (the union of male and female aspects in honour of the Lifeforce – see the chapter *Spin that Wheel*' for more details), the athame represents the male force.

Pentacle

ALIGNED WITH EARTH

This disc is usually made of clay, brass or other metal, ceramic or wood, and carved with a pentagram and sometimes other symbols. I actually made my pentacle myself. I had been looking

at expensive brass pentacles in esoteric supply stores but another Witch gave me a great hint. She suggested I go to a flower shop and buy one of those unglazed, orange clay flowerpot bases, turn it upside down, draw a pentagram on it in black texta and voila! A perfect pentacle! The pottery also represents the element of earth. I use my pentacle to rest my athame upon and sometimes place objects for blessing upon it. It can be used as a plate for the Cakes and Ale ceremony as well (see page 111). A new tradition has emerged in the last few decades which involves using a spherical stone as a type of pentacle. Possibly this shift in consciousness and symbolism occurred once pictures of the Earth from space became widely available; we know that Earth is a spherical rather than a flat object. (But obviously you couldn't use it as a plate for cakes!)

Cup/Chalice

❋ ALIGNED WITH WATER ❋

Usually a chalice will contain some wine or other liquid for the Cakes and Ale ceremony. In the symbolic enactment of the Great Rite, the chalice represents the female element.

Wand

❋ ALIGNED WITH FIRE ❋
(or Air in some traditions)

The wand is used for conjuring (i.e. attracting spirits and pres-

ences), as well as channelling and focusing energy. Some Witches use a wand to cast Circle and don't actually have an athame. Other Witches use both, seeing the athame in a role of penetrating the ether and the wand as conjuring it. I have a wand and I use it in conjunction with my athame. I use the athame to cast Circle, consecrate objects, as a part of the symbolic Great Rite and to close Circle; and I use the wand in spell casting – to whip up extra energy and send it where I want it to go. For ages I did without a wand and just used my athame for everything, which was totally effective, but I enjoy having both now. My wand is made of ash wood with an amethyst set in the tip, which is good for general magickal work. Specific woods are considered best for certain requirements; for example, willow for use in lunar rituals, oak for solstices and elder for exorcisms. Personally I find my ash wand suitable for all work. The next wand I make will most likely be of eucalyptus, which I will save for use at Sabbat rituals. A lot of magickal supply

stores sell wands, but it is fun to make your own; usually wands are about eighteen inches long and not too thick. You might find a stick on the ground that appeals to you; or if you cut one from a living tree, do it at midnight (preferably on the night of a full moon), after which thank the tree and pour a libation of wine at its roots. Try to cut the stem in one stroke – don't hack at it! Remove all little twigs and leaves and then peel away the bark. Sand the wood until it is smooth and whittle one end to a point (if you are planning to bind a crystal to the tip, flatten the end). Oil the wand well with a mixture of three tablespoons of mineral oil (get it from the chemist) plus five drops each of frankincense oil and rosemary. If you desire, bind a crystal of your choice (check out the *This Goes With This ...* chapter) to the tip with leather or suede (leather shoelaces bought from a shoe repair store work well) or a strip of cloth (e.g., silk) if you don't like the animal factor. You can paint or carve your Witch name in runes along the base plus any other symbols you consider appropriate. To determine your magickal Witch name you can meditate for inspiration or choose a Goddess' or God's name whose qualities you relate to: whatever feels right. When a name comes to you and you get shivers down your spine, you'll know it's the one!

Bowl of Water

❋ ALIGNED WITH WATER ❋

A few pinches of salt added to the bowl of water make it a purifier – plunge the blade of your athame in this before you cast Circle, charging it (and the water) with your energy as you do so; be aware that the athame is an extension of you and pour your energy into it. Get passionate about it. You are not dunking a biscuit into a cup of tea! You can also sprinkle the charged water around the perimeter of the Circle to consecrate it.

Incense

⊛ ALIGNED WITH AIR ⊛

Incense is used to enhance a magick-al atmosphere, clearing excess energy (pass an object through the smoke) and purifying the space. Incense sticks are OK but it's better to blend your own and burn them on a charcoal disc that sits in some sand (or salt) in a heat-proof bowl.

✦ *Note: to light those pesky charcoal blocks, hold them aloft with eyebrow tweezers and pass a flame at the edge until it starts to spark. Keep holding it with the tweezers until the whole thing has sparked up.* ✦

Bowl of Salt

⊛ ALIGNED WITH EARTH ⊛

Pour a little salt in water for purification. You can also sprinkle salt around the edge of the Circle to represent Earth when you are casting.

Candle

⊛ ALIGNED WITH FIRE ⊛

Candles are often used in spells – you can anoint them with certain oils and carve symbols into them. They represent the element of Fire on your altar.

Goddess/God
Symbols or Images

It is appropriate to have representations of the Goddess and God on your altar. I have two candles permanently on my altar in stands which represent the Goddess (Moon base) and God (Sun base). My altar is not all that huge so some meanings and symbolism overlap (Fire is represented here as well). You can have statues representing particular deities, too. I have a gorgeous pewter statue of a naked maiden leaping with her arms outstretched and head thrown back. I bought her a few years ago when my heart (and my body!) were heavy and sad and she seemed to embody some of the joy and abandon that was then missing from my life. Her lithe yet strong limbs and movement bring to my mind the Maiden aspect of the Goddess. Also on my altar are various items from nature that I have collected over the years. For example, I have a couple of small cowrie shells that I found diving (the little creatures that had lived inside them were long gone). Cowrie shells are often thought to resemble female genitalia and so are very appropriate symbols of the Goddess.

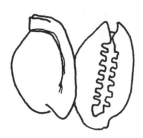

Basically, the above items will get you going. Below are a few extras that will fill in the corners of your altar.

Sword

❋ ALIGNED WITH AIR ❋
(or Fire)

Generally used only in a coven situation (the Coven Sword). It is used for casting Circle in coven work, during Initiations and Rites of Passage, i.e. very formal events.

Boline

Traditionally, a boline is a white-handled knife used for cutting herbs for magickal use only, and for carving symbols in candles, etc. It's seen as the practical working knife that the athame is not. I don't have one of these – they're not essential, though if you're really hung up on keeping all your rituals and spell-castings super-magickally hygienic you may like to have one of these. Sometimes I think if you get too hung up on everything being 'untainted' you forget about the magick, so I'm reasonably fastidious about 'pure' magickal tools and ingredients, but if I end up cutting something with a plain old pair of kitchen scissors it doesn't wreck anything for me. Actually, lots of Witches are not too precious about how they use their tools – I'll go so far as to contradict what I said earlier and note that some 'Kitchen Witch' types are quite happy to use their athames to cut up the veggies. In fact, very earthy Witches would not so much use their athame as a kitchen knife as vice versa! My friend Liam Cyfrin's initiatrix had a traditional athame but had also charged up her Swiss Army Knife for boline and athame duties, while also using it for everyday

123

jobs. After all, magick is meant to permeate every aspect of a Witch's existence!

Cauldron

The ultimate Witchy accessory! Use it for holding water for scrying, initiation rituals and for boiling up potions (you know, eye of newt, bat's blood and all that sort of stuff!). You can also use it to contain fire for exorcisms and Sabbat celebrations; for example, the tradition of jumping over the flaming cauldron (and frying your backside) and for throwing small children into for hexings ... *only kidding*! Seriously, the cauldron is a symbol of infinite wisdom. It is a multi-faceted tool only limited in its uses by your imagination.

Altar Cloth

I have a very old square silk scarf, black and printed with stars and crescent moons. At the moment I'm not using it, I just have a white wooden table because I'm in the mood for simplicity and cleanness. Different coloured altar cloths can be good for different purposes (check out the *This Goes With This ...* chapter) and as they are portable you can happily set up altar on any surface after putting your cloth down.

So, in a nutshell, when setting up your altar (especially for the first time) you'll need your athame, your pentacle, a bowl of water and a bowl of salt, a candle, some incense and something to represent the Goddess and God. Everything else can be gradually incorporated as you go along. Just remember, however, that all the tools and implements I have discussed are props to assist you in tapping into your personal magick and fusing it with forces around you. The power is not in your tools – it is in *you!* Lots of Witches have done some of their best workings on beaches or out in the countryside somewhere, with no ritual tools, no altars, no clothing or jewellery (magickal or otherwise) – just us, a few friends perhaps, and the Universe. Magick comes from within you and the props just help in the process of drawing it out!

Consecrating Your Magickal Tools

New tools need to be consecrated before doing any magickal work. There are a few different methods but my favourite is quite simple and takes place outdoors.

First make an incense mixture from two small handfuls of sandalwood chips, two of dried rosemary and two of thyme, mixed well. Go somewhere where you have access to a body of water, can safely have a small fire and won't be disturbed; for example, the beach, a water hole, riverbank or lake. You need to go there either at midnight under a full moon, or at sunrise, so it needs to be somewhere relatively safe as well. If only your backyard or balcony is appropriate, have a large bowl of either sea water or water you have collected from a river or spring, nine red candles if you can't have a fire and a heat-proof bowl half-filled with sand for burning four charcoal discs and incense (you need a lot of smoke).

Make your fire or light the candles, and spread your tools on a cloth in front of you – you may have your athame, wand, chalice and pentacle. Still your mind and focus on connecting with the presence of the Goddess and God and the sacredness of Nature and Life of which you are an essential part. Think about how you as a Witch work within the realms of this world and beyond, about the role your tools will play in the unleash-

Book of Shadows

A Book of Shadows is a Witch's magickal diary, a spell book and anthology of ritual. Every Witch should have one – it's your own personal record of magickal experiences and accrued knowledge. It doesn't have to be some big, gothic tome with parchment on which you write only with a quill pen and magickal ink (though it can be if you like!). My current BOS is a plastic folder with replaceable sheets of paper. It features polaroids of rituals stuck next to written notes, computer discs with spells on them tucked into front cover pockets, plastic inserts enclosing feathers, twigs and lace from ritual ... there's even purple streamers from when I last saw Madonna perform and I got a seat virtually in the front row! Now *that* was a magickal experience! So don't be afraid to get creative. My girlfriend has recently bought me a beautiful new BOS in the classic Witchy style, with a lock and beautiful recycled paper – I'm going to use that for extra special magickal notes (though they're all pretty special). By the way, don't make a habit of showing your BOS to people. Contain its energy for your needs.

ing of your magickal powers and how they are your weapons against fear and spiritual ignorance.

One at a time pick up each tool, take it to the water's edge and sprinkle water over it three times (or plunge your athame blade into the water) as you say: '*I consecrate you, (name of tool), in the eyes of the Lady and Lord with the sacred element of Water. May you assist me in my magick with harm towards none and for the greatest good of all.*'

Now throw a handful of incense onto the fire (or charcoal discs) and pass each tool through the smoke three times, saying: '*I consecrate you, (name of tool), in the eyes of the Lady and Lord with the sacred elements of Air and Fire. May you assist me in my magick with harm towards none and for the greatest good of all.*'

If you are working with candles have them in a semi-circle around the bowl of incense.

Now lay each tool on the earth (you could stab the blade of your athame into the ground) and pressing your hands into the earth next to them, say: '*I consecrate you, (name of tool), in the eyes of the Lady and Lord with the sacred element of Earth. May you assist me in my magick with harm towards none and for the greatest good of all.*'

If you like you can say a more elaborate, personalized blessing; for example: '*In the eyes of the Lady and Lord and with the pristine element of Water – the blood of my planet – I consecrate you, athame, weapon of Air, in the sacred art of Witchcraft. I charge you with the radiant forces of Light and Dark, Creation and Destruction. Assist me well in my Craft causing harm to none and for the good of all.*'

Substitute the elements:

'... with the dynamic element of Fire – the heart of my planet ...'
'... with the ethereal element of Air – the breath of my planet ...'
'... with the sturdy element of Earth – the body of my planet ...'

It's a good idea to do a ritual straight away with the consecrated items. Cast Circle and perhaps do a spell for general empowerment (check out the *Having Your Wicca'd Way!* chapter).

SEVEN DAYS TO A MAGICKAL NEW YOU!

A MAGICKAL MAKEOVER

If you really want to enhance your magickal self, taking a week off work or other commitments is certainly the way to do it. But remember, it takes dedication! You're not taking a holiday. Some of the work you'll undertake won't be easy, but some of it will be a breeze.

The aim of the week is to give novices a full grasp of basic Witchcraft and gain more experience of Witches' general skills, plus generally enhance a massively magickal sense of self. The whole experience should be approached with a sense of fun and adventure!

Also, be aware that everything set out here is intended to inspire you and give you ideas. You can follow everything to the letter if you want, but I always emphasize that the most magickal experiences are usually the ones that you create yourself. So experiment and change things around to suit your ideas.

Try to time your week around the waxing and full Moon. However, even though there are rituals that are enhanced by these phases, it's certainly not essential. By focusing properly you can make this week very potent regardless of what the moon is doing.

You will be spending a lot of the week alone and somewhere private where you can perform your magickal work without interruption. I would suggest stocking up the fridge and pantry with lots of fresh, nutritious foods – however, this isn't a diet programme, so don't plan to double your magickal week with a weight loss programme. It will only be distracting and anyway, what you are attempting to do here is rise above society's pre-conceived notions of appropriate appearances and accept how amazing you are unconditionally. Fresh, simple foods will allow easy digestion and provide the brain and body with lots of nutrients, which will help you work magick more effectively. Have a good read through this chapter and make a list of what you'll need: herbs and oils for the spells and potions, candles, books (bought new or borrowed from the library) etc, so try to stock up on all these at the start. If you choose not to be skyclad or it's just too cold for bare bodies at the time, buy or make a brand new, special garment to swan around in all week. The only time you'll need to leave your environment is to perform one of the suggested nature rituals and to go for a nice walk in a park, forest or along the beach, or perhaps to stock up on a few extra magickal props that you might find you need. Also remember to turn off the mobile and take the phone off the hook when you don't want to be disturbed!

Getting Started

These general guidelines will be your structure for each day; then substitute the appropriate magickal tasks that follow for each day. These tasks set a framework into which you can intersperse other magickal activities of your choice amongst them.

On Waking

Slowly stretch in your bed, luxuriating in your body. Think about what an extraordinary being you are: a human being capable of magnificent things, a Child of the Universe. Just before you rise, think about how you have set this week aside for yourself, to explore and expand your magickal self. Have a *dream diary* by your bed and write down anything you remember and consider significant so you can analyse your dreams at the end of the week.

When you are ready, deeply inhale and exhale five times. Get up, rinse your face, and head outside to your garden, balcony or perhaps just an open window. With the sun and fresh air on your face, perform the Pentagram Salute to the Sun.

Pentagram Salute

With the right forefinger, touch your third eye (between the eyebrows), left breast, right shoulder, left shoulder, right breast and third eye again to complete the Witches' sacred five-pointed star. As you do this, say either silently or out aloud, 'I dedicate myself in Perfect Love and Perfect Trust to my Goddess and God and to the Universal forces of Magick.'

Get Clean

Purifying Elixir

You will need:
1.5 litres of spring water
3 teaspoons of almond essence
11 drops of rose geranium essential oil
1 piece clear quartz crystal
Mix the above together in a glass container, drop the crystal in and seal (either with a lid or waxed paper and rubber band).

Shower or bath with the intent not only to purify your body but to remove any excess energies you accumulated whilst surfing the night planes (i.e. dreaming!). Douse yourself with a cup of Purifying Elixir at the end of your shower, or add it to the bath. Dry yourself and either remain skyclad or put on your special clothes. If you choose to wear make-up or go to a lot of trouble with your appearance at this point that's fine! Stir up those creative juices and exult in yourself! Alternatively, be as bare as the day you popped out into the world.

Chakra Meditation

The following meditation is not only to focus and centre you for the day but also to empower you by actively re-establishing the connection of your life force with that of the Universe.

   You will need:

❋ A long sarong or piece of material in a light colour (pearly, pale blue would be good), long enough for you to lie stretched out on;
❋ 1 white candle;
❋ 1 red candle.

✦ Note: you might like to consider making a guide tape by recording yourself slowly reading through the meditation, so you don't have to try to remember anything and can just lose yourself in the visualizations. ✦

Lay out the sarong and light the candles, placing the red one at your feet and the white one at your head. Make sure they will each be at least a foot away from your body when you're lying stretched out.

   Lie down on the sarong with the backs of your hands resting on the ground so that your palms are face up. Relax your

133

body. Take seven deep, slow breaths, feeling the air move not only through your lungs but through your whole body.

❋ Concentrate on the first chakra at the base of your spine: the Root chakra. See it as a kind of 'wheel' in an earthy deep red colour – and feel it pulse. When that is clear, sense the wheel starting to spin in a sunwise (deosil/clockwise) direction. Feel the strong centring action of this first chakra as it spins. Now, see it extend as a beam of red light deep, deep down into the earth, grounding and connecting the core of your being with Gaia, the Earth Mother.

❋ When you sense your connection to be really strong, move your attention to the next chakra: the Base Sexual chakra, which is just above the pubic bone. See it as a clear, yet intense, orange, like a huge spark from a volcano, spinning and pulsing.

❋ Move to the next chakra, the Solar plexus, located at the base of the ribcage, the home of 'gut' feelings. See it spin and pulse, its colour pure yellow like marigolds.

❋ Next is the Heart chakra; see it spin and pulse a soft green, the colour of delicate new blades of feathery grass.

❋ Move up to the Throat chakra, and see it spin and pulse the azure blue colour of a fresh, clear daytime sky.

❋ Next is the Brow chakra, or 'third eye'; see it spin and pulse a rich, dark blue – the colour of a deep tropical ocean.

❋ Finally, move your attention to the Crown chakra, a crystal-clear light purple, like a violet sky at sunrise. Concentrate on it spinning and pulsing, and as it does, feel the top of your head tingle as you open your Crown chakra to the Universe. See a bolt of infinite diamond white light come from the heavens and connect with your Crown.

See the light charge through your glowing chakras, intensifying their colours and making them spin faster and faster. Then, see the white light shoot through the red cord of your

The Chakras

The first chakra is the Root chakra found at the base of the spine. Its energy colour is deep red, denoting physicality, life force and the sense of physical safety and groundedness.

The second chakra is the Sexual chakra; it is located at the front of the body just above the pubic line and its colour is clear orange, denoting sexuality and all other sorts of personal creativity.

The third chakra is the Solar Plexus chakra; it is located above the navel and below the ribcage and its colour is bright yellow, denoting personality and power.

The fourth chakra is the Heart chakra; it is located at the heart and its colour is soft green, denoting love and related emotional sensitivity.

The fifth chakra is the Throat chakra and its colour is azure blue. It is located around the larynx and is related to communication, speech and expression.

The sixth chakra is the Brow chakra or 'third eye'. It is located between and slightly above the brows and its colour is dark indigo blue. It is related to psychic thought, intuition and visualization.

The seventh chakra is the Crown chakra and it is located at the top of the head. Its colour is clear violet or white and it denotes connection with the Universe.

Root chakra descending into the earth and feel how grounded you are as you are charged with the purest of energy. See your chakras glowing like a string of beautiful coloured pearls and feel your whole being suffused with power.

When you are ready, slowly close your Crown and Root chakras. Take three deep breaths and open your eyes. You will be charged and centred and ready for an amazing day!

At the End of the Day

Before you go to bed, stand out under the moon or face an open window and again perform the Pentagram Salute. Take a good Witchy novel to read in bed (perhaps *Queen of the Witches* by Jessica Berens or Phyllis Curott's autobiographical *Book of Shadows*) and have your dream diary next to the bed with a pen, ready for you to make notes on your dreams first thing in the morning.

Monday

Monday is ruled by the Moon so today will be a day for you to increase your skills of divination: looking into the future, or between the worlds, for guidance and insight. Put a large pot of mugwort tea on the stove, but don't brew it too strongly as you will drink at least four cups throughout the day. Make an anointing oil of two drops of lemongrass oil in one teaspoon of a base oil (jojoba or wheatgerm) and anoint your third eye area to increase your psychic sensitivity.

Assemble your chosen tools of divination – Tarot cards, crystal ball, runes, whatever. Treat the day as a time for study;

Brewing Herbal Tea

Use roughly a small handful of dried herbs, or a large one of fresh herbs, and add to a four-cup pot. Add almost-boiling water and let it stand for five minutes.

spend the morning reading reference books and stocking up on more knowledge. Today is a peaceful and reflective day, so move slowly and if you can, allow your mind to wander; be in a semi-meditational state all day. A cup of mugwort tea sweetened with honey and drunk at intervals of every three hours will help you achieve this.

In the afternoon, blend some divination incense. Grind together two teaspoons of sandalwood, one teaspoon of orris root powder, four cloves, half a teaspoon of nutmeg and four drops of lemon oil.

As the sun is setting, meditate on one or two particular Tarot cards or runes that you feel drawn to. Light a white candle and place the cards or runes in front. Burn a stick of myrrh incense (save your divination incense for the ritual) and meditate by staring at them. When you are ready make any relevant notes on insights gained in your Book of Shadows.

The Ritual

After sunset, set up your altar with white and silver candles and white flowers to honour the Moon Goddess. Place amethyst, moonstone and black obsidian crystal on your altar and have your divination tools and incense ready. If you like, have a bath with a few drops of lemongrass oil added and drink another cup of mugwort tea to ready yourself for your ritual.

Cast Circle, calling on the Triple Goddess: *'Diana, Selene, Hecate – Maiden/Mother/Crone – Great Goddess of the Moon, illuminate my consciousness with your radiant glow.'*

Meditate on your divinatory goals – do you want insight into a certain problem? Do you want a general reading concerning your life's direction? Do you want to do a reading for a friend who needs guidance? Do your reading from your chosen tool of divination as the divination incense burns, taking your time and allowing your intuition full rein. Keep burning the incense as you make a written record of all insights gained.

When you are satisfied that your reading is complete, thank the Goddess and close Circle.

Tuesday

Today is ruled by the planet Mars, so it's a good day to be courageous and do rituals and activities to let go of anything in your life that just doesn't serve you anymore.

Get up early and brew some ginseng tea with a little ginger-root added. Make an anointing oil of five drops of pine oil in a teaspoon of jojoba and anoint your pulse points – wrists, crooks of arms, ankles, behind the knees and ears, the base of the throat and over the heart. This anointing will work to purify and centre you.

Have a really big clean up of your house and be brutal! Throw out everything that is trapping you to the past and holding you back: old letters, old photos, even clothing and furniture. Organize for the Salvation Army or another charity organization to come by (don't forget to put something on if you're doing your magickal retreat skyclad!) and collect all the nicest items that you are letting go of for needy people to enjoy. Before you give them away, do a small purification ritual by lighting a stick of frankincense incense. Circle the goods three times deosil (clockwise) saying: *'I banish any negativity stored here.'*

Then circle the goods widdershins (anti-clockwise) three times and say: *'I imbue these gifts with love and good will.'*

When you have finished your clean up, rearrange your furniture, or if that's not appropriate, rearrange any knick-knacks or tidy up cupboards, etc. Put a breath of fresh air into your home.

Make a purification incense of one teaspoon of dragon's blood powder, three pinches of tobacco, one teaspoon of frankincense and three drops of sandalwood oil. At sunset open all the windows, doors, cupboards, drawers, wardrobes etc, and perform this ritual:

In a heat-proof bowl, light two charcoal discs and sprinkle them with your purification incense. Walk from room to room, fanning the smoke outward with your hand saying: *'I release the past. I put all sadness and negativity to rest as the sun sinks below the horizon of the past and draws with it everything that no longer serves me.'*

When you have completely fumigated your space and the sun has set, close all the doors and windows – anything you opened. Then do a final ritual of release:

Decorate your altar with orange and white candles, and red flowers. Burn an incense made of two teaspoons of sandalwood with three drops of cypress oil. Have a cauldron with a fire lit within, or one black candle lit. Have a red paper and a black pen ready.

Cast Circle and call on the God Thor – the Nordic God of Thunder, who wields a huge hammer. *'Great God of Thunder, Thor – aid me with your mighty presence, avail me of your strength as I crush all obstacles that block me.'*

Close your eyes and feel Thor's power roar through your veins. Recognise the things in your psyche that are blocking you – old fears, old desires – and write them down on the paper as Thor crushes the bonds that bind them to you. When you have purged everything, crush the paper into a ball and throw it into the cauldron and sprinkle some of the incense on top. Otherwise, burn it in the flame of the black candle.

Thank Thor for his presence and enjoy the sense of clarity and peace you feel now. Rest now that conflict is gone. Meditate on the qualities of courage, endurance and optimism. When you are ready close Circle.

Wednesday

Today is ruled by the planet Mercury and is therefore a day to store up on more knowledge – read books about the Craft and go to the library if necessary or browse through some Witchy bookshops. Focus on familiarizing yourself with the origins of the paths of Witchcraft that appeal most strongly to you. Get a school project book and make notes, and cut out pictures from magazines and travel brochures that illustrate your information.

In the evening do a ritual for knowledge:

Blend an incense of three bay leaves, one teaspoon of mace and three drops of ginger oil. Prepare a tea of sage, with a few drops of lemon juice added. Decorate the altar with gold and purple candles and bunches of lavender or other purple flow-ers. Have your project book nearby.

Cast Circle and invoke the Greek Goddess of Wisdom, Athena, and the Greek God of Intelligence, Hermes. *'Ancient Goddess and God, Athena and Hermes, witness and bless this rite of knowledge. I vow to pursue wisdom and truth and to always learn and grow in my Craft.'*

Consecrate and bless your project book with the four ele-ments. Fan incense smoke over it for Air and say: *'Blessed are my efforts by Air.'*

Sprinkle the book with salt for Earth and say: *'Blessed are my efforts by Earth.'*

Sprinkle it with a little water for Water and say: *'Blessed are my efforts by Water.'*

Then hold it up to the light of the candles for Fire and say: *'Blessed are my efforts by Fire.'*

Sip your tea and read your project book, acknowledging your efforts and your continuing desire for knowledge. When you are finished thank the Goddess and God and close Circle.

Thursday

Thursday is ruled by the planet Jupiter. Today take advantage of the planet's 'wealth of spirit' aspect to charge up rituals of communing with the elements and nature.

Wake up to watch the sun rise and prepare to go on a break-fast picnic. Choose a beautiful place and one where you can easily access not only air and earth, but fire and water; a secluded beach, a lovely old park with a pond – somewhere you can get to reasonably easily and (if you're female) not so remote that you won't feel safe (an unfortunate part of living in today's violent society). Perhaps if you have a lovely garden which has a pond or something similar, you may choose to stay at home, it might even be raining, in which case, great! You can stand skyclad in the rain to connect with Water. Pack your picnic basket with not only food and drink, but candles, incense and your Witch's tools. I suggest making a thermos of peppermint or dandelion root tea and taking plenty of fresh fruits and bread and cheese.

For your 'communing with nature' incense, mix together three teaspoons of sandalwood and five drops of rose geranium oil and use when casting Circle. Take four dark blue candles and a green cloth for the altar.

When you arrive, set up an altar on a rock or flat surface and place the four blue candles in the Quarters to mark the perimeter of your Circle. Provided the place you've chosen is sufficiently secluded but safe, work skyclad to increase your contact with the world around you. If you can, light a small fire, and then cast Circle, taking extra time to focus on calling in the Quarters.

Invoke the God of Nature, Pan, and the great Earth Mother, Gaia: *'Great nurturing Mother Gaia and fertile Lord of the Forests, Pan, I give thanks as I am surrounded by your beauty and abundance; I am blessed as I am cradled in your embrace.'*

Eat your breakfast, then crumble some food and pour some drink on the earth as an offering. Soak up the natural environment and, as you eat, be aware that you are born of the same elements of everything that surrounds you. Feel your deep and innate connection to the land.

When you have finished eating, it is time to align with the

elements. Lie flat on the earth and absorb the ancient energy of Earth. See in your mind's eye the reality that you are lying on a huge planet, floating through space. When your body is resonating with Earth's vibrations say: *'I am born of Earth, I am blessed by Earth.'*

Now stand up, close your eyes and sense the air around you. Be aware of any subtle breezes or strong gusts of wind. When you are ready say: *'I am born of Air, I am blessed by Air.'*

Now sit in front of the fire (or hold a candle from the altar in both hands). Feel the warmth of the flames (cup your hand around the candle flame if necessary) and watch their movement. Allow yourself to be mesmerized. Think of the molten flames at the core of the planet you stand on and the fiery form of the Sun that is above you. When you are ready say: *'I am born of Fire, I am blessed by Fire.'*

Now if necessary, open a doorway in the Circle to be able to get closer to Water. Do this by slicing down through it with your athame saying, *'The Circle is open but unbroken'*, and then when you have walked through, slice your athame back up (like a zip) saying *'The Circle is closed but I carry its protection'*. See yourself with a glowing sphere of protective white light around you. Now go for a swim in the ocean, or dip your feet in a pond, or stand out in the rain – commune with Water in the way you have chosen. Think of oceans of the planet; think of your body, composed of 70% water, feel yourself immersed in its flowing and healing qualities. When you are ready say: *'I am born of Water, I am blessed by Water.'*

When you are ready, go back to Circle, again, using your athame to open and close it, and meditate on how you are evolved of this planet, how its life is your life. After your

143

meditation, close Circle and keep enjoying the great outdoors! When you get home take the necessary steps to join an environmental conservation group (if you're not already a member).

Friday

Today is ruled by Venus and so is a day to devote to self-love and love for all humanity. Start by doing lovely things for yourself. Perhaps make some of the Witchy cosmetics suggested in *'Cosmetic Conjurings'* and give yourself a facial (yep, guys too you need pampering as much as women do!) Spoil yourself and have a massage (perhaps get a mobile masseuse to come to your house), lie around and eat delicious foods. Drink strawberry tea.

Make a personal shrine to the Goddess/God within. Collect photos of yourself of when you were a baby right through to the present and arrange them attractively, perhaps wreathed by garlands of ivy leaves and flowers. Burn some sticks of musk incense. When your collection is complete, meditate on your photos; look at a baby photo and gaze into your young eyes. Think about all the things you've seen and done since that photo was taken. Take the time to acknowledge how you have grown and all the phenomenal things you have done – from learning to walk, to learning to speak, through to your teenage and adult achievements. Focus on how, despite the difficulties of life, you are one of the Universe's biggest success stories!

During the day, also read a book on human biology, to more fully comprehend how your body is one of the most incredible things in Creation.

Make an unconditional love incense by grinding together two teaspoons of vervain, one teaspoon of dragon's blood powder, one handful of dried rose petals, three drops of lavender and two of clary sage oil.

At sunset do this ritual:

Set your altar with three pink candles and three light green candles, pink roses or other lush, pink flowers and a mirror, either small or full length. Cast Circle calling on the Goddess Aphrodite: *'Sweet Goddess of Love, Aphrodite, who magnifies the joyful energies of love. Witness and bless my rite of love and healing.'*

Gaze at your reflection in the mirror and feel unconditional self-love. If you have troubles doing this, ask for help from Aphrodite again and know that you have every right to feel love and appreciation for yourself within your sacred Circle at this time. If you have hang-ups about your physical shape, do this ritual skyclad and be accepting of your body for its uniqueness and the fact that it's yours. When you're ready, keep looking at yourself and say: *'(Your name), You are blessed by the Moon, the Sun and Stars, you are a Child of the Universe, I love you.'*

Raise power within Circle by passionately focusing on the feelings of love that you feel for your loved ones and favourite things. (Some Witches raise power by masturbating to orgasm.) When you feel sufficiently full of love, send the blissful, ecstatic energy outwards to all people on the planet, acknowledging that we are all one, and say:

'From me flows the ecstatic and holy joy that is the spark at the core of all Creation. I offer this energy up as a gift of love to all people.'

Now meditate for a time on the sacred gift of sexuality and

145

carnal pleasure, and on the holiest of all feelings, unconditional love.

When you are ready close Circle.

Saturday

Saturday is ruled by the planet Saturn and there are a couple of options here. It can either be a day that you devote to absorbing more occult wisdom, by reading books on magickal theory and/or it can be a day that you exorcise any very strong feelings of anger and hatred. The ritual I have suggested is for people who feel capable of tapping into their darkest feelings and unleashing them as a purging experience.

Make an incense to honour the Hindu Goddess of Destruction and Creation, Kali. Grind together four teaspoons of comfrey, one teaspoon of henbane (if you have it; otherwise use horehound if you don't), one teaspoon of myrrh and eight drops of patchouli oil.

A lot of current information about Witchcraft paints the Witch to be white and shiny, benevolent and good, bestowing blessings and good fortune on everyone – but that denies half our powers. Today is the day that you get mad and allow yourself to feel the power of your rage. Before your ritual, think about what makes or has made you incredibly angry: harbour enormous resentment and probably sadness (anger and sadness are often the same thing), allowing it to build inside you. Listen to music that fires up your fury; when I did this I listened to American band, VAST. Their debut album played super loud is very moving. I thought about those who had hurt me deeply, physically, mentally and spiritually: ex-boyfriends, ex-school mates, even criminals like rapists whose crimes had horrified me.

If you feel it is appropriate, further facilitate the altering of your consciousness with wine or herbal tea (perhaps a weak brew of guarana with a pinch of cayenne added), whatever is your choice. However, don't blot yourself into oblivion – you want your blood so hot that it burns your veins, but you want to be in control and able to gauge your limits before you transcend them.

If you don't feel like doing this today, that's fine – but only to a degree. These powers of anger and resentment and hatred are as valid as the powers of love and compassion and should be respected and acknowledged, and a Witch should be able to tap into them on call. So this ritual can be very cathartic and a vehicle for self-growth.

When night has well and truly fallen, get ready for this ritual. I suggest you do it in the bathroom as you need some-where you can get messy and get clean. Prepare your altar and environment with black candles; you may wish to continue playing evocative music. Have one white candle, anointed with neroli oil, put aside. Have ready either black, water-based paint or if your skin may react, a tube of cosmetic mud mask, black or dark green in colour. You also need some beautiful soap – I recommend a natural soap, particularly with almond, sandalwood or lavender oils. Some lovely rich moisturising lotion might be a good idea too, especially if your skin is dry.

When you are ready cast Circle invoking the Goddess Kali: *'Kali, Goddess and Queen of Retribution, Queen of War, who strikes fear in the hearts of those who harm. Avail me of your powers of destruction and help me to destroy the pain I feel.'*

Sit and meditate on the things that have caused you sadness and fury, and as you do so acknowledge your inner pain by marking yourself with black paint. If you have physical scars from any cruelty inflicted on you, swipe them with black paint as well. Bring all of that pain that is inside up to the surface and cry and scream; lose yourself in your pain, in your fear, your anger. When you are ready, acknowledge yourself in the mirror and again call on Kali: *'Kali, Goddess and Queen of Retribution, Queen of War, who strikes fear in the hearts of those who harm. Avail me of your powers of creation, So that I may be cleansed and whole.'*

Turn on the shower so that the water is fast and hot. Stand under it and watch the blackness drain away. As it goes down the drain you will probably feel like crying again but it will be tears of release. Let them wash away in the cleansing water too. Soap yourself in a rich, creamy lather rinsing all traces of negativity away.

When you are ready, get out of the shower and snuff the black candles. Light the white candle and gently towel yourself dry. Massage the moisturizing lotion gently into your body, feeling free and cleansed and healed.

Thank the Goddess, close Circle and just relax for the rest of the evening.

Sunday

Ruled by the Sun, today is a day to actively re-dedicate yourself to Witchcraft. You will do two rituals, one dedicating yourself to the God and the other to the Goddess.

Make Sun incense by grinding together two teaspoons of frankincense, one teaspoon of copal, one teaspoon of rosemary and four drops of orange oil.

Dedication to the God

Prepare the altar with gold cloth and gold candles, yellow and orange flowers, and have a chalice of spiced mead ready; if you don't drink alcohol, try some warmed apple cider, spiced with cloves. Have anointing oil ready by blending one teaspoon of jojoba oil with two drops of frankincense oil.

At noon, when the sun is peaking, cast Circle and perform the Pentagram salute, dipping your finger into the anointing oil as you do so. Then invoke and honour the God:

> *Great Lord, powerful God who blesses all with his potency;*
> *who surrounds us with many names:*
> *Lugh, Cernunnos, Ra,*
> *Apollo, Odin, Zeus,*
> *Bacchus, Mercury, Pan.*
> *You activate all life with your dynamic essence;*
> *I acknowledge your presence*
> *within and without me.*
> *As I stand here, Witch and devoted acolyte*
> *of all the forces of Magick in this world and beyond*
> *and all worlds in between.*

Toast your dedication with a few sips of mead and pour some on the ground as a libation. Finish your mead as you make notes in your Book of Shadows about your growing magickal goals and aims.

Before you close Circle, once again honour the God by saying: *'Great Lord, I carry your passion in my heart; I am eternally blessed by your Divine presence.'*

149

Dedication to the Goddess

If you've timed your week perfectly, it should be a full moon tonight. If not, it is best that the moon is in the waxing phase – but whatever phase it is in on your part of the world, the Lunar energy is present.

Make Moon incense by grinding together two teaspoons of sandalwood, one teaspoon of orris root, a small handful of dried gardenia petals or dried jasmine flowers, and three drops of lotus oil.

Do this ritual when the moon is well risen in the sky. Prepare the altar with silver cloth and silver and white candles. Decorate it with lots of white flowers, especially ones that bloom under the moon's glow like jasmine and gardenia. Have a chalice of beautiful sparkling white wine, like champagne, ready; or if you don't drink alcohol, perhaps a glass of sparkling, pale grape juice. Prepare anointing oil by blending one teaspoon of jojoba oil with two drops of sandalwood oil.

When you are ready, cast Circle and perform the Pentagram salute, dipping your finger into the anointing oil as you do so. Then invoke and honour the Goddess:

> *Great Maiden, Mother, Crone, divine Triple Goddess,*
> *from whom all things proceed and to whom all things return;*
> *all powerful Queen of Life and Death, who*
> *embraces us with many names:*
> *Diana, Selene, Artemis,*
> *Hecate, Isis, Demeter,*
> *Cerridwen, Kali, Hestia.*
> *You nurture and permeate all life with your radiant essence;*
> *I acknowledge your presence within and without me*

as I stand here, Witch and devoted acolyte
of all the forces of Magick in this world and beyond
and all worlds in between.

Toast your dedication with a few sips of sparkling wine and pour some on the ground as a libation. Finish your wine as you make notes in your Book of Shadows about the wisdom you have gained as a Witch and the ethics of your Witchcraft.

Before you close Circle, once again honour the Goddess by saying: *'Great Lady, my soul radiates your omnipotence, I am eternally blessed by your Divine presence.'*

Finally, I would just like to remind you that all these activities, rituals and incantations etc, are suggestions to fire up your imagination. Be creative and expand on or change things as you feel compelled. After all, it's *your* magickal week!

151

HAVING YOUR WICCA'D WAY

SPELLS TO SORT YOU OUT

Throughout this book I have mostly encouraged you to create your own spells as often they will be the most meaningful to you and thus the most powerful. However, there have also been a few 'spelled out' conjurings and here are a few more, created by me, to inspire you to create your own!

Before you embark on trying any of the following spells remember that:

The Magick is Within You!

A spell will only be fuelled by your desire for it to work. Of course, you draw on natural forces, Goddesses and Gods and elemental energies to propel things along, but the spark that ignites a spell comes from *you*. So get passionately involved in what you are doing, and I urge you to have *a thorough under-standing of the meanings of the symbols and tools being used.* For example, you should understand why the candles are dark blue, why the herb vervain is involved and why you are calling on the assistance of Hecate in a particular spell. Do your research – you'll find plenty of information in the '*This Goes With This ...*' chapter, but don't stop there, start building your magickal library (see '*The Library*' chapter for suggestions) to have a solid base of knowledge to work from.

All the spells suggest to cast Circle, but if you are stuck for time and feel sufficiently experienced you can visualize the Circle in your mind. However, the full ritual will probably empower your spell to be more effective. You decide.

Finally, enjoy! Even if you are doing a healing spell for a very sick friend, enjoy your power and your choice and your ability, don't censor yourself and don't doubt yourself – you are making magick!

Preparing Yourself ...

When you prepare for a ritual or spellworking it's important to cleanse yourself of all distracting accumulated energies. While a full ritual bath is best, sometimes it's just not feasible to take the time to douse yourself in a purifying herbal infusion. One thing you should always do before magickal work, however, is wash your hands. Not necessarily with soap and water, better it be salt (preferably sea salt) and water. Take a palmful of salt and under a running tap, rinse your hands thoroughly massaging the salt into them and visualizing any accumulated energy that could interfere with your spellcasting rinsing away. It can also be good to make an infusion of rosemary and rinse your hands in this, but if you can't get salt or rosemary at least let fast running water flow over your hands and visualize the psychic junk flushing away.

Another important preparation for a ritual, especially if other people are involved, is to have a rehearsal before doing the real thing. Try to memorize as much of the spoken stuff as you can, so you can concentrate on the meaning of the words during the actual ritual rather than just reading them out of a book. Also if you are doing elaborate outdoor rituals at night it's a good idea to familiarize yourself with the area in daylight, so that while madly running around raising power you don't accidentally fall off the edge of that cliff that drops away just outside the circle of firelight!

When doing rituals at home remember to take the phone off the hook or turn the ring volume down and, if you have one, turn the volume on the answering machine down too. Though to be honest, I have never been interrupted during ritual by a phone ringing – it's as if everyone can pick up the vibes that I don't want to be disturbed.

A 'Give me the Money!' Spell

Money is something everyone wants; and this is a spell not only for enough money, but for lots of money! It requires strong powers of visualization and a firm belief that you deserve prosperity.

Do this spell on a Thursday at midday when the sun's energy is peaking, and during a waxing moon phase.

You will need:

※ 3 green candles;
※ A colour photocopy of a blank recent personal bank statement (first photocopy, then liquid paper out the balance amounts, then photocopy again so that you have a blank statement);
※ 1 green ribbon;
※ 9 drops of bergamot oil;
※ 1 teaspoon of dried dill;
※ 1 teaspoon of dried sage;
※ A typewriter or word processor and printer.

155

Before you start your spell ritual, have a good think about money and your relationship with it – do you feel it is hard to get? Do you feel that the more you earn, the more you spend? Do you have enough to live comfortably, but you want to live *more* comfortably? Are all your friends not very well off, so you feel you can't be either? Erase any thought processes that are limiting your prosperity.

Now, decide exactly what sort of money you want to have. When I did this spell I summed up my situation by realizing that I only ever dealt in $100s – I would earn $100 for a show with my old band; $200 for an article I wrote; $600 for an old guitar that I sold; my bank balance only ever had an amount in the hundreds (or less!) in it. I decided that I wanted to deal in $1000s. It's worth pointing out that there's no point in being greedy when doing this sort of spell, not just because it's tacky but because greed only exists in a mind that is constantly in a battle against poverty. And that attitude is going to undermine the belief that the spell will work; that is, it's going to enormously lessen the chances of it working. Often money spells work best when they're either for a special purpose (for example, a trip you feel you really need to take, or a car if you're in genuine need of one) or as a continuing thing just to keep the income coming in. A clear attitude that acknowledges that resources can always be called in when needed, rather than a panicky, one-off 'major Lotto win' kind of approach, is going to be more effective.

Bearing all this in mind, decide what your money goals are and type up a new bank statement, like this,

Transaction	Cash	Cheque	Current Balance
–			$2,000.00
Deposit	$2,000.00		$4,000.00
Deposit	$1,300.00		$5,300.00
Withdrawal		$2,000.00	$3,300.00
Deposit	$5,700.00		$9,000.00

or however your statement is presented. Make it look real, use your typewriter or computer and printer, so that it convinces you that *this is possible.*

When you have completed this, get ready for your ritual by showering (wash away the past) and dressing in your favourite clothes and perfume or aftershave. You want to feel fantastic and capable of taking on the world!

Cast Circle and anoint each of the green candles with three drops of bergamot oil, then set them up in a triangle on your altar. Place your new bank balance statement in front of these and sprinkle the dill and sage in a deosil (sunwise) circle on it as you repeat until all the herbs are on the paper: *'Prosperous is my rightful state, there is no limit to the money I make.'*

Now, raise power in whatever way you choose, for example: chanting 'money, come to me, money, come to me' over and over; sense your desire start as a burning sensation in your feet, and building through you until you feel you are going to explode. At the point where you can't take it any more hold your hands over the triangle of candles, channelling the energy into their flames and the bank statement. Say: *'Fire, speed my wish to me.'*

Now drip three drops of wax from each candle in the centre of the circle of herbs on the bank statement.

Fold the statement into a wallet shape, sealing the herbs

157

within, and wrap the ribbon around it three times, tying it off with nine knots. Keep the money charm where you file your bank statements and for the next two Wednesdays before you go to bed light the candles again, hold the charm and repeat the mantra, 'Money come to me' for three minutes or so. As you do this visualize yourself going to the bank to deposit your desired sums of money. At the end of those two weeks leave the charm with your bank statements and go about your business.

When I did this spell I noticed a distinct turn-around in my financial situation within three months. All of a sudden I started getting offered more money for the same jobs. I found myself not being so 'tight', and realizing that the more I spent, secure in the knowledge that I was prosperous, the more money came my way.

A 'Get the ***** Out of my Life' Spell

One of the most popular, scary images of Witches is of the cackling old hag stirring a cauldron of foul-smelling brew made up of things that would shock a serial killer. It is generally assumed that if she is engaged in something like this, she is hexing someone. Now, spunky modern day Witches know that hexing someone is going to bring with it too much karmic detritus and so is not worth the effort. But occasionally you need to get rid of someone who is *really bugging you*! Following is a karma-free spell guaranteed to get rid of the unwanted sexual advances of that creepy boss, the harassing and obsessive interest of that neurotic ex-boyfriend and the annoying work/school mate at the next desk who keeps pinching all your pens! But just so that no-one gets their hackles up, this isn't a hexing spell – you're just aiming to get them out of your face, not harm them or even bind them to any significant degree.

You will need:

- ❋ 9 rusty nails;
- ❋ 9 drops of black pepper oil;
- ❋ 1 knob of garlic with the top cut off;
- ❋ 1 red candle;
- ❋ 1 black candle;
- ❋ 1 cup of sea salt;
- ❋ 1 ice cube tray;
- ❋ Water;
- ❋ A freezer;
- ❋ Paper and pen;
- ❋ A photo of the one who's got to go.

Sprinkle a circle of salt about five feet in diameter on a flat surface (perhaps the kitchen floor). Sit in it with all your goodies. Light the candles, placing the red one in front of you and the black one behind. Take seven deep breaths, stilling your mind. Now, focus on the photograph and take the garlic and rub it on the photo 'crossing out' the person. Say: 'I release you from my life, I banish you from my space, this I do in good grace. So Mote It Be.'

On small pieces of paper, write down all the things this person does to bug you and place them in each cube of the tray. Then pour water into the tray. Take the nails and drip the drops of oil on them saying three times: *'Barred are you from my sphere, my will is strong, my thoughts are clear.'*

Now stand up and say, 'It is done'. Open the circle of salt by pushing it aside and place the ice tray in the freezer. As the water freezes, that person's actions will stop against you. How long you keep the cubes is up to you. Permafrost them if you want! However, if a month later you feel that the action taken is sufficient, carry the cubes outside, dig a hole, drop them in and pour boiling water over them. As they melt sense it all fading away into the past. Cover the bits of paper with earth, brush your hands off and move on.

Place the nine nails under the doormat of your front door. The person will not be able to enter your home, nor will thoughts of them haunt you once you step over the threshold. Bury the photo in some earth – a garden or pot plant will do. The person will leave you alone.

A 'Can't Help Myself!' Spell

Yes, you can – with Witchcraft! Following is a very effective, yet simple binding spell for breaking bad habits.

You will need:

* ❋ 1 black candle;
* ❋ 3 frankincense incense sticks;
* ❋ 1 brand new, large, compact mirror;
* ❋ 1 piece of black paper;
* ❋ 1 heavy red texta (so that the ink shows on the black paper);
* ❋ 4 sewing pins;
* ❋ Black tape;
* ❋ Scissors;

❈ Old compact mirror;
❈ Rock salt.

Do this spell at midnight and during the waning moon (which is just after a full moon). Dress in something black that covers your arms and legs and wear no make-up or jewellery. Sweep or vacuum a space about three feet in diameter for you to sit within. Light the candle, burn some frankincense incense sticks and assemble your tools. Still your mind, inhale the incense deeply and with your right hand sprinkle a circle of salt around you in an anti-clockwise (against the sun/widder-shins in the Northern Hemisphere) direction. Think about your bad habit – biting your fingernails, overeating, smoking, procrastinating, laziness, moodiness, whatever.

Write your bad habit centred on the top half of the black paper, for example, 'I am lazy and I procrastinate, which lets down not only myself but also my work mates;' or 'I smoke too much and it is not only ruining my health but also my children's;' or 'I bite my nails and it is an ugly, unhygienic practice.' Be harsh and write down exactly what you can't stand about your habit. When you have done this, fold the paper in half twice with the words on the outside and pin the corners together. Place it in the compact mirror with the words resting against the mirror so that they reflect back onto themselves. When you have done this, snap the compact shut firmly and wrap the black tape around it eight times. When you have done this, open the circle by pushing the salt in a deosil or clockwise (sunwise) direction. Take the compact outside and bury it. You will notice an eradication of your habit immediately, and it will be completely gone by the next full moon.

Getting Through Work (School, University, A Gig, etc) When there's No Way You Can Throw a Sickie

You will need:

❋ One white candle;
❋ St John's Wort oil;
❋ Sea salt;
❋ A stick of sandalwood incense (or the actual woodchips or powder) to be burnt on a charcoal disc;
❋ A small handful of fresh marjoram and another of thyme;
❋ A small piece of amethyst;
❋ A piece of pale blue or white cloth (about the size of a handkerchief or use a new one);
❋ Blue or white ribbon or thread.

The night before you have to go to work or, if you have time, in the morning, have a shower and scrub your whole body with handfuls of the sea salt. The salt will purify and cleanse you and assist in washing away any accumulated negativity and weakness associated with the illness. Better yet, if you live near the sea, go and jump in and ask Mother Ocean to wash away your ills.

Assemble everything on a table, bench top or altar space and, if you feel comfortable with it and are reasonably adept, cast Circle and call in the Quarters.

Rub the candle down with a little St John's Wort oil. This oil has enormous healing and purification powers, both medicinally and metaphysically. Light the sandalwood incense and deeply breathe in its purifying and protective essence. Next, light the candle and calm your mind. Gaze into the flame and call on the Goddess Diana to assist your rite with these words: 'Diana! Goddess of Vitality, Nurturing and Strength, Holy Moon Goddess who shines on us all, I bid you to witness this rite of healing and avail me of your Divine energy.'

Now, close your eyes and visualize a giant, swirling funnel of light above your head extending up into the heavens and beyond. See a stream of silver energy lighter than air pour down that tunnel, and enter you through your crown chakra. Feel it penetrate every cell in your body and let the heaviness of your illness lift away.

Open your eyes and see your hands glowing, infused with healing energy. Lay the cloth out flat and place on to it the mixture of marjoram and thyme. Marjoram has protective powers, can assist in lifting depression and also has money-attracting powers, so your day will be a fruitful one. Thyme encourages good health and when smelled gives energy and courage.

Put three drops of oil onto the herbs and rest the amethyst on top. Now place your hands over the mixture and charge it with Diana's energy by visualizing the silver light flowing from your hands into the herb mixture, and being further amplified by the crystal.

When you can sense the energy has been transferred, with the index finger of your right hand trace a pentagram in the air over the cloth to further bless and seal the energy. Now, take the corners of the cloth and bring them together, wrapping the ribbon or thread around the top deosil (clockwise in the Northern Hemisphere) three times. The number three

163

reflects the sacred triple manifestation of the Goddess Diana as Maiden, Mother and Crone. Tie it off with nine knots – nine knots are used to reflect regenerative and restorative energy. The number nine will always reproduce itself when it is multiplied by any number, for example: 9 x 4 = 36 and 3 + 6 = 9. It symbolizes that which cannot be destroyed and so imbues the charm with strength and tenacity.

Now it is time to close the ritual. First thank the Goddess: *'Divine Diana, I gratefully acknowledge your presence here. I now reflect your endless strength and fortitude. So Mote It Be.'*

Rest your palms against the floor to ground any excess energy. If you cast Circle, bid farewell to the Guardians of the Quarters and close it down.

Snuff the candle and incense and either go to bed or get ready for work. If it is bed you are bound for, place the charm under your pillow while you sleep and then take it to work the next day. At work place your health and endurance charm in a pocket, as you need to keep it next to your body so that you can be infused and strengthened throughout the day by the energy it exudes. The charm will also be working on your aura, renewing any weaknesses and purging negativity. During the day when you need an extra rush, crush the charm in your fist a little to agitate the herbs and deeply breathe in their scent to clear your head.

You'll sail through the day!

A 'How to be Irresistible' Spell

If the object of your desire isn't returning your interest, it's more than likely you're aiming for the wrong guy or girl.

They're not for you, so don't bother about them. Do some magick on yourself instead. The following spell will help to sort you out.

Cast this spell on a Friday, which is ruled by Venus, the Goddess of (self) love. Start by doing something radical – get up to watch the sun rise on the morning of your spell and even more radically, do it in the nude! Spells for self-empowerment are always given a good boost when performed skyclad. Let those pure morning rays warm you and charge up your inner power. (If you can't comfortably perform this one skyclad, wear something simple and white.)

You will need:

❊ A piece of orange paper (for optimism and empowerment);
❊ A silver pen (for intuition);
❊ A red rose (passion and love);
❊ A red ribbon;
❊ Scissors.

Close your eyes and connect with the Earth by charging your elemental energies. Imagine the ocean's waters in your blood, the planet core's molten fire in your heart, the world's winds in your lungs, and the mountain's strength at your feet. Let your spirit soar.

Now compose a poem or ode to yourself about your attributes. Say what you long to hear from another. Read it three times slowly and then scatter the rose petals on it. Put a lock of your hair in the centre, fold the paper into a triangle sealing its contents, and bind it with a ribbon by tying seven knots. Hold your charm to your heart and say: *'Venus charge my*

165

A Visualization Exercise

Being able to visualize things clearly with your mind's eye is a skill. Sometimes it happens easily and spontaneously, and at other times it seems impossible. When I was first starting out I would do basic 'mind's eye training' exercises every chance I got. I used to do the following one sitting on the bus for half an hour going to and from work every day. This circle exercise is a really good discipline to learn. It helps you get very good at focusing your mind unwaveringly on only one thing which is a handy ability to have for spellcasting.

Close your eyes (everyone will just think you're another sleepy commuter) and 'look' at the blackness of the back of your eyelids. See it as a tangible screen and 'watch' the interplay of dots and shades of light that move across it. To create more things to watch, gently press the palms of your hands against your eyes for a few seconds, remove them and watch the light. When you are fully in touch with the 'movie screen' of the back of your eyelids (this can take some practice) it's time to draw a picture on it. Starting at the top of the screen 'see' an electric blue dot appear, and when it's clear 'see' it move in a clockwise direction, leaving a trail of blue light behind, tracing out the shape of a circle. When you reach the top again, see the blue circle complete for a few seconds before seeing the dot start to move in an anti-clockwise direction, this time 'rubbing out' the circle. When you reach the top again and the circle is gone, see the blue dot hover in the blackness and then start drawing the circle again.

Do this for as many times as you can. It takes a long time to get a tangible, clear image and in some cases you'll only ever feel you are 'imagining' seeing it. That's OK – I have had visualizations during ritual that are so clear it's like a movie in my head and at other times the visions are not 'seen' but are more ethereal and only suggestive of things and events. The important thing during visualization is how deeply you are affected by and involved with the whole proceedings.

heart with strength, so that my charms are better spent, on someone for whom I am meant.'

Kiss it three times and keep it with you for seven days. It will align the energies of your head and heart and help you make the right choices in love.

A Spell for Personal Healing, Confidence or Self-Esteem

This is a simple spell that can give an immediate pick-me-up when your vitality is lagging, or you're nervous about a job interview or a first date – or whatever! (This one's best done skyclad as well.)

You will need:

* ❋ 1 piece of paper;
* ❋ 1 black pen;
* ❋ 1 glass of mineral water;

❋ 1 teaspoon of sandalwood chips or powder;
❋ 1 cauldron (or something you can burn the paper in – even a saucepan);
❋ Matches and 3 charcoal discs.

Cast Circle, either with a full blown ritual, or by standing and inhaling deeply three times, holding your right arm at a 90 degree angle to your body and clicking your thumb and fore-finger three times. Visualize a sphere of bluish-white light around you.

Light the charcoal discs and place them close together in the cauldron. When they are hot and glowing, sprinkle half the sandalwood over them and write down your fears on the piece of paper, for example, 'I'm scared I'll make an idiot out of myself in front of Mark/Mary;' 'I feel like I'm coming down with the flu;' 'I'm scared I'll forget the answers to the test,' etc.

When it is written, read it three times, then scrunch the paper into a ball saying loudly, '*Begone*!' and toss the paper on top of the charcoal discs. As the paper flares into a flame know that your fear is burnt away. When the paper is just ash, sprin-kle the rest of the sandalwood onto the discs, take three deep breaths and loosely cup the palms of your hands together. Imagine yourself to be brimming with confidence and health – almost ridiculously so. Concentrate this energy into a ball of rose-coloured light between your palms. Feel it grow hot and empowered there. When it is very tangible, place your hands over the glass of water and drop the revitalizing energy ball into it and then gulp all the water down. Don't waste a drop!

Now stand with your arms held out slightly to your sides with your palms upward and close your eyes. Feel vitality and confidence tingle through you. Say, 'I am unique (healthy/intelligent etc) and blessed' and then click the fingers of your right hand three times to open Circle; or open normally if you did the full ritual.

A 'Have a Good Trip' Spell

This spell will ensure a safe journey and safe return. If you don't want to come back (or the person travelling doesn't) don't do the burying part of the spell and leave out the bit about the lunar tide in the spoken charm. This spell can be done up to a week before you or the person leaves. If you delay your trip, do the spell again.

Do this spell on a Wednesday at sunrise and invoke the God Mercury when you cast Circle.

You will need:

❋ 2 small pieces of driftwood or petrified wood
❋ 2 pieces of dried kelp (seaweed). If you can't get some from the beach, get some from a Japanese food store (it is used for rolling sushi);
❋ 1 sprig of rosemary;
❋ 1 glass of white wine (if it's air travel) or red (if it's land or sea travel);
❋ Make an incense blend of lavender, sage and 5 drops of almond oil;
❋ 1 red candle;
❋ Yellow piece of paper, red ribbon and red pen.

Just before sunrise, wake and shower or bathe. As you do so think about your upcoming trip.

Set up an altar either outside, on a balcony with pot plants, or near an indoor plant. Assemble your tools and cast Circle. Light the incense and candle and place the rosemary in the wine.

Take a small sip and tear the paper in half, writing on one half your point of departure and on the other your destination. Place a piece of wood and piece of kelp on top of each half. Take another sip of wine, placing your hands over the paper and say: *'Mercury, be with me as I travel over land and water. Bless and hold me safe as I, propelled forth by the fire of the rising Sun and drawn home by the lunar tide of the Moon, undertake my journey.'*

Take another sip of wine and pour a libation onto the ground (or on the soil around the plant). Wrap the other half of the paper around the stone and kelp, and tie with red ribbon. Then, if you like, finish the wine (pouring a libation for the Goddess and God), and ponder your trip. If you're worried you'll get a bit boozy drinking wine at sunrise (unless you've been out all night at your going away party, in which case this would be a hair of the dog!), pour all the wine as a libation onto the ground. Close Circle and, if you can, mail the rest of the talisman to your destination. If you can't, carry it with you in your hand luggage or pocket.

An 'I'm Sick of Dwelling in the Past/Feeling Guilty/ A Failure' Spell

Do this spell when you can't stop regretting something you've done. It may be the fact that you went out with such a loser for three years, or that you didn't bother to study for the test which you failed, or that you lied to your partner/mum/friend about where you were last night.

The best time is during the waning moon at midnight and preferably on a Saturday. Also, it is best to do this spell where you can lie down on the earth. If this is impossible, you'll have to be ready to use firm powers of visualization. (This spell is adapted in part from Marina Medici's *Good Magick*.)

You will need:

❁ 2 drops clary sage oil;
❁ 2 drops of lavender oil;
❁ 2 tablespoons of arrowroot gel (check out the '*Cosmetic Conjurings*' chapter for instructions on how to make it);
❁ An oil burner with 3 drops of lavender and 3 of clary sage;
❁ 4 white candles;
❁ 1 large bowl of warm water;
❁ 1 white towel;
❁ 1 hand mirror.

Just before midnight blend the clary sage and lavender oils with the gel in a glass or china bowl and place the candles so that you can lie with two either side, one below your feet and the other above your head. At midnight cast Circle, light the candles and sit in the centre with the bowl in front of you. Either shut your eyes or look up at the waning moon and think about what you want to let go of. Let the guilty/ashamed/ embarrassed feelings crawl through you and see them amass around you like storm clouds gathering. Now paint your face with the gel (avoid your eyes) and lie down on your back with your palms resting downward. Let yourself sink deeply into the earth and watch the dark clouds float away or even see them being blown apart and dissolved by strong winds. Feel anchored and safe as you lie and as the clouds disappear know they will never darken your day again. Don't think specifically about your hang-up, just see it as clouds being drawn down and away. If it starts creeping up inside you, externalize it as a cloud and see it sucked away and neutralized.

As the clouds disappear, inhale deeply the beautiful, clarifying scents around you and know that you are nurtured and loved by Mother Earth, and that she has healed you. When you feel ready, sit up and rinse your face, patting it gently dry. Take the mirror and look at your face, glowing in the candle light and know that you are cleansed and ready to move on.

Close Circle and sleep well!

An All Round Healing Spell

This spell is really good for any kind of healing, whether the person or animal is near or far away.

You will need:

※ A photograph of the person/animal receiving the healing;
※ 9 light blue candles;
※ 1 very sharp knife;
※ Needle and red thread;
※ 1 clear quartz crystal;
※ 1 rose quartz;
※ 1 handful of a combination of dried rosemary, rue and vervain;

❊ 2 drops of eucalyptus oil (enormous healing powers);
❊ A piece of light blue cloth and white ribbon.

Cast Circle, burning frankincense incense. Make a circle on the altar with the candles and place the photograph on the light blue cloth in the centre. Drip two drops of oil – one on the head and one on the heart – of the poppet/photograph and say, '(Name), you are to be healed'. Now raise power by chanting the Wiccan Goddess chant: 'Isis, Astarte, Diana, Hecate, Demeter, Kali, Innana' over and over, faster and faster. As you are doing this you are calling on the powers of all these Goddesses to heal. When you feel the Circle brimming with energy stop chanting and say again, '(Name), you are to be healed.' Sprinkle the herbs over the photograph and lay the crystals on top.

Place the photograph in the centre of the candles and hold both your hands over it, closing your eyes and calling on the presence of the Goddesses in Circle saying, 'Great Goddesses, move through me so that my friend is healed.' Feel them pour their healing powers down through your crown chakra and into your hands. In your mind's eye, see their energy and your love combine to bathe the photograph in a glowing colour (which colour it is will spontaneously manifest, depending on the illness or injury). When all the raised power in the Circle has poured into the image, take your hands away and place them on the ground to earth any excess.

Say 'It is done,' thank the Goddesses and snuff the candles. You can either give the image to the person requiring healing to put under their pillow, or you can place it somewhere in a safe place.

A Bunch of Really Old Weird Spells and Illness Remedies

Last year in a second-hand bookshop I found a wonderful tome called *Cures and Curses* by Dorothy Jacob. It was originally published in England in 1967 and Ms Jacob has done a wonderful job researching weird and wonderful, Witchy titbits. Here are a few of my favourites:

❋ A charm to cure hiccups: Have a cup of tea ready and say; 'Hiccup, hiccup, rise up, rise up, Three drops in a cup, are good for the hiccup.' Then drink three sips of tea from the far side of the cup.

❋ If you have spilt salt, avoid ill fortune by throwing a pinch over the left shoulder.

❋ Never light three cigarettes with one match (better still, don't smoke and don't encourage other people in this putrid habit by lighting them for them).

❋ Touch the earth before starting a long journey to ensure safety.

Ms Jacobs also gives examples of 'quaint' animal magick. Describing how cats are 'soaked in magic', she explains:

The blood from a severed tail of a black cat will cure shingles or any other skin disease. Styes on the eye can be cured by stroking with a black cat's tail – use a tom for a woman, a queen for a man. At the same time this charm must be repeated: 'I poke thee, I poke thee, I poke the queff that's under the 'ee O qualy way! O qualy way!'

> ✦ *Note: in offering the above as an interesting Witchy titbit, I am not condoning the abuse of animals!* ✦

She also offers this gem from 'The Prescriptions of the Physicians of Myddfai':

> *A Way in which things can be seen which are invisible to Others. Take the gall of a cat and hen's fat mixing them together. Put this in your eyes and you will see things that are invisible to others.*

The Welsh legend of the 'Physicians of Myddfai' dates from pre-medieval days. This race supposedly derived their magickal skill as it was handed down from father to son, from a fairy mother who had married a Welsh mortal named Rhiwallon. Following are some more of their pronouncements:

> *A cold mouth and warm feet will live long. Suppers kill more than the Physicians of Myddfai can cure. A light dinner, and a less supper, sound sleep and a long life. To make someone confess what they have done wrong: take a frog alive from the water. Extract its tongue and put it again in the water. Lay this same tongue on the heart of the sleeping person, and they will confess their deeds in their sleep. To know whether someone who is ill will live or die: anoint the patient's heel with some pig's fat and give the remainder to a dog to eat. If the dog will eat it, the patient will live, if not the patient will die.*

Finally – a few magick cures for warts from Marcellus of Bordeaux:

175

Touch your warts with as many little stones as you have warts; wrap the stones in an ivy leaf, and through [throw] in the thoroughfare. Whoever picks them up will acquire the warts.

A bit nasty, eh? Here's a couple of kinder options:

Blow nine times on the warts when the moon is full. Catch the moon's rays in a dry metal basin and wash the hands in it.

Here are a few of Ms Jacob's referenced sources in case you want to find out more about ancient practices of healing using superstition, sympathetic magick, Witchcraft and a little bit of medical knowledge!

The Compleat Herbal, Nicholas Culpeper, 1653

English Folklore, Christina Hole, Batsford, 1940

From Witchcraft to Chemotherapy, Sir Walter Langdon-Brown, Linacre Lecture, Cambridge, 1941

The Golden Bough, Sir James Frazer, Macmillan, 1948–51

Health's Improvement, Dr Thomas Muffet, *1655*

The Housekeeper's Receipt-Book, Anon, 1816

Power in Numbers

Witches realize there is an effectiveness in numbers. The traditional coven of thirteen has more to do with the collective power of a group of people working on a spell rather than any great spooky significance of the number thirteen. Healing, for example, is often undertaken during coven meetings. If the person needing healing is not available to attend in person, it is still possible to perform a healing for them. Several years ago I attended a coven meeting of the Eldergrove Coven in Sydney's western suburbs. The first Friday of every month is open night, when uninitiated members are allowed into the Circle. On these nights anywhere from twenty-five to fifty people meet in a rented hall.

On this particular night, healing was high on the agenda and after we had performed the opening ceremony of casting Circle, the High Priestess informed us we would be doing two healings that night. The first was for a man suffering with cancer. At this point a thin, hunched over man was led into Circle by one of the coven members. The High Priestess approached him and said, 'Welcome. Are you here of your own free will?' The man nodded, and then she asked, 'Do you wish to be healed?' Again he nodded and the High Priestess motioned him to sit in the centre of our Circle. She then explained to the coven the method of healing we would be undertaking, namely, a 'laying on of hands'.

First we raised a Cone of Power. The High Priestess led us

in a rapid dance moving deosil (anti-clockwise in the Southern Hemisphere) around him, calling out the names of various Gods and Goddesses which we repeated. Faster and faster we went until everyone was running, loudly chanting all the while. I could almost see a silvery, hazy sphere begin to glow around the perimeter of our Circle as the power was raised. I don't know what the poor sick guy was thinking, sitting there with his head bowed and surrounded by a bunch of dancing, yelling Witches with hair and black robes flying everywhere! Finally the High Priestess shouted, 'The power is raised!' We all stopped running and placed our hands on the man. I could feel immense heat as I placed both my palms on his back and I didn't know whether it was coming from him or from me. As we clustered around him he literally disappeared under a sea of hands. I was aware of a vibration that seemed to take over the whole room, and above the sounds of heavy breathing and words of healing muttered by different coven members, I was sure I could hear a strange buzzing sound.

After about two minutes we removed our hands from the man and were instructed to rest them on the floor to ground any excess energy. The atmosphere of the room seemed to shift – as if a cool breeze had blown through it, whisking away the dregs of the power we had raised. Then we sat back in a circle and the High Priestess took the man by the hand as he stood up. I noticed he was standing straight and tall, his expression relaxed and his eyes clear. She asked him how he was feeling and he said much better and thanked the coven before being escorted by a member out into the foyer.

The High Priestess told us the next healing would be a planetary one. This was around the time of the horrific nuclear testing at Mururoa Atoll and all of us agreed our Mother Earth needed lots of loving, healing energy as those awful bombs ripped through her stomach. Again we ran around the perimeter of our Circle raising power and chanting a charge led by the High Priestess. As the cone reached its peak we all dropped to the floor and pressed our hands hard against it channelling the healing force that we had raised deep into the Earth, willing it to race through her body to the location of the blasts. The High Priestess intoned in a deep resonant voice, 'Mother, accept our love and healing. We acknowledge your great sacrifice in the face of human fear and ignorance.' I felt my hands dissolve into light and I became aware of an awful sense of sorrow. Almost to my astonishment tears welled up in my eyes and poured out, dripping off my cheeks onto the carpet. In my mind's eye I saw great aching cracks and chasms appearing in layers of honey coloured rock, and as they appeared I tried to imagine them closing back up again. The voice of the High Priestess faded away and I didn't open my eyes again until all the cracks were closed.

We sat around the Circle, spent. Some coven members also had tears on their cheeks and the High Priestess said, 'Well done, everyone.' Then we performed the 'Cakes and Ale' ceremony and had some general discussion and a little bit of food to ground ourselves before closing Circle.

THE LABYRINTH OF LOVE

HOW TO FIND YOUR WAY IN AND OUT

Everyone deserves love, but I'm wary of love spells because so many of them are manipulative by nature. There is a common misconception that the main power you can want as a Witch is the ability to get someone to fall in love with you. Also, books with a proliferation of love spells lead the reader to think that being single is a lesser state of being, whereas to me Witchcraft fosters a sense of self-respect and self-reliance to the point where romantic partnerships are not the be-all and end-all of living.

Witchcraft is such a hands-on religion that the time I've spent single over the last thirteen years I've poured into developing my Craft – as a Witch there's always a ritual to do on a dateless Saturday night! Still, love is a basic human need of course, and every Witch I know has done some kind of love spell at one time or another, whether it's to assist an ailing relationship, find a new one (or help someone else to) or to end one.

One of the main tenets of Witchcraft is 'Don't interfere with another's free will'. So if you're doing a 'Come to Me' love spell it's really important not to specify one particular person as this is both manipulative and potentially disastrous. You need to focus only on someone coming to you who will fulfil your needs and desires and let the Universe decide on who is most appropriate. Aiming your spell at someone you have a crush on, but perhaps has shown little interest in you, and trying to 'get them' is interfering with their free will and your spell is bound to backfire in some way. They might turn out to be a loser pot-head, a violent psycho, or just completely boring. After two weeks you may want to get rid of them, but since you did such a damn good job with your spell, you can't!

I have a good friend, Jason, who was always ringing me up with tales of woe about the disastrous relationships he kept getting himself into. He would get these crushes on boys who were not gay and kept getting his heart broken. Jason is gorgeous, very intelligent but doesn't always make the best choices when it comes to relationships. The final straw came when he got a crush on an acquaintance of mine – a straight guy called Andrew – and the phone calls became more desperate: 'Can you tell him I like him?,' 'Do you think he likes me?' I love Jason and I didn't mind him calling me up and asking these things, but I just didn't want to see him wasting all the love he has to give on some guy who would never return it.

So, I did a little spell – nothing too fancy. I got two small pink candles, the kind that go on birthday cakes, and melted them into a pile of wax. I declared one of them to be Jason and the other a companion that would fulfil his needs. Then I rubbed both of the candles with a blend of ylang ylang, ginger and jasmine oil. Ylang ylang is often used in spells of love and sex as it has the effect of making you irresistible to the gender of your choice. I used ginger to represent the kind of pure passion experienced when you are happy and at ease in your body. It is also suited to a generally high, young male sex drive. Jasmine (which is bloody expensive!) is good for attracting love as opposed to sex: it possesses a very high spiritual vibration and is great for spells involving friends and family relationships.

I set up a special altar by creating a circle of dried rose petals and dragon's blood powder on a piece of white cloth and placed the two candles, the bases of which I'd melted slightly so that they would adhere to two small chunks of rose quartz crystal, inside. Rose quartz is very good for amplifying energies of love and friendship. I also placed inside five apple seeds. Apples are the fruit of love and the seeds represent the eternally regenerative qualities of love. Outside the circle I placed a bowl of water, a pile of sea salt, some love-attracting incense I'd made from dried gardenia petals (for ecstasy) and sandalwood powder (for protection) on a disc in the burner, my athame on the pentacle and a pink ribbon.

Then I cast Circle and called in the Guardians. I specifi-

Flowers and herbs have been used for centuries for making magickal potions for both beauty and healing

Give Yourself a Magickal Makeover!

(See Seven Days to a Magickal New You)

Good morning!

The Pentagram Salon

Nature in my street!

Brewing up a Witchy Storm

Chakra Meditation

The future is divine!

Dreaming the Dark

A Wiccan Ritual

Draw on the energy of Fire when you need the qualities of independence, self-confidence, and swift, effective action

Draw on the energy of Water when you need to draw on wisdom, when you feel the need to be nurtured and when you would like to have greater emotional harmony

ential in the working of magick.
n nature and our place on the planet.

Draw on the energy of the Earth when you have physical work to do, if you need physical nourishment and sustenance, and when you need to feel more 'grounded' and secure

Draw on the energy of Air when you are working with dreams or mysteries, or when you need to free trapped energy

The Four Greater Sabbats are Imbolc, Beltane, Lammas and Samhain

Top far left: **Samhain Oct 31st** – The beginning and end of the Witches Year, this is a time to honour the dead as the veils between the worlds are at their thinnest. Place apples and pomegranates on your altar and say goodbye to the year that has passed

Bottom far left: **Imbolc Feb 2nd** – The end of darkness and a time of growth, cleansing and renewal. Decorate your home with snowdrops or other white flowers and light a white candle

Bottom left: **Beltane May 1st** – Traditionally a time for handfastings and for physical and spiritual celebration. Hold a ritual outside with plenty of flowers and succulent seasonal fruits

Top left: **Lammas August 1st** – A time of joy and abundance and celebrating the harvest. Gather with your friends for a feast of freshly baked bread, cakes, berries and grapes

Top right: There are many Pagan and Wiccan Gods and Goddesses, it's up to you to decide   which ones you are particularly inspired by. This is one of my favourites, the Egyptian Goddess Sekhmet, the Lioness Goddess, whose name means 'powerful'

Bottom right: The chakras are centres of energy located at various points throughout the body. Each chakra has its own magickal associations

Far left: Many Western Witches mark themselves with tattoos, much like the shamans and witchdoctors of old. I have four tattoos, each one representing a major Witchy turning point in my life

Left: This Wiccan altar was prepared for a handfasting. The Goddess and God are represented, as are the four elements. There is also a chalice, incense, ribbon, mead, biscuits, a rose quartz crystal for love, a broom for the couple to jump over and a special candle for the couple to keep. You can tailor-make your own altar however you wish

Crystals are used for divination, meditation and healing, and are often worn as ceremonial jewellery

cally invited the Goddess of Love, Aphrodite, into the Circle to assist me, feeling her presence as a general sense of benevolence and good fortune.

I closed my eyes and meditated for some time on my friend, focusing my mind's eye very clearly on his face as I deeply inhaled the sweet, musky incense. Then I lit the two candles standing closely together and said the following enchantment:

'With intention true of spirit I ask you lovely Aphrodite
To bless these candles pure and create of their light a lover's fuel
To speed the passage of one to another
So that two loving caring people are joined together.'

I watched the candles burn rapidly, their wax dripping down over the rose quartz and fusing the two crystals together. When the flames went out and the wax cooled, I gathered the corners of the cloth together, so that the rose petals, dragon's blood powder, the apple seeds and the fused crystals were enclosed, and sealed the charm by tying the pink ribbon around the opening with five knots. As I tied each knot I said:

By one this spell is done
By two it will come true
By three So Mote it Be
By four for the good of all
By five so shall love thrive

I used five knots because it is said that 'Every woman and man is a star' and over the five-pointed star-shaped pentagram you can stand a human with her or his head at the top point and outstretched arms and legs marking the other points. Five is a number that is mystical and magickal, yet essentially human. To tie off the charm with five knots seals the magick drawn from between the worlds and encourages it to manifest swiftly in the everyday world. The shape of the pentagram is also the way apple seeds are arranged at the core of the fruit so the five knots also reflect this and further enhance the love attracting potential of the spell.

After sealing the charm, I thanked the Goddess Aphrodite and the Guardians for their help and attendance and closed the Circle. I put the charm on my altar and waited for news from Jason.

Sure enough, two days later I got a phone call from him. He excitedly told me that he had met this gorgeous guy, who was gay, available and seemed really nice. They were going out on the weekend. Now, the interesting twist in the way this spell manifested in his life is that he rang me after his date and said that he'd decided the guy wasn't quite right for him. He had all the things he usually falls for – long hair, young body, cheeky personality – but that was just it. Every guy he'd fallen for before had screwed him around and he was learning to spot the warning signs.

I took this as a sign that **the spell was working in his life in a far more constructive way than if the 'perfect' guy had just walked in the door the next day.** Jason was learning to be discerning and true to himself and manifesting these qualities would ensure that a more appropriate person would ultimately be attracted to him. The spell has definitely attracted more guys into his life – he has changed from being a wallflower to having a different date every week. He's having fun being with lots of people and slowly making up his mind about what he really wants in a romantic companion.

This spell can be adapted to use for yourself. When you start to meditate, think of what you really want and need in a partner and when you are ready, write down a list of your requirements on a pink piece of paper. Place the list in front of the candles and as they burn, after the enchantment, read your list out loud. When the candles have burnt down close the charm with the list inside and keep it on your altar. Or you could try sleeping with it under your pillow for a few days and see if you dream of your future partner. When I tried this I ended up dreaming about an old girlfriend whom I hadn't seen for years and a week later we bumped into each other at a gig and a month later I was living with her! On my list I'd stated I needed a companion who could offer me unconditional friendship and support, someone who was intelligent, attractive and patient. My girlfriend was all these things, and though it wasn't a romantic, sexual union, we spent a year-and-a-half happily living together, supporting and inspiring each other. I felt all my needs were indeed fulfilled.

I've had a few disgusting boyfriends in my time who have treated me badly. As you grow through your twenties it's easy to get stuck in a rut with the kind of relationship you manifest in your life and I kept attracting arseholes and finding them attractive. There was always the initial three-month blissful period followed by their true colours showing, my panic setting in, and then the relationship would descend into hell. One of the guys I went out with in my early twenties was a particularly nasty number. After a few months the usual pattern of a violent relationship established itself – daily hysterical fights followed by tearful, passionate repatching, weird mind games,

185

things being thrown around the room, him convincing me it was all my fault, etc. But what convinced me that it wasn't my fault was when I found out he'd been injecting cocaine and sharing needles with his less-than-salubrious junkie friends.

It was bad enough that he was lying to me about his drug taking, but when I found out he'd been sharing needles, I finally woke up. As a 'monogamous' couple we regularly had unprotected sex, so when he hit up he was not just exposing himself to the risks of HIV/AIDS and Hepatitis B and C, but putting me at risk also. This was the final proof I needed – to know that despite his declarations of love (in between the fighting) he really didn't care about me.

I wanted out. I did the obvious thing and broke up with him, but in the following weeks I bumped into him when I went out, he started calling me and leaving messages, and he even came over and mooched around the front of my house a couple of times. Worse still, I'd started reminiscing about the 'good old days'. I felt lonely and was starting to think that perhaps if I'd been a better girlfriend he wouldn't have been drawn to taking the drugs, and maybe if I tried harder we could get back together, and ... *madness!* All the typical patterns of thought for a woman addicted to violent relationships. So, in a moment of lucidity I did a spell to break all ties here, and between the worlds, with him.

I gathered up every photo I had of him as well as photos of us together – carefully cutting my image out – every note he'd written me and every card he'd given me over the year we were together. I put them in a pile in the backyard where I could have a bonfire. Then I put thirteen garlic cloves and three handfuls of pine needles in a glass bowl and placed it next to the pile. This is an excellent banishing mixture that an elderly, hereditary Witch told me about. There was a pine tree in my street so I was able to get dried needles from under the tree, but if you can't find any, twenty-seven drops of pure pine oil can substitute. Garlic and pine have immense banishing and protective powers – remember the tales of old when people would hang garlic on their doors to keep vampires away and pine needles were sprinkled on floors to exorcise negativity. I did this spell at midnight on the fifth night of the waning moon, but you could do it any time, though night is best.

To prepare myself for the spell I had a shower and rubbed myself down with sea salt. I then removed my jewellery and tied my hair back off my face and put on a long white, cotton nightgown. My yard wasn't that private and I didn't want nosy neighbours poking their heads over the fence to see who was having a fire at midnight ... and seeing a naked Witch! For this spell I didn't cast Circle as I did not want to contain the energies I was about to release. Instead, I sat in the dark a few feet from the pile and focused on my breathing for some time to calm my mind. Then I did a meditation where I pictured my ex-boyfriend and I sitting opposite each other out in space. As I concentrated on this I started to see a cord of light develop that joined us from solar plexus to solar plexus. I became aware of a sucking sensation just above my stomach as I sat there and I knew this was where our energies were attached and that he was draining mine like a vampire. (A couple of girlfriends of mine have also done this spell after and experienced different attachments for the cord: one saw herself attached to her boyfriend at the third eye, and the other at the heart chakra.)

At this point I knew I had to break the cord and so I called on the Archangel Michael to assist me. I was introduced to the energies of this Angel by another Witch who often called on him when she needed the powers of his huge sword to slice through any psychic debris. Even though Archangel Michael is a Judeo-Christian angelic force I have never felt any conflict when calling upon his presence. Whether he 'really' exists is irrelevant to me because the bottom line is that he always turns up when invited and with the element of fire fuelling his presence, he comes swiftly and acts fast.

As I sat there hovering in space and joined to my ex, I called out, 'Divine and Powerful Archangel Michael, I respectfully ask for your assistance to end my plight.' In my mind's eye I saw him appear in a swirl of blinding yellow light and heat. He was incredibly beautiful and awesome, naked and androgynous, hairless but with huge sweeping wings of glowing white feathers. In his left hand he brandished an enormous sword, its handle made of red, molten steel and its blade a long, unwavering flame so hot that it was blue-white, like a laser light.

He raised the sword high over his head and swung it down slicing the cord. At once I felt the pressure on my stomach ease, but in my mind's eye I could see a tenuous glow start to reappear. Again, I saw the Angel raise his sword and this time repeatedly slice it down between us until the cord was all but tiny filaments of light that floated away. The Angel came and hovered behind me enfolding me in his soft downy wings as I saw the image of my ex fade to a speck and disappear. I stayed floating within the Angel's embrace feeling at peace and pure, and in the 'real' world I lay down on the grass and fell into a light sleep.

After some time I awoke and got up. I walked over to the pile and tipped the garlic and pine needles over it. I took a match and lit the edges of some of the cards and photos. Then

I sat down about four feet away, made a protective circle of sea salt around me, and watched the pile flare up. I still felt the phantom wings of the Archangel holding me and I felt protected, safe and unattached as I watched the flames destroy and purify the remnants of my past with my ex.

After about twenty minutes all that was left was glowing red embers and I breathed in the cool night air deeply. I felt really cleansed and free. I opened my circle of sea salt by pushing some aside, picked up a spade and began to turn over the earth where the fire was, burying the embers. I scooped up as much of the salt as I could and sprinkled it over where the fire had been to completely nullify any remaining energies. Then I went inside to bed and slept deeply.

Dare I say, **'like magick!', from the next day there were no more phone calls, visits or confrontations in the street. No longer was I going over the relationship in my head; instead I was thinking solely about myself and getting on with my life.** I did bump into my ex about five years later and as soon as I saw him I felt Archangel Michael's wings about me again. As we made brief small talk, I thought to myself, 'God, what did I *ever* see in you?'

If you want to try a spell like this yourself but don't have a backyard, maybe you could go to a remote beach and have the fire on the sand, but only if your memorabilia is just paper so you're not polluting the environment. If you have a fireplace you could do it at home and gather up the ashes, and put them in the outside bin (once they are cold!) for collection (this also applies for outdoor burnings where perhaps some items are made of plastic). After the fire pick out any remaining non-biodegradable objects and wrap them up in white cloth or paper and also put them in the outdoor bin.

189

* * *

Often long-term relationships need a bit of spicing up and there are a few little magickal tricks that can help. If you're fighting, seven drops of basil oil in an oil burner will clear the air between you both. If you tend to argue a lot at home, especially if you share a small space, stale negative energies can build up and need to be cleared to make way for better, empathic communication.

Buy a wooden-handled, straw broom that you will only use for the purpose of 'energy sweeping'. When you are alone at home and know you won't be disturbed, bathe and rub yourself down with sea salt, put on some simple, clean, white clothing or perhaps stay skyclad, and open all the windows and doors. In a bowl, make a mixture of two cups of purified or spring water, a handful of sea salt and seven drops of camphor oil. With your right hand sprinkle this mixture over the straw end of the broom and then go to the room where you argue the most, maybe the bedroom or the dining room, and start to 'sweep' – not the floor, but the air! Start at the top corner of the room and work through 'sweeping' all the stale energies out the window. When you have completed the first room, sprinkle the broom with more of the 'cleaner' and 'sweep' the other rooms.

When you have finished wrap the straw end of the broom in white cloth (I put it in a white pillowcase) and stand it in the back of your wardrobe or somewhere where no one is going to find it and use it to clean up crumbs off the kitchen floor! 'Sweeping' like this really does clear the air but also, when I run around the house like a mad woman swatting away flies with a big broom, I also often crack up with laughter which improves my mood. Then when my grumpy loved one comes home I feel cheered and can avoid any repetitive arguments and get on with establishing friendlier vibes.

If your relationship is lacking in sexual oomph try placing a few bowls of dried galangal root around the house with a few drops of ylang ylang in each. Galangal is commonly used in Indian and Thai cooking but most New Age and Witchcraft supply stores sell it as it promotes lust; and ylang ylang encourages sexual passion and harmony. As you place each bowl around the house, for a few moments place both hands over it and focus on your breathing, stilling your mind. When you are ready, focus on your sexual chakra centre and see it pulse a deep orangey-red within you. Draw the energy up to your heart chakra, which is glowing green, and see the two colours blend like an oil wheel. Now let this light suffuse your whole body and think about all the fun, raunchy times you and your loved one have spent together, or you would like to spend together. Let your imagination run wild! See those images being swept up by the swirling colours, and tumble down your arms, through your hands and into the bowl, infusing the contents with your desire.

Exotic tropical flowers like birds of paradise, orchids and hibiscus can add a luscious, passionate energy to any environment, as can lots of red candles lit just before the sunsets and left burning to illuminate the evening. I set up a great seduction scene for a new lover once by doing this and cooking a meal using lots of 'love foods'. I made a

191

baked tofu casserole with apple and cinnamon chutney and we drank lots of warm honey mead that I spiced up with extra cloves and ginger. For dessert we gobbled each other up! Scott Cunningham's excellent *The Magic of Food* has lots of suggestions and I often refer to it because I find cooking quite a spiritual experience.

To me the process of preparing food – blending flavours, textures, colours and energies – is an empowering, magickal act of creation that can nourish and enchant. A book (and the movie based on it) that perfectly illustrates this is Laura Esquivel's wonderful *Like Water for Chocolate*. In a poignant and yet funny scene the heroine, Tita, weeps as she prepares the wedding cake for her sister's marriage to the boy that she, Tita, is in love with. Her tears fall into the mixing bowl and bewitch the cake. At the wedding after eating the cake, the bride, groom, family and all the guests can only cry and cry and cry! The book has food, love and magick interwoven all the way through and is one of my favourite novels.

I've left the best love spell for last and it's one that most people find very difficult to do. It's a 'Self-love' spell and I think this is the most important kind of love spell of all – for when self-love is present, all other kinds of love follow.

You will need:

✳ A beeswax candle (or a vegetable wax white candle can substitute);
✳ A mirror that you can sit in front of;
✳ A stick of Nag Champa incense or any other possessing a really pungent, heady scent.

You will also need to memorize this enchantment which is adapted, in part, from the infamous *Desiderata.*

I am a Child of the Universe
No less than the seas and the stars
Beautiful and Complete in Myself
Blessed, Essential and Perfect

Carve your full name into the candle with the tip of a pointed knife. When you have done this, anoint the candle with your spit using your right thumb and forefinger and place it in a holder in front of the mirror. Sit with the lights turned off and light the incense, close your eyes and quietly breathe in and out. Feel any tension draining away through the soles of your feet, through the floor and down into the earth. If you are in an apartment, see the tension make its way through the struc-ture of the building and down into the earth.

When you feel very calm and relaxed, open your eyes and light the candle. With its flame illuminating your face, gaze into your own eyes in the mirror. Try not to think anything – just stare until your face in the mirror goes out of focus and your eyes become all that you see. When this happens say, 'I love you'. You'll probably find at this point that your face will immediately jump into focus and you will feel uncomfortable and maybe even silly. Persevere, saying calmly over and over again, 'I love you, I love you'.

Once when I was very depressed I did this spell, and at this point I started crying and feeling pathetic, but it's important to let any emotions that surface like this to pass. Just let them flow out your feet and down into the ground.

Continue to look into your eyes but now start saying 'I love you, _____ (your full name)'. Keep saying this over and over and let any rising sad, or even angry, emotions drain away. After a while you should start to experience happy and ecstatic feelings. Even the most depressed people who have tried this spell have found that this happens. Keep repeating the love mantra until you feel suffused by the loving energy of unconditional self-acceptance. If you feel unhappy and uncomfortable in your body, you could perform the spell sky-clad. After spending some time focusing on your face and repeating the words, 'I love you', you could stand back from the mirror and focus on your whole body reflection, still saying the mantra.

Then, when you feel ready, take a deep breath and passion-ately and purposefully say the enchantment. Feel the words permeate every fibre of your being with complete conviction.

Now, snuff the candle with your fingertips. The spell is complete. Keep the candle on your altar or wrap it in white cloth and put it away somewhere. It has absorbed the magick-al, restorative energy you emanated while doing the spell, and so over the next four days if you need to reaffirm feelings of self-love at any time, light the candle and gaze into the flame for a few minutes, breathing deeply and letting tension and fear drain away through the soles of your feet. After four days, if you are still feeling a bit up and down, it's a good idea to do the spell again with a new candle. Bury the old one in the ground, don't throw it in the bin. Usually, however, this spell works fast and can often be an immediate catalyst for new, happier times in your life.

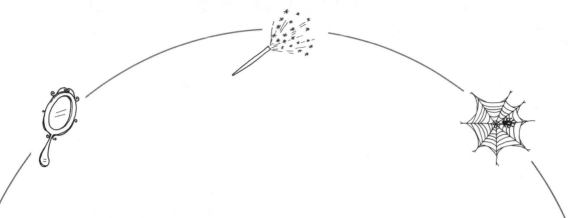

BITCHCRAFT

HEXING, PSYCHIC ATTACK AND PROTECTION

Hah! I bet this is the first chapter you turned to! I have one opinion about hexing – in 99.9% of cases, I don't do it. Not because I can't or because I don't want to, but because hexing someone ties them to you. It becomes your responsibility to make sure their life is miserable or they meet an early demise (or whatever) and it's a bloody hassle. If I have a problem with, for example, an ex-lover, the last thing I want is to have to devote to them the huge amount of time and effort it takes to effectively hex them.

I'd rather just make the break and get on with my life.

Some might find it quite thrilling to picture themselves standing over a cauldron of boiling bat's blood, tossing in the fingernail clippings and locks of hair of their despised one, stirring the concoction with the leg bone of an ox and watching evil black smoky demons rise out ready to do their bidding. However, real, effective hexing spells aren't about gothic theatre props: they're generally very simple in practice and as I reinforce in this book, the real power behind any spell, hexing or otherwise, comes from the passion and emotion it is fuelled with.

To stop someone from harming and hurting others on a physical level, it is far more effective and bad karma-free to use a good binding spell. You need to make a doll (a poppet) from plain cloth stuffed with cotton wool. Make this before your ritual and don't worry if you're not a sewing expert – something with a body, head, two arms and two legs will do.

You will also need:

✳ Some red ribbon or thick thread
✳ A black candle
✳ Patchouli leaves and frankincense
✳ A charcoal block
✳ A piece of white cloth

At your altar cast Circle (if you don't have an altar, just cast Circle in a private room) and create a sacred space between the worlds by burning the patchouli leaves with frankincense on the charcoal block. Usually patchouli is used in love spells, but its dark, pungent aroma is also associated with the arcane, all-pervading power of Hecate, Witch Queen of the Underworld, seen in the dark moon and at midnight, and avenger of all crimes, particularly those against women.

Light the black candle and pass the poppet through the incense smoke saying, *'Hecate, Great Goddess of Life and Death, I ask you to acknowledge that this creature of cloth be known now as the flesh and blood of _____ (name of person or if you are binding a criminal, their title eg: 'the rapist')'.* Take the poppet in your hands and wrap it firmly with the red ribbon, tightly binding any limbs that could harm. For example, if you are binding a rapist make sure you bind it particularly tight over the groin area, and if you are binding someone who harms with words wrap it tightly over the mouth area. As you do this repeat the charge: *'Between the worlds in Hecate's eyes you, _____ (insert name), are bound powerless. In the eyes of this world you are bound harmless.'* When the poppet is firmly bound, lay it down in front of you and visualize white light like a heavy fishing net dropping over and clinging to it like glue, and binding the person completely from committing any harmful action.

Wrap the poppet in the white cloth and bury it somewhere close to where the bound person lives or frequents. Or if you can't get there, bury it by the ocean and bid the sea to bless the spell. If you bury it in sand, make sure you bury it really deep, so that little kids building sand castles don't dig it up the next day.

From experience, I have often found the best binding spell in everyday situations to be tolerance and forgiveness. Foster within yourself the ability to walk away from petty and vicious confrontations. People who are out to hurt you, or scare you, need you badly – for without you there's nothing for them to

Hexing and Healing – A Magickal Ethics Ramble

I cannot stress enough, it really is best *not* to hex. To hex will bring into play **the Threefold Law – that which you send out returns to you threefold.** So if someone has hurt you or someone you love already, do you really want to go through more hell? (Not that your only deterrent from doing harm should be that you don't want to be done over yourself). Do a binding spell instead to stop them from committing further harmful actions, pick up the pieces and move on.

Healing is one of the most traditional Witchy skills. Healing is something all Witches feel called to do – whether it's healing yourself, your pet, your friend, the planet, or warring peoples in other countries. Being able to cast a healing spell is infinitely more satisfying than hexing for the same reasons that being a skilled doctor is a more impressive calling than being a hit-man. While there has to be a balance in our lives between the positive and negative, it doesn't mean that we need to spend equal time on constructive and destructive activities! The negative is hard at work already – death, disease, injury and violence are always out there waiting to attach themselves to us and the people we love.

At this point in our development, our greatest challenges are in protecting and healing. Destructive behaviour is so easy. It's the arena of the idiot. Think about the millions of years of evolution that produced a fly and the brainless response that lets us flatten it without a qualm. Or think of a couple conceiving a child in love and passion, protecting, educating and nurturing him for years, only to see him dragged into someone else's war and blown away by a gun – a millisecond squeeze of a trigger and it's over. Any imbecile could have pulled the trigger but the raising of the child took years of care, intelligence and creativity. Imagine if the bullet did hideous damage but didn't kill the boy; that a surgeon put him back together, using every fraction of her skill and training to repair the boy's broken body and bring him back from the gates of death. It's crystal clear – destructive action is generally as challenging as scratching your backside, while nurturing and healing can test us and strengthen us beyond what we might have thought possible. That's genuine power.

199

unleash their cruelty and ignorance on. If you don't take their bait, if you don't hang around for them to be horrible to, then what can they do? Nothing! Effectively you have rendered them powerless, and rather than you spending time on casting spells on them, you can start casting spells on your own life to repair the damage done, empower yourself and move on.

It has been said, however, **that a Witch who cannot hex, cannot heal.** Most experienced Witches respect and understand the role that hexing can play in the Craft. Many Witches do not 'turn the other cheek', so rapists, child molesters, and other violent criminals can be considered worthy recipients of a particularly lethal hexing spell. In fact, a good analogy for hexing is physical revenge: if a loved one is raped and you know who the culprit is, it can be very tempting to take the law into your own hands and dispose of the culprit. You might decide to do this, but you'd do so in the full knowledge that you'd be likely to spend time in prison as a consequence. The same applies to hexing. A particular person might warrant it, but you'd have to be prepared to bear the unpleasant consequences in your own life.

In cases of love, or more specifically disgruntled lovers, I don't think hexing spells are warranted and ask for trouble, but for interest's sake coming up on the next few pages is a hexing spell that an acquaintance of mine performed on an ex-lover who had hurt her deeply. It worked in that he had quite a bit of bad luck befall him – but so did she: her next boyfriend turned out to be worse than the one she hexed. She knew better than to hex again. You can try this spell out, and I have actually included appropriate things to do if you are hexing a criminal, but first a few words of warning: one of the basic rules of Witchcraft is, **'Do what you will if it harm none.'** All Witches accept that if you do something to deliberately harm someone, then another (karmic) Witches' rule comes into play: **'That which you send out, returns threefold.'**

In other words, if you give someone a hard time, you're most likely to have three times as hard a time as them. Of course, you could get on the karma roundabout and think, 'Oh, I'm paying them back for the hurt they've caused, so it's their karma I'm dishing out here and not mine.' Not so – the nature of life is cyclical and eventually everything comes back around. Even though it can be argued that by hexing a rapist/criminal you are protecting the innocent and doing something positive, you still have to accept that there will be some kind of repercussion in your own life.

As I mentioned earlier, however, the ultimate show of power is the ability to forgive and to heal. You will do far better to forgive the person and even do a healing spell for them. People who hurt are usually suffering themselves. But if you're absolutely sure you have to hex then something else to consider is that the most effective spellcasting is done when the mind is passionate but also *very* focused. If you feel the need to hex someone, especially an ex-lover, then it is quite likely that you are on a bit of an emotional roller-coaster. Your spell will either not work, or be likely to ricochet around the hexed one's life and then back into your own like a bullet fired in a small room.

You've been warned ...

A Hexing Spell

The first things you need for this spell are body bits. I mean fingernail clippings, or hair, or spit from the person you are hexing – the more the better. How you get these I'll leave up to your own devious methods. My acquaintance was hexing an abusive and cheating ex-lover so it wasn't too hard for her to get a few bits and pieces, like hair from a brush and bits of toenails off the carpet (her lover had the revolting habit of picking off his nails in bed and dropping them onto the floor!). One good trick is to get fingerprints on a glass – just be sure the glass is only imprinted with the victim's prints and not yours.

Once you've assembled the body bits, you'll also need:

❊ Two black, vegetable wax candles
❊ A double-boiler saucepan

❋ Two pieces of black cloth
❋ A packet of pins
❋ A piece of black paper
❋ Perhaps a photograph of the
individual. This isn't really
necessary if you have the body bits,
but having a photo can help you
focus your energy.
❋ Some frankincense oil, pure not
perfume.

On the first night of the waning moon, just before midnight
take everything into the kitchen as this is where you'll be conducting your spell (not very glamorous, I know, but you need
to use the oven). On the kitchen table or bench top lay down
one piece of black cloth and on it place one black candle in a
suitable stand. Lay out the body bits, a pile of pins, the paper,
oil and whatever else you have. Put a little water into the
saucepan and place the boiler over the top.

Just after the stroke of midnight, light the candle, take a
deep breath and still your mind. Think carefully about what
you are planning to do and know that whatever harm or mis-
fortune that will befall your victim will also befall you, but in
ways you cannot envisage now – the universe is full of
unpleasant surprises when it comes to this kind of stuff. If
you decide you still wish to go ahead, remove all your clothing, including jewellery, hair ties – everything. Leave it all in a
pile on the floor beside you. Now, anoint your chakra points
with the frankincense oil – the crown of your head; your third
eye (between the eyebrows); your throat; over your heart; your
solar plexus; just below your navel; and the base of your

spine, over the tailbone. In doing this you are attempting to seal off your auras to help protect you against the repercussions you are likely to suffer from doing this spell. In addition to protecting your aural self with the oil, it's also a good idea to seal and protect your physical self by applying salt water on your body 'openings', the eyes, ears, nostrils, genitals, and even the so-called 'blind' openings, i.e. nipples and navel. There are twelve openings in males and thirteen in females.

My acquaintance who originally did this spell cast a Circle at this point, inviting various nefarious entities in to help her conduct the spell. I'm not going to give you the methods and incantations for this as it is potentially far too risky. I don't personally believe in self-aware demonic entities but I do believe in destructive negative energies, and to wield these volatile forces in a focused and directed way requires extensive knowledge and training. It would be irresponsible of me to encourage experimentation with this energy. If someone decided to hex a rapist or other violent criminal, rather than calling on negative energies it is far better to invoke balanced deities who have associations with defence or justice. The Goddess Nemesis welcomes the opportunity to bring justice to an offender and restore the balance of nature, as does the God, Thor, who will wield his mighty hammer and crush those who deserve it.

When you are anointed, breathe deeply again and focus calmly on the image of the despised one. At the same time take the unlit black candle, snap it in half and place it into the double boiler. Gently turn up the heat so that the wax starts to soften – you don't want it to become runny, just very pliable. When it is soft enough, pick out the wick and focus again on the image of the despised one, pushing the body bits into the soft wax. Remove it from the pan and as best you can mould it into the general shape of a body.

As you squeeze and shape the wax, think intensely only of the despised one – not yourself, not what they've done to you or anybody else – just them, their face, the sound of their voice, the smell of their body. If you feel any emotion, channel it into anger but keep a lid on it for now, just let it build up inside you. If you do this spell for someone who had committed a violent crime against someone else, then you would focus on the crime they committed as you create the wax effigy.

Also it's unlikely that you would have the criminal's body bits and in this case any remnant of their physical presence will do. If you have none then carve the word 'rapist', 'murderer', or whatever is appropriate, into the wax body.

When you are satisfied with your creations, take one of the pins and while the wax is still a little soft, stick it into where his or her heart would be. As you do this, feel your anger and hatred reach boiling point. Say out loud, '_____ (insert their name or title), as the moon's light fades to black, feel your Life Force drain into a bottomless pit from which you cannot crawl.' As you say 'cannot crawl', jab pins into the figure's legs and in your mind see your victim collapse in a heap. As you see them on the ground, stab more pins into your creation's back saying, 'I will you to suffer as I (or your victim/s) have suffered!' While you're doing this it is very important to pour your anger and hatred into the wax image – if you're doing this spell properly you would be sweating and shaking by now.

If you are hexing a rapist or other criminal it is now appropriate to hold the effigy between your hands and say, 'May justice prevail, so that your own ignorance and ego is your *downfall.'* Visualize the criminal being captured by police and locked up in jail with no hope for release.

Now it is yourself you must jab a pin into. Draw blood on the tip of the index finger of your right hand and with the tip write your victim's name (or name the crime) on the black paper and then your own under it in blood. As you do this say, *'Bound to me are you by blood, may no other release you from this spell than me.'* Take the paper and the poppet and wrap them in black cloth. Now snuff the candle with your fingertips – the spell is complete. Turn on the lights and clear up everything. You may notice a strange, unpleasant vibe in the air – if so burn some frankincense incense and open the windows.

You have few choices here. One is that you can mail your horrible little wax thing to the person you have hexed – this is likely to make them either freak out or laugh their heads off. Or perhaps you could take a polaroid of the doll and mail that to them in an attempt to intimidate them. Most amateur hexers' spells work best when the victim is susceptible to suggestion. Planting a seed of paranoia, in the sense that 'someone is out to get them', makes the victim more likely to become nervous, fearful and clumsy. They may start to have sleepless nights, get depressed and even do something stupid like walk out in front of a bus.

In the case of a criminal whom you cannot approach, keep the effigy in a dark cupboard for three days so only you know where it is. At midnight on the third night burn the doll outside, and as the flames die down to embers, see the criminal's Life Force fading away. Bury the remnants and sprinkle sea salt over the ground and then walk away without looking back.

There is an Aboriginal method of hexing called 'pointing the bone': if a certain bone is pointed at an individual by an empowered tribal elder, the individual knows they are cursed to die. Apparently there is a case where an Aboriginal man was taken to western doctors by his family in a desperate attempt to restore his fading Life Force (after a bone had been pointed at him) but the doctors could not determine what was wrong with him. The man grew more and more listless and after a few weeks he died. Some would consider this working purely by the power of suggestion; others, especially Witches, would think that, indeed, the power of suggestion had something to do with it – but more important is the 'psychic attack' that comes with the spell.

When my acquaintance cast her hexing spell a big part of it involved creating a spectre-like form. The job of this entity was to haunt her ex-lover at night in his dreams. Now, my acquaintance is convinced that she actually saw a dark form manifest in front of her as she was conducting the spell, and as far as I'm concerned that's as real as it needs to be. Whether it went and haunted her ex-lover – well, there's no definitive proof, but the poor hexed one had insomnia for weeks and was a nervous wreck after the spell was performed.

Image magic is to be treated with respect. If you're very clear on your intention (and, to repeat, healing is far and away the least murky motive) it may be very effective. The danger is that it may also be effective if your motive is not clear.

Remember **most of the human race is emotionally rather fragile. Handle with care.**

Psychic attack is a popular catch-cry for some Witches, like candida and irritable bowel syndrome is for many naturopaths. As soon as something goes wrong for which there isn't an obvious explanation, then it must be a 'psychic attack' from some rival Witch or enemy. Traditionally psychic attacks can be anything from vermin infestation of your home to a run of bad luck, an illness, injury or a general feeling of uneasiness. I never worry about psychic attack for a couple of reasons. Firstly, I don't believe in good and evil, God and the Devil. I believe Universal Energy is neutral and it is the way it is shaped and used that colours it as a positive or negative (or somewhere in between) force.

I also believe that as I am 'a child of the Universe', I have the same power and potential within me that exists outside me. So, if someone is giving me a hard time and sending me negative energy, I am well equipped to transform that energy into one that is more agreeable for me. Psychic attack in everyday life is probably not going to involve ghosts haunting you at night; it's more likely to be a scenario such as having to go to a meeting at work and experiencing hostility from your fellow workers. As you walk into the boardroom you can feel a very chilly and unwelcoming vibe directed at you. Or you walk into class at school and, although they don't say anything, the 'toughies' up the back are ganging up on you, and you sit in your seat and feel their eyes boring holes in your back.

Sometimes feeling bad vibes is not so much someone psyching you out, it is a matter of falling prey to your own insecurities and lack of confidence. If, however, you are positive that people are out to get you, there are a few things you can do. Creating a protective shield around you is a good start. You can do this by visualizing a sparkling, diamond-white egg-shaped aura around your body starting about three centimetres from your skin and extending out about fifty centimetres. Use your mind's eye to see any destructive energy directed at you being absorbed by it and transformed into constructive and harmonious energy. With a bit of practice you can develop a shield that can even deflect cruel words, angry looks and nastiness on the physical plane. The task of focusing to visualize a protective sphere can calm your mind and centre your physical actions to the point where you can resist getting involved in arguments and other distressing situations. You can actually render those situations neutral, again either by walking away or by exuding a calming energy.

You can create another protective sphere by extending your left hand out from your body and clicking your index, third finger and thumb. As you snap them, see a thread of deep violet/blue light whizz out and circle your body like a skipping rope. The purplish light is reflective of the deepest spiritual universal energy and is good to use in conjunction with the white sphere when you're feeling particularly snowed under. See it whip swiftly around you, briskly deflecting any strikes of negative energy. You can click it on and off with your fingers as you need it. It's also good to say a few affirmations. As you imagine your shield you could also say out aloud or internally, *'I am loved and protected by all that is divine and pure in the Universe.'*

One old method of ridding your house of negative psychic energy is to place an egg (free range of course!) in a corner of every room. Replace them once a week and continue to use them until you feel the negative energy gone. Eggs are considered mystical symbols of creation. In many myths and legends they are mentioned to represent the Life Force itself and are always sacred. Placing eggs in rooms allows them to absorb unpleasant and destructive energy and start to restore it to neutrality again – but when you replace them, don't eat them!

Bury the eggs in the garden to help neutralize the negativity, or, if you have to, throw them away in an outdoor bin and as you do so, say a few words of acknowledgement for the role they have played in ridding your life of that negativity. Of course, if you want to be nasty and confuse your attacker, you could always bake them a cake with the eggs and take it to them. They'll be so surprised at your friendly gesture that they'll happily munch out and get a good feed of their own nastiness. The law of 'That which you send out, returns three-fold' would be giving them their just desserts.

There are many formal rituals and spells for protection and purification and many of the books listed in the Library have interesting and effective examples. The following record of ritual work is taken straight from my Book of Shadows circa 1989. I did this ritual a week after moving into a new home and sensing that there was something not quite right about the place!

Midnight, Wednesday, 4th September, 1989, Moon in Cancer
PURIFICATION AND DEDICATION OF MY HOME

Tonight I made an infusion of sage (by steeping a handful of the herb in boiling water) then I lit a blue candle and placed it in the bathroom. I showered by candlelight, visualizing the dross of everyday living being sloughed off me and getting swept down the drain with the swirling waters. I then doused myself with the infusion, visualizing it healing and closing any holes in my aura and helping to realign my chakras.

I set up my altar in the living room. I lit two white candles with the flame from the blue candle that had illuminated my purification. Using my mortar and pestle I made an incense of benzoin gum and sandalwood for purification and added Dragon's

Blood for protection and dedication. I cast Circle to encompass the whole apartment and called in the Quarters. While burning incense on the altar I took a bowl of salted water from room to room, sprinkling it with my fingers and repeating my purification charge: 'Goodbye, goodbye to the past that dwells here; goodbye, goodbye to you spirits and ghosts, it is time for you to move on and away. Good luck and farewell.'

Back at my altar I then added more incense to the bowl and walked from room to room fumigating any negative energy, saying, 'In this space in this world and all the worlds between, I release all negativity directed at me. Here in this space I am divinely protected and safe.'

Finally at my altar I performed the following dedication of my home: 'I dedicate this home to me. I fill its rooms with my energy. In this space all things creative and peaceful shall reign, especially love, health and financial gain. This home of peace and fun and love vibrates now in my name. So Mote It Be.'

Then I closed Circle, put everything away and went and had the first really good sleep in a week!

Of course, this ritual is personal but it provides an idea of how you can go about purifying your space and aligning its energies with your own. It's also adaptable for purifying and protecting working environments, not only your own but that of others – you can tailor the purification and dedication enchantments by substituting the name of the person you are doing the spell for and the appropriate location.

It's a good idea to align the energies of any environment you are spending a lot of time in with your own. In magickally marking out your personal territory you are ensuring that you will be protected and supported in all your endeavours there.

COSMETIC CONJURINGS

MAKING YOUR OWN WITCHY COSMETICS

When I first started getting really passionate about Witchcraft I had more free time on my hands than I do now. I would spend evenings mixing up incenses and oils, potions and ointments. I became an expert at whipping up Witchy cosmetics for face, body and hair care on the inside and out. Following are my notes from my Beauty Book of Shadows! They are all tried and tested and pretty damn good, if I do say so myself! I found Alan B. Hayes book, Beauty from the Garden *(Sally Milner, 1994) very helpful, amongst others, and made additions and adaptations according to my instincts and experiments.*

✦ *Note: all these products need to be stored in glass and any jars or bottles you use need to be boiled and sterilized. Just pop them in a saucepan full of simmering water for five minutes and then let them dry by themselves.* ✦

Hestia's Honey Sweet Lotion

This is the lotion to use when you want to put your house in order! By this I mean cleanse and balance your skin so that it feels supple, and comfortable and easy to live in!

You will need:

❈ **6 tablespoons of arrowroot gel;**
❈ **30 mls strong chamomile tea infusion;**
❈ **2 teaspoons honey;**
❈ **8 drops of lemon juice.**

Combine all the ingredients in a suitable bottle and shake thoroughly. Keep it in the fridge and shake before use. Use it whenever your skin is feeling stressed, clogged and tired – instantly brightens and smooths.

Arrowroot Gel

Combine 1 teaspoon of arrowroot with 4 tablespoons of distilled water. Heat gently, stirring until mixture thickens and clears. Remove from heat.

Diana's Dose of Divinity

This light facial mask makes your skin glow like a Goddess!

✦ *Note: boys, don't get this on your beard stubble whatever you do!*
Use it an hour after shaving. ✦

You will need:

❋ **250 ml of egg white;**
❋ **50 ml glycerine;**
❋ **2 drops of orange oil;**
❋ **2 drops of neroli oil;**
❋ **2 drops of thyme;**
❋ **10 ml vodka.**

213

Thoroughly mix the ingredients and allow to stand for three days so that the liquid becomes clear; then decant into a fresh bottle. Massage a teaspoon of the mask into your skin and leave for twenty minutes before rinsing.

Persephone's Perfection

Like Persephone's return from the Underworld which brought the sleeping wintery land blooming back to life, this cream will restore radiance to a dry, dull face.

You will need:

* ❋ **15 g beeswax;**
* ❋ **30 ml almond oil;**
* ❋ **20 ml avocado oil;**
* ❋ **5 ml virgin olive oil;**
* ❋ **5 ml jojoba;**
* ❋ **40 ml distilled water;**
* ❋ **8 drops lemon juice;**
* ❋ **5 drops of rose geranium oil;**
* ❋ **¼ teaspoon triethanalomine (get it from the chemist).**

Melt the beeswax in a double-boiler saucepan over a low heat. When it's completely liquid, stir in the distilled water, then the oils (except the rose geranium) and triethanalomine. Remove from heat and add the rose geranium and lemon juice, beating with a spoon until mixture cools. *Warning!* It looks a yucky brown colour until it cools and then it turns a beautiful pale yellow. This small amount goes a long way – take a pea-sized amount and warm between your fingers and then smooth over your face.

✦ *Note: if you have oily skin, exchange the avocado oil for wheatgerm oil and the rose geranium for lemongrass.* ✦

Medusa's Makeup Remover

This stuff can scare the make up off a goth!

You will need:

❋ **1 teaspoon each of dried sage and yarrow;**
❋ **20 ml of liquid witchhazel (from the chemist);**
❋ **15 g beeswax;**
❋ **30 ml avocado oil;**
❋ **40 ml virgin olive oil;**
❋ **3 drops eucalyptus oil;**
❋ **20 ml aloe vera juice;**
❋ **¼ teaspoon triethanalomine.**

Finely grind the herbs together in a mortar and pestle, or coffee-grinder. Melt the beeswax in a double-boiler saucepan over a low heat and add oils, aloe vera, triethanalomine and herbs – stirring well until mixed. Remove from heat and beat continually until cooled and then stir in the liquid witchhazel.

This is a lovely green colour and works best by warming some between the palms of your hands before spreading over your face. Wash it off with a warm cloth.

Rhea's Rough Treatment

This Greek Mother of the Universe can smooth over any problem – this gentle facial scrub is brilliant!

You will need:

- ❋ **4 tablespoons of finely ground oatmeal;**
- ❋ **2 tablespoons hazelnut ground meal;**
- ❋ **4 tablespoons mixed ground herbs – rosemary, yarrow and mint (put all the above in a coffee grinder);**
- ❋ **1 tablespoon olive oil;**
- ❋ **½ cup of natural yogurt;**
- ❋ **12 drops lemon juice;**
- ❋ **2 tablespoons aloe vera juice.**

Mix the above ingredients together, adding the lemon juice and aloe vera last. Keep it in the fridge, giving it a quick stir before use.

Hade's Herbal Helper

This dark brew is a fantastic skin tonic, especially for men after shaving.

Blend the following amounts of herbal teas (make the teas by using one teaspoon of dried herb to one cup of water):

- ❋ **¼ cup sage;**
- ❋ **¼ cup chamomile;**
- ❋ **¼ cup yarrow;**
- ❋ **¼ cup rosemary;**
- ❋ **½ tablespoon glycerine;**
- ❋ **20 ml rosewater;**
- ❋ **10 ml witchhazel;**
- ❋ **1 drop of patchouli oil.**

Shake well and store in the fridge.

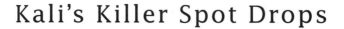

Kali's Killer Spot Drops

These drops chop the heads off the bacteria which cause pimples, and heals the damaged skin.

You will need:

* ❋ **a strong brew of comfrey tea;**
* ❋ **2 tablespoons comfrey tea infusion (steep comfrey in water overnight so it's a strong brew);**
* ❋ **11 drops lavender oil;**
* ❋ **7 drops of tea tree oil;**
* ❋ **12 drops of lemon juice;**
* ❋ **1 egg white.**

Whip the lot together and store in the fridge. Rub a drop gently on spots and watch them disappear!

Lilith's Lovely Lippy

A lip balm that will make your lips as lush as the Garden of Eden.

You will need:

* ❋ **15 g beeswax;**
* ❋ **50 ml almond oil;**
* ❋ **20 ml virgin olive oil;**
* ❋ **40 ml rosewater;**
* ❋ **2 teaspoons honey;**
* ❋ **2 drops wintergreen oil.**

Melt the beeswax in a double-saucepan over a low heat. When it's completely liquid stir in the oils and rosewater. Remove from heat, but leave the top pan over the water and stir in the honey. Pour the contents into a glass bowl and beat until cool. This stuff thickens and goes creamy white. It works fantastically and doesn't go cakey on your lips.

Pan's Peppermint Paste

Pan, being the lusty God he is, needs fresh breath – and this toothpaste does the trick! It really freshens and leaves teeth smooth. The fact that it's brown isn't off-putting at all!

You will need:

* ❋ **2 drops of peppermint oil;**
* ❋ **10 ml of virgin olive oil;**
* ❋ **2 tablespoons powdered orris root;**
* ❋ **1 teaspoon of sandalwood powder;**
* ❋ **1 tiny pinch of cayenne pepper;**
* ❋ **1½ tablespoons arrowroot gel.**

Mix the peppermint oil with the olive oil and then add the rest of the ingredients. Mix to a putty-like consistency. Store in the bathroom cupboard where it is dark and cool.

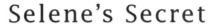

Selene's Secret

These hair rinses make your hair *shine*! They are especially good for people who have dreadlocks – they condition and disinfect the scalp, helping to keep dandruff at bay.

Wash your hair with your normal shampoo and rinse well. If you have dreads just pour the rinse through and let it dry. If you don't have dreads but would like your hair to have a bit of texture, don't wash it, but just pour the rinse through as well.

B a s e   R e c i p e

You will need:

❋ **2 teaspoons tea tree oil;**
❋ **3 teaspoons glycerine;**
❋ **3 cups of the herbal infusion (see below) strained really well;**
❋ **5 drops of the appropriate essential oil (see below).**

Herbal infusions for fair hair (including red hair)

You will need:

❋ **2 tablespoons chamomile;**
❋ **2 tablespoons yarrow;**
❋ **1 tablespoon elderflower.**

Simmer above dried herbs in 2 litres of water for ten minutes and then steep overnight.

Herbal infusion for dark hair

You will need:

❋ **2 tablespoons rosemary;**
❋ **2 tablespoons nettle;**
❋ **1 tablespoon borage or sage.**

Simmer above dried herbs in 2 litres of water for ten minutes and then steep overnight.

Essential Oils

❋ **3 drops frankincense and 2 of clary sage for a warm scent (good for autumn and winter);**
❋ **3 drops of thyme and 2 of marjoram for a cool scent (good for spring and summer).**
❋ **Invent your own blend!**

DIVINE DEALINGS

GETTING A GRIP ON THE PAST, PRESENT AND FUTURE

Divination is something that every Witch is drawn to practise – but it's not only about looking into the future. **It's about being grounded in the present, learning from the past and evolving into the future.** *Any reading using the forms of divination below will give you an idea of most likely outcomes based on where you sit in the Universal scheme of things at the time of the reading.*

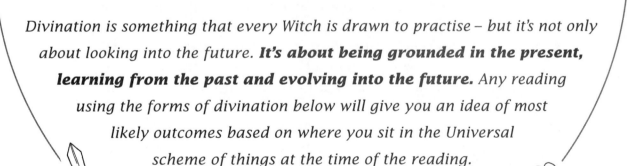

This can all change in the blink of an eye though as the Universe is in a constant state of flux – however don't become a divination addict! By this I mean if you don't like the results of a reading, don't do another one straight away. I usually won't do a reading more than once a month and my favourite methods are described below.

If you are just starting out as a Diviner, take your time and trust your intuition – the methods below are not only tools to tap into the subconscious but also keys to open the doors to the worlds between the worlds that lie beyond. How well you navigate your way (that is, what you divine) will be determined by how receptive and open you are.

Let's Look Into it

Scrying is a method of divination that is often very revealing and meditative. Using a 'facilitator' you defocus the conscious senses and let the deeper ones have their say. Crystal balls, black mirrors, bowls of 'Black Water' and pieces of opaque crystal such as black agate and obsidian are all

useful. You can buy crystal balls, black mirrors and the opaque crystals at Witchcraft and New Age supply stores. I especially like using the bowl of 'Black Water' because it can be created as you need it and tuned specifically to your needs. Here is what you do:

Black Water

Fill a glass or crystal bowl with water, at least nine inches in diameter. Into this put 22 drops of black india ink (from a stationery supply store) or more if required, until an unfathomable swirling blackness is achieved.

Ritual for Effective Scrying

Set up the bowl with two small white candles either side, making sure that there are no reflections of the flames in the water – the water must seem like a bottomless tunnel. Cast Circle and add the condenser to the water after the Circle is cast. Take seven deep breaths and still your mind. Gazing into the Black Water say, 'My mind is clear, my vision pure.' This statement is to assist you in achieving a blank, unquestioning, non-judgemental, ego-free state in which to tap into your visions. Let your eyes drift out of focus as you gaze into the water and release expectations. When I do this, gradually shapes and images seem to appear suggesting different outcomes to situations I have queries about. When I get really deeply into this, all else seems to fade away and I no longer know whether my eyes are open or closed. Most of what I am seeing seems to be playing across a theatre screen set somewhere out in the middle of the cosmos – or maybe inside my mind!

If you are having trouble scrying, burn sandalwood incense and anoint your temples with a little nutmeg oil.

A good tip is don't try too hard – just chill out and let the visions come, whether they appear as specific visuals or thought suggestions or whatever. I have had some pretty

225

profound visions while scrying, but sometimes all I experience is a calming meditation rather than a great revelatory session. It's a good idea by the way to keep a written record of your visions in your Book of Shadows.

✴ *Note: Another good training tip is to look at a lot of those 'magic 3D pictures'. They are great trainers for opening the inner eye, seeing beyond the obvious and through the veils of the worlds between the worlds.* ✴

It's on the Cards

Tarot reading is considered a basic Witch skill. I have spent some time becoming familiar with the Tarot but I have not made it a pivotal point of my Craft although I own two decks – the recently created *Celtic Tarot Deck* and the classic pack created by A.E. Waite. I've had revelatory and helpful experiences with the Cards, however, in personal terms I only use Tarot as a confirmation tool. Any Tarot reader will tell you that it is virtually impossible to do an accurate reading for yourself as you

cannot be objective enough. However, if I am feeling a bit torn and un-centred, the ritual of laying the cards out and meditating on them is a pleasing and fortifying experience. I feel calm and centred afterwards, and somewhat purged if there has been something bugging me. Inevitably the messages the Tarot provides are accurate reflections of what I know in my heart is happening, beyond ego and desire.

There are many different Tarot decks around now with most of the cards having a wealth of imagery, incorporating lots of different archetypes and spiritual themes. These can be visually absorbed and with the assistance of an explanatory handbook you can create a reasonably good general reading. This is a good starting point if you are in the process of getting in touch with your psychic powers, though real Tarot reading starts when you put the handbook away and let your subconscious navigate.

✦ *Note: There is a degree of psychic ability required for an accurate Tarot reading, but often a creative connection with your intuition is enough to start with.* ✦

The key to becoming an able Tarot reader is to spend a lot of time with the cards and becoming very familiar with their imagery. This can take some time as the Tarot deck consists of seventy-eight cards! Fifty-six are the Minor Arcana which is divided into four suits – usually Cups, Wands, Swords and Pentacles (or Coins) – and from which the modern day playing deck has evolved. Twenty-two are the 'trump' cards of the Major Arcana – these deal with the deeper karmic and soul-based mysteries of life and they don't have anything to do with the modern playing deck except for one, the Fool, whose descendant is the Joker – though the role of the Fool in Tarot is held in much higher esteem than that of the Joker. Besides becoming familiar with the Deck you also need lots of practice to become an accurate reader – preferably on people you don't know very well. As a fledgling reader, if you do a reading for

A Bit about Psychic Powers

Highly developed psychic powers are not mandatory when practising Witchcraft. My experiences are often not of the fairytale kind – I don't see pixies and goblins, nor talk to spirits. However, I did see a dragon sitting on my shoulder once: it was about three inches high and steam wizzed out from its nose like a kettle on full boil, and its tail thrashed around like a raptor bird out of Jurassic Park! It appeared the day I decided to have a water dragon tattooed on my upper left arm and stayed until the tattoo was done. Whether it was 'imaginary' or 'real' is irrelevant – I've learnt that imaginary is as good as real when it comes to magick and spellworking. In fact, psychic power isn't as vital to magickal practice as is a good, unfettered creative mind.

someone you know very well it can be hard to separate your personal opinions and expectations of them from the Universe's. Working with strangers can help hone and sharpen your psychic and intuitive skills.

There is a lot more to the mystery of the Tarot than just fortune telling – individual cards can be used for inner spiritual exploration or 'Pathworking', especially those of the Major Arcana, which can be used in conjunction with the Qabalistic Tree of Life. The Tree is a vast and complex subject that I am not going to attempt to delve into here, except to say that it provides an ancient Hebrew map to deeper and deeper levels of consciousness and spiritual development. It is something nearly every Witch ultimately feels the calling to understand.

I can recommend Dion Fortune's *The Mystical Qabalah*, as a good investigative starting point.

Life in a Tea Cup

Tea leaf reading is another form of divination that I have recently been drawn to – partly because of a friendship I have struck up with a wonderful Scottish woman and professional tea leaf reader named Grace. Below she gives you an insight into the magickal world of tea cups!

My granny did tea leaves and my mother did tea leaves – all the women in my family were a wee bit spookish. My granny saw ghosts and spirits and to me growing up in that environment was normal. When I was about four or five I started dreaming about fairies and ghosts and I could actually touch them and sense them around me. My granny was a character; she used to read tea leaves in this wee tobacconist shop in Glasgow. I was about nine and I would go over after school and she'd have some old woman sitting beside her and there would be clouds of smoke – my granny smoked like a chimney – and she'd be reading the tea leaves. I couldn't help but take a look and say 'Oh granny, I can see this and that.' The people my granny did the readings for would turn to me and say, 'What else can you see – are you fey?' And granny would say 'Oh aye, she's fey.' When you're "fey" it means you can see, but I was never taught the leaves, I just picked it up.

When I was sixteen I worked as a junior in a bookshop and one of my jobs was to make the tea – you only had tea leaves back then and I used to love spooning them out into the pot. I would serve the customers tea and when they'd finished I'd have a look in their cups. I'd see all sorts of things, musical notes, people running away from something, numbers, letters and sometimes full names. I remember asking one person 'Have you got an Uncle Jimmy? He's going to win some money', and then they came back a couple of days later and said he'd had a win on the horses.

It's just in my blood.

When I do readings I feel like I'm helping people to get through their problems and onto better things – to move on. Often when people come to see me they are stuck in a rut. I can't work miracles, but I can help. If I look in the cup and the pictures are really dark and no good I try not to scare people by telling them the worst – but I have to be honest and tell them there's a bit of a challenge ahead. People are vulnerable so I never tell them anything to encourage a problem. If I see, say a health scare for someone, I'll encourage them to have a check-up rather than saying 'you're going to be sick'. Most importantly, I get people out of that 'stuck' feeling and they go away feeling fantastic. It's how you present it.

I've never read a book to understand the images I see, I use my intuition and my psyche and my common sense. Animals are always good to see, birds especially – they are free to fly wherever they want. A house can be a safe place; a ship moving can be good news coming towards you. But a still ship can mean stagnant energy. Little dots mean lots of money and a bright cup with lots of space between the images is a sign of good fortune.

If someone's drawn to reading the tea leaves and perhaps is using a book to guide them, I have some suggestions to help. Start by sitting quietly. Maybe burn some aromatherapy oils and have a candle lit. I always have a small amethyst crystal ball nearby, to hold if I'm having trouble seeing things clearly. Follow this little ritual: after the person has drunk their tea, have them swish the

*leaves around to coat the inside of the cup and then have them
turn the cup into the saucer with the handle pointing towards
them and spin it three full circles. Then have them pick it up and
blow into it to put their breath in it and hand it to you.*

*Hold the cup in your left hand, focus your mind and look into
the cup and at the position of the images – where they are in the
cup and the relation of one image to another. When you hold the
cup in your left hand and the handle's pointing up and out, to the
right will be the past, to the left the future and down at the bottom
is the long-term future. The pictures that you see are in your own
mind. I might look in the cup and see a house and a garden and
another might look at it and see a big lion. The images will form so
that you can interpret them and relate them to what's happening
to the querent at that time.*

*Reading the tea leaves is one of the simplest things you can do;
it helps to be naturally psychic, but you can develop the gift and
become a good reader with practice. I have been reading for
nearly fifty years – you'd want to be good after that long!*

BED, KNOBS AND BROOMSTICKS

MAGICKAL SEX

Most sex practised by Witches when working magick is suggested, not actual. As I describe 'Spell Boundaries', the ritual of Cakes and Ale – celebrated at every coven meeting and most personal rituals – is a symbolic representation of the Divine sexual joining of the Goddess and God. This ritual is otherwise known as The Great Rite. **Witches do not have any hang-ups about sex – we worship the forces of life and as such sex is sacred and can play a very important role in some ritual work.**

The energy of an orgasm can be the most powerful fuel to help propel a spell along to fruition; in fact virtually all power raising in a Circle is based on the build-up/release/wind-down pattern of the orgasm. Orgasm can also be used as a tool to achieve transcendental states – the ancient Eastern practice of Tantric sex attests to that.

Sex is not something Witches take lightly and to use the energies it creates in magickal work, especially in groups, requires training and preparation. It usually occurs only occasionally amongst the most experienced of Initiates who are very comfortable and familiar with each other. Wiccan sexual magick usually occurs in three forms: couples working privately; couples working with a group who leave them to themselves whilst the actual sexual part of the Circle is happening; and (probably most commonly) solo energy raising.

Solo energy raising involves masturbating to orgasm to raise power. Most find when using orgasm in Circle it is not appropriate to rely on lusty thoughts to get there as these can be too distracting and draw your mind away from the magickal work at hand. I concentrate on the awesome power that I, as a woman, am able to create, carry and nurture life within me. I meditate on the sacred gift of orgasm, the pleasure being a personal reflection of the infinite Divine joy found at the core of the Universe. I concentrate deeply on that aspect and find that when I do orgasm at the peak of the ritual, I experience the energy as a force that pulses from my lower chakras, surging up through the others before blasting out of my crown chakra, at the top of my head.

Because most people's upbringing encourages them to feel a bit awkward and uncomfortable about sex, or to relate to it in a destructive way, sex magick can take some practice to get right, particularly if it involves working with other people. Sexual energies are volatile and to aim and 'fire' them accurately requires the ability to distance yourself from how you would normally experience sexual acts and pleasure. If you are interested in trying sex magick, the best place to start is at home, alone.

A basic solitary sex magic ritual using orgasm as the primary magickal force goes something like this:

First, bathe with the intent to purify yourself of all built-up tension and distracting energies. If you do not have a permanent altar, make sure you have the four elements represented in your Circle – incense for Air (one that I have used to stimulate the sexual force is made from patchouli leaves, some powdered cinnamon stick and a few drops of cypress oil), an orange candle for Fire, a bowl of spring or sea water for Water and a clear quartz crystal for Earth. Depending on your ability to focus, accessorize your space as decoratively or simply as you feel appropriate. However, for your first few attempts avoid setting up with traditionally 'sexy' accessories – keep the Circle simple. Sex isn't the issue here, the magickal power of orgasm is. Perhaps have a beautiful cushion upon which to sit (it's best to be sitting upright when raising solo power).

Cast Circle and sit in the centre. Now close your eyes and state your aim out loud, for example : 'I wish to manifest a new job in my life.' Now meditate on that aim for as long as you feel you need to until you have a very clear picture in your mind of what you wish to achieve. When you are ready, keep your eyes closed and, as you want the energy to flow right through you, stroke your whole body to awaken it to subtle sensations before beginning to masturbate. Try to focus all your thoughts on your aim – this can be quite difficult but anytime your mind wanders, gently coax it back to visualizing your desired outcome. Feel the urge to orgasm build-up inside you, but delay it for as long as you can – having to think about your goal can help here! The longer you can hold off, the more power will be generated.

When you feel the ultimate peak approaching, focus as hard as you can on your aim and then release the orgasmic energy. See it rise up like lightning through your body, shooting out of the top of your head and into the cosmos to fuel the manifestation of your wish. Sometimes it can help to open your eyes right at the point of orgasm and stare at the flame of the candle, seeing the energy pour into the flame, and seeing in that microcosm, action in the macrocosmic fiery, churning Cauldron of Creation.

After orgasm, take a deep breath and say out loud, 'It is done.' Now stand up and close Circle as usual, remembering to ground yourself with some wine and cakes (or the like). The spell is complete.

Another, easy method of tapping into orgasmic energy as a magickal force is to dedicate each and every solo orgasm you have to someone or something as a sacred blessing. Performance artist and modern-day Goddess of Love, Annie Sprinkle, expounds this policy and it's a great start towards reinstating the sexual as sacred in a society that often encourages individuals to think that masturbation is 'dirty' and 'perverted'.

When you get comfortable working with sexual energies in this way you might like to try sex magick with a partner. They need to be familiar and comfortable with working with sex energy as well – it is important to be able to align yourselves at the point of orgasm. Set up the space as you would for a solitary working, with rugs and cushions for comfort, but again – keep it simple. Intercourse or mutual masturbation can be used for couple or group orgasmic power raising. A woman who is menstruating (a particularly potent time for sex magick) may prefer not to be penetrated, so masturbation is appropriate here. In fact, as this ritual honours the divine power of orgasm but is not specifically a fertility ritual, mutual masturbation can be the most effective way to work with collective orgasmic energy.

Before casting Circle you and your partner need to clarify completely that which you are working towards, because it is really important that you are both thinking the same things at the same time. If you can manage this, the energy created can be astounding and work very fast in creating your desired out-come. It is also important to decide whether you will look at the candle flame when you orgasm or at the psychic centre of each other's Third Eye (between the eyebrows).

If you can, bathe with the intent to purify together – this starts the magickal bonding process. Here, it is probably appropriate to make a special note for the boys. Often when you're about to do a sexual ritual your erection will start up way before the Circle and stay there all the time the casting and setting up is going on. This is fine! Sometimes the old clash between sex and religion can creep into the male mind when this happens and make men feel that they can't cast Circle in that state. Wicca honours the sexual drive as sacred and as such it is entirely OK if a guy (or a girl) is in a state of sexual arousal during magickal work.

OK, back to the ritual. Cast Circle and sit facing each other. Gently hold hands and close your eyes and meditate for some time on your aim. You will probably both feel ready to start raising power at the same time and this can be signalled by a gentle squeeze of the hands. Keeping your eyes closed, both of you start to caress each other with intent to create sexual arousal. At this stage it is important to keep your minds focused on the spell, and if thoughts wander, bring them back. When you both feel ready, begin to masturbate or start to have intercourse. For intercourse, it is best to be sitting upright and facing each other. Sometimes having a single chair in the centre of the Circle can make this easier.

Still keeping your eyes closed start to build up orgasmic energy again, holding off for as long as you can and both of you focusing intently on the aim of your spell. The trick here is to align yourselves with each other's energy so much so that you will be able to peak simultaneously together. When this moment arrives, open your eyes and stare at each other's Third Eye and see the energy streams of your orgasms leave the top of your heads, meeting and entwining above you both, and spiralling off into the cosmos. If you want, rather than looking at the Third Eye, you can rest your heads together at that point and with your mind's eye see the energy streaming away to do its job. If you have chosen to look at the candle, make sure you both look at it at exactly the same time – so that the energies are like two bolts of lightning charging the flame.

When the peak of orgasm has subsided, look into each other's eyes and say together, 'It is done.' Now close the Circle and do not speak of the ritual until the desired outcome manifests. It is not necessary to save any body fluids released at orgasm when doing this type of work, although you may want to because they will be blessed with the sacred energy of the rite. If you do collect them, perhaps give them to a plant that will benefit from the cosmic and organic nutrition. It's also appropriate to mention here that when you do get very familiar with working sex magick you can incorporate more exotic and stimulating objects and processes into the ritual, which can increase the amount of energy released, but while you're getting used to focusing on orgasm as an energy source, keep it simple.

To become really proficient in sex magick as a couple, it will probably take a lot of practice and a lot of 'accidents' – but all acts of love and pleasure are sacred to the Goddess, so don't worry if some attempts just collapse into a lovemaking session. However, **learning to work with sexual energies in a disciplined, magickal way is very empowering and can positively affect your whole life** – particularly if you are in a partnership as regular practice of sex magick can profoundly celebrate and deepen a couple's relationship.

The Pink Witch

At its core, Witchcraft embraces the magnificent diversity of humanity in all its colours, shapes, sizes and preferences. We encourage evolution and change and one of the most dynamic modern aspects of the Craft is its challenging of patriarchal gender roles.

Witchcraft is a religion that honours the Life Force as sacred and is primarily matriarchal though many Wiccans are tending more and more to a Taoist-like balance of female and male energy. The Goddess is still often given extra emphasis but that's largely to help correct the masculine imbalance many of our cultures have. As the gap between men and women's power in society becomes narrower, the need to exult the Goddess above the God becomes less necessary. Witches do not see the emotional and physical union of heterosexual couples as superior to that of lesbian and gay couples. Love and pleasure are sacred to Witches and all Witches are free to explore these in whatever way they choose. Reproduction of the species is not the only expression of love or pleasure, nor the only form of fertility. We also acknowledge that absolute masculinity and femininity exist only in the abstract. In practice, each of us has male and female elements to our personality and energy. Not surprisingly, gay and bisexual culture took the rainbow as the symbol of the richness of variety in our species.

The polarities of male and female qualities exist in both sexes – the human being is a complex animal! Ancient Eastern religion comments on this: in Taoism there is a concept expressed as 'the Ten Thousand Things', in which nothing is purely Yin or purely Yang, but rather a complex blend of the two; not black, not white, but grey. Also, consider the actual Taoist symbols of Yin and Yang – each contains the essence of its opposite.

In many ways, especially in the past, Witches and homosexuals have a lot in common. Throughout history both groups have often been treated as outcasts and minorities to be hunted down and persecuted. In these modern times, Witches and homosexuals have been increasingly encouraged to come out of our individual 'closets' (for a Witch, the broom closet of course!) and though there is still prejudice directed at us, there is considerably more freedom for us to express ourselves.

In fact, prior to the dominance of the Western patriarchal religious mindset, there is a rich history of the profound role the homosexual has played in the spiritual evolution of humanity. It is only since the Christian era that the idea of a woman or effeminate man as a spiritual leader has been denigrated (funny, though, isn't it that priests still seem to have a fondness for long flowing skirts!).

In ancient temples and primitive cultures the homosexual, effeminate man and virgin Priestess (virgin meaning complete unto herself) were seen to have great psychic and magickal abilities. Also, if you do a bit of research you'll find many of the Goddesses and Gods of old had lesbian and gay encounters. Hermes, the Greek God of magick, medicine, intelligence and communication was portrayed as androgynous and bisexual. And going further back in time, one of the greatest ancient Syrian Gods, Baal, was often portrayed as being one with his female counterpart, Astarte, and invoked as 'Baal – whether God or Goddess'.

The infamous isle of Lesbos was colonized by Amazons in the 6th century BC. The women of this island were revered as poets, musicians, artists, lovers and Priestesses in service of the great Greek Goddesses, Artemis and Aphrodite. Even though during the early Christian era most traces of this colony were destroyed, today some Wiccan covens exist as female-only – the roles within the coven being based on the perceived structure and function of these ancient temples.

Some traditions in the Craft teach that energy polarity is like a battery and to raise power during magickal ritual it is essential to have the 'opposites' of male and female acting together. But these energies are given gender-specific definitions based on archetypal behaviour and roles of women and men in our society, not on some profound universal truth of what it is to be male and female. We all have the Goddess and God within us. A perfect example of this is raising power as a solitary Witch – when firing up alone you are expounding the totality of your personal being, celebrating the fact that all things exist within as well as without.

In Witchcraft, gay, lesbian, bisexual, and transgendered humans can find a sense of spiritual peace and integration. There are inspiring role models, Gods and Goddesses to relate to, and a tolerant and compassionate magickal community to be a part of. Everyone can turn the Wheel of the Year, dance the spiral dance of the Cosmos and take their rightful place as divine children of the Universe.

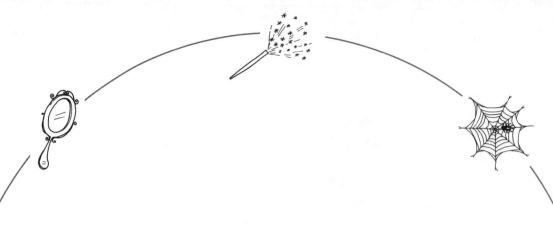

FLYING HIGH

MAGICKAL DRUGS

Drugs have been used in ritual for thousands of years. Ancient Shamans, Priestesses and Priests used different herbs, liquors and foods – like magic mushrooms – to enter trance states and merge with the Nature of this world and the Nature of other worlds. Within most traditional cultures, drug use in ritual is usually taken very seriously.

The Shamanic rituals of indigenous peoples like the Australian Aborigines, the Amazonians, the North American Indians and some African Tribes have very strict specifications as to the preparation and environment of the individual and amount of the substance taken. Certain drugs can open up gateways in the brain that lead to very intense and sometimes overwhelming out of body, out of mind and out of this world experiences.

Drug taking in ritual is not to be compared to 'popping a pill' at a nightclub or getting paralytic at the pub – which are completely removed from ritual drug taking. When you have created a space between the worlds using the sledgehammer effect of drugs, you are inviting all sorts of presences and energies into your mind and soul and if you are not sufficiently prepared with knowledge, training and support, you are asking for trouble. Some may say 'Good! I like trouble, give me the drugs!' but these people are the ones that give drug use in ritual a negative reputation, because most likely they are irresponsible, attention-seeking losers.

In this strange society, consumption of deadly drugs like alcohol, tobacco and certain prescription medications is encouraged and yet far less dangerous substances like magic mushrooms and marijuana are illegal. Don't get me wrong, I think people who abuse these substances and become paranoid trippers and brain-dead potheads are losers but I do think it's worth addressing in this book how drugs can be constructive in the evolution of the spiritual self – but only for the experienced Witch!

I do know that in some smaller gatherings of initiates organic drugs are sometimes used for certain ritual work. For example, on Samhain, when the 'veils between the worlds' are lifted, some Witches will take a light hallucinogen or narcotic

to further facilitate communication with the spirits of departed loved ones. The experiences they have in private and
sacred spaces are far less outrageous and damaging than the
actions of violent, moronic, intoxicated people after a night
spent drinking in a bar.

Magic mushrooms can sometimes be used to open door-
ways to other levels of reality, especially with past and
future divinatory work, as they can assist in transcending
the constructs of linear time sequencing. However, much
training and preparation is required for lucid experiences.
Going into a field and picking a bag of magic mushrooms in
the morning sunshine after a light overnight rain and then
gobbling them down will most likely just have you giggling
and throwing up all day, not visiting other worlds. I am not
advocating their use, magic mushrooms are illegal (tell that
to the spores and the cow dung that they grow in!) but if you
are interested in reading up on their use in indigenous
Shamanic practices and present day ritual, as well as some
interesting new theories on human evolution, I highly recommend Terence McKenna's books. *Food of the Gods* and *The
Archaic Revival* are two of his works that are particularly
educational and thought provoking.

Drug taking for magickal purposes is a very personal thing.
No coven forces an initiate Witch, or any other for that matter,
to take drugs. In fact, most discourage it and some covens will
not even use any form of alcohol in ritual work, substituting
fruit juice instead. **Drug taking is also not a pre-requisite
for spiritual and magickal development; it is entirely
optional or in certain covens and paths, forbidden.** In
fact a lot of Witches with highly developed psychic powers
don't want to take drugs in ritual because as one said to me,

'My psychic powers are developed enough, if I became any more open I would go nuts!'

Personally, I think drugs have the potential to be too distracting. I have had profound transcendental experiences in ritual, especially during guided meditations, but at the same time I have been focused and grounded. I have had clear memories of the experiences in ensuing days, and been able to integrate the wisdom gained into my regular life and ongoing magickal practices more effectively than if I'd been off my face and left with a druggy hangover the next day. Regular use of drugs in ritual can lead to dependency on them, which is ultimately debilitating and can severely inhibit magickal development. Aleister Crowley, for example, was undoubtedly quite a brilliant magician for a period of his life. He used a variety of drugs, like opium, in high quantities to presumably enhance his magickal abilities; however, what contributed in a small way to his prowess became his downfall. Crowley died alone, an opium addict and an alcoholic.

One of the myths about Witches perpetuated in the Middle Ages was that they flew through the air. Far more likely is that they flew through the air in their dreams and meditations, probably propelled by the use of certain herbs applied to the skin in the form of ointments. There is a recipe for 'going to a Sabbat in the imagination' recorded in 1615 by Jean de Nynauld in his book *Lycanthropy, Metamorphosis and Ecstasy of Witches*. The main ingredient is supposedly the fat of a child, but we can forget about that ridiculous assumption; the other ingredients, though, seem quite appropriate for an ointment to induce an altered state. The herbs aconite, water parsnip (hemlock), cinquefoil and deadly nightshade (belladonna) were steeped in a base of pig's fat or other animal fat,

245

to which was added soot. When applied to the temples, wrists and other areas where the skin is thin, a highly intoxicated state was achieved resulting in the user experiencing 'journeys out of the body'. In the book it is also noted that an ointment 'to produce the sensation of flying' consisted simply of animal fat and belladonna.

Aconite and deadly nightshade are highly poisonous in relatively small doses and hemlock can also be deadly (but not as deadly as nicotine in comparative amounts). These 'baneful' herbs should only be used by experienced and trained Witches, as it is really easy to have too much and make yourself very, very sick. Datura is another highly toxic plant that is sacred to some Witches for use in divination and which is also referred to as 'Jimsonweed' by American Indians and used by their Shamans to induce visions.

A few years ago a couple of male acquaintances of mine (not Witches) decided to have a 'visionary' experience with datura. They did a bit of research to do with methods of preparation and ingestion but little else. They decided for twenty minutes they would boil fresh datura leaves into a pulpy tea and would each drink a cup (comprising of about two handfuls of leaves) and eat the pulp. I was a bit worried about them and said I would 'babysit' them during their 'vision quest' and, if necessary, help navigate through any gnarly bits.

They were both laughing and bursting with bravado as they drank the foul tasting brew. We had prepared the lounge-room with cushions, incense and soft lighting and soon after drinking the tea they both lay down saying they felt a bit nauseous. Ten minutes later they seemed to fall asleep. I checked to see if they were still breathing, which they were, so I sat back and watched. After about twenty minutes they both sat bolt upright looking very strange. One was trying to speak to me but his words were coming out all garbled and the other had his hands over his ears and was yelling at me, 'It's too loud! It's too loud!' The other then vomited everywhere (I managed to get out of the way but had to clean it up), and the other got up and started  stumbling around the room, still with his hands over his ears. Then the guy who had vomited started panicking and choking on his breathing, before screaming that he couldn't breath. He was thrashing around so much that I couldn't get near him and I considered calling an ambulance, but he calmed down after five minutes and then lay on his side moaning like a sick animal.

For the next three and half hours I watched them both have really bad trips, full of panic, pain and unpleasant delirium, capped off by one of them defecating in his pants. Finally they fell asleep. The next day neither could remember anything profound or significant, they just both had really bad headaches and felt sick. The reason I have mentioned all this is because it perfectly illustrates how insufficient knowledge and preparation can have extremely unpleasant and potentially fatal results.

Two legal herbs which can be safely used to assist in reaching out to 'between the worlds' are damiana and ephedra. The leaf of the damiana plant can be steeped in water to make tea and also smoked in small amounts. This produces a feeling of relaxation and in some can induce erotic sensations and facilitate ecstatic visions. For this reason it is a herb traditionally consumed at Beltane as a part of the Fertility Rite celebrations and can also be burnt with lavender during Full Moon rituals to honour the Goddess. Herbalists often prescribe damiana medicinally as it is an effective kidney tonic. Approximately two teaspoons of the herb per person can be steeped for up to ten minutes (not boiled) in hot water, and one cup, strained, perhaps with honey, is all that is needed.

Ephedra is traditionally used in Chinese medicine as a treatment for asthma and bronchitis. It is the herb from which the chemical ephedrine is derived, otherwise known as 'speed'. So its effects can be quite stimulating, especially if taken in large amounts which isn't great for ritual. To experience a subtle, ecstatic sensation that can be very good for deep trance work and ritual dance, I can recommend a brew of ephedra with some guarana added. Steep three level teaspoons of the herb with two teaspoons of guarana per cup in hot water for ten minutes only, but don't boil. Strain, stir well and perhaps add some honey.

For me, the most valuable aid I have for trance and ritual work is the technique of Vipassana Meditation which I learnt several years ago. I have described the technique in the '*Witches Britches'* chapter, as it inspired me to get a body piercing as an outward expression of the intense inner experience. The ten-day Vipassana retreat really is a crash course in advanced meditation that gives you the life-long skills to easily, legally and safely achieve a heightened state of psychic sensitivity whenever you need. There is also a three-day course called Anapana which teaches you to calm your mind by focusing on your breathing, but I would really recommend the full course: it will be one of the most amazing things you will ever do. Vipassana Meditation is a Buddhist method but is non-denominational though they don't suggest learning the technique to assist in the practice of Witchcraft.

It can be tempting to seek druggy 'short cuts' to spiritual and magickal enlightenment but ultimately you are only cutting yourself short. The key to real and enduring magickal powers is desire, discipline and determination. However, I've never found the occasional tipple of mead, spiced wine or the exotic Strega to go astray at a Circle gathering. Mead in particular is a favourite liquor among Witches, being one of the oldest fermented drinks known, and credited with magickal and medicinal properties. My friend, Nick Felgate, is an Assistant Winemaker and Meadmaker for Maxwell Wines, the largest mead producer in the Southern Hemisphere based in McLaren Vale in South Australia. He gave me some fascinating information on this sacred drink made from fermented honey, as well as the dirt on some other special Witchy drinks:

249

Among the Ancients mead had magickal and, indeed, sacred properties. Honey was considered a 'giver of life' and the bee was associated with the souls of humans and was considered a messenger of the Gods. Mead making preceded wine making among the Aryans; however, not only was it the liquor of the Gods throughout the Aryan world, it was also honoured by Mediterranean cults which would seem to have had an indigenous origin rather than Aryan. They worshipped the ancient Gods Bacchus or Dionysus with Bacchus being traditionally known not only as the God of Wine, but also the God of Mead. Mead was also drunk in honour of the Great Mother Goddess whose worship preceded that of the Mediterranean Gods.

Associated with the cult of Dionysus were the Gods Priapus and Pan (the latter clearly being continuous with the present day

Witches' Horned God) and in the festivals to honour them mead
was offered in sacrifice. It was probably the close association
between mead and the Great Mother Goddess (and Priapus and
Pan, etc.) that resulted in there being very few references to honey
and bees in the Bible.

From the earliest times it was recognized that honey, and
particularly mead, has strong revitalizing qualities and healing
virtues. Mead is believed to be an elixir to prolong life; in fact, the
magick mead of heaven was thought to confer immortality upon
the mortals who partook of it.

The strong aphrodisiac qualities of the liquor are appreciated
and mead was not only made for strength, virility and length of
life, but also for recreative powers. Among our ancestors it was
custom at marriage, and for a month afterwards, to feast upon
mead. This was called the honeymonth – which became the
modern day honeymoon. Apparently some wedding celebrations
were sex-orgies in which the guests were given honey and honey-
wines until they were drunk!

The peculiar properties of mead as the first wine drunk by
humans and the qualities inherent within it have never been
surpassed by any substitute liquors to this day, though there
are certainly beverages that have similar profound medicinal
and magickal properties. Benedictine is a liquor developed
in medieval times by French monks as a medicinal tonic for
various ailments, as well as having sacred properties, and
Nick was involved in creating a particularly special brew with
his friend Paul Kern, who is a naturopath. I sampled the
Benedictine and found it superbly fortifying and intoxicating!
Below are some of Nick's personal notes on his method of
making Benedictine.

We 'started' our Benedictine with straight alcohol before adding a 90% infusion of mint leaves, lemon verbena, sage, basil, lemon, bay leaves, rosemary, juniper berries, chamomile, cloves, elderflower, cinnamon, saffron, stinging nettles, pimentos, coriander, lemon balm and Chinese jasmine tea. Horehound was also added and the brew was aged in French and American oak for seven months. When the maturing process was completed we added honey and spring water to dilute it to 40% alcohol. After this we strained and collected all the herbs and flowers that went into the brew and burnt them in a crucible, reducing them to a fine ash. By burning off the carbon life-form the insoluble mineral salts and trace elements of the plants can be extracted. The ash was then added back to the original brew so that the Benedictine contained absolutely all the healing properties possible of the plants involved. Most of the ingredients were organic and grown at my close friends', the Parkinson Brothers, biodynamic farm, situated at Mount Jagged in South Australia. The resulting brew was light in texture with a complex flavour and intense magickal presence.

Finally, one of the most legendary of Witches' brews is the Italian Strega Liqueur. Strega means 'Witch' in Italian and is made in Benevento in Southern Italy. On the label of the bottle is a picture of a Witch astride a broom and a picture of the Horned God, Pan, leading three maidens around a tree. Like Benedictine, Strega's flavour is largely derived from a secret mixture of herbs, however, with the liqueur having a flavour similar to Sambucca, they would most likely include anise or licorice. Strega can be ordered through bottle shops that specialize in imported wines and liqueurs. It tastes quite incredible and the bottle is aesthetically appealing in

251

that there is a Witches' head and broomstick etched into the glass!

So, as you can see, Witches have plenty of reasons to imbibe our favourite liquors, but excess is not appropriate when doing magick – we save our partying for after our spellworking.

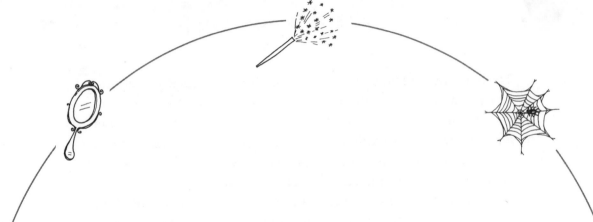

CYBER-SORCERY

MAKING MAGICK WITH YOUR COMPUTER

*Witches and computers make magick together! In fact, the Net is such a profound and magickal phenomenon that I'd go so far as to say in the next fifty or so years every Witch will have a computer on her or his altar! I really feel that **the Internet is the closest humans have come so far to creating psychic thought-transference via technology.** Much of the Internet is connected via fibre optic cables along which information is transmitted as light, and mystics have predicted throughout time that humans are evolving to a point where we can exist as pure light: pure consciousness.*

The way the Internet can unite people regardless of considerations and prejudices about gender, race and creed also reflects the Wiccan attitude of unity and tolerance. There is a huge amount of magickal and esoteric knowledge accessible on the Internet and occult chat rooms are everywhere. There are easily as many on-line covens now as off-line!

Computers are becoming more and more a part of people's lives, a trend that can only continue. Curiously, Wiccans and computer skills seem to have been closely linked for decades now. Certainly by the late 1970s, San Francisco's Silicon Valley area was known for its Pagan community as well as its computer whizzes. In the first edition of her classic study of American Paganism, *Drawing Down the Moon,* Margot Adler observed that 'A striking number of Neo-Pagans [work] in scientific and technical fields, and all [feel] there is absolutely no conflict between their scientific work and their belief in, and use of, magick.' In the book's revised edition the intertwining of these two strands had become even more pronounced and Margot devoted a section of the book to analyzing the link between magickal computer-oriented thinking. The way in which various Wiccans and Pagans related to computers and magick varied, some feeling that working with both provided balance between the right and left brains, and others believing that the new technology was, in itself, virtually magickal; in fact one interviewee said that 'Computers are elementals in disguise'! Of course, in the 1980s when Ms Adler was writing, it was still very early days in the computer revolution. The 1990s will be remembered as the decade of the home computer and Internet boom and predictably, Witches were very quick to take this new magick on board. Pagan bulletin boards came along well before the World Wide Web and it wasn't long before many Witches moved from a Book of Shadows to a DOS (Disk of Shadows).

Not all Witches and Pagans are ardent tech-heads though. There are still many thousands who prefer a less-intensely technological lifestyle with maximum closeness to the earth and live quite happily without televisions and phones, let alone own email addresses and home pages. It's probably fair to say that, although the number of tech-head Pagans out there is likely to keep on growing for some time to come, we're an eclectic breed and tend to use whatever magick works! For me, though, I've found **computers can be used to assist in spell-working and a general magickal head-space.**

Maybe you can't stand being in your stuffy office, cut off from Nature and anything magickal. Maybe you feel your computer is an evil robot staring blankly at you and taunting you! For starters, get a great screen saver. Find one that stimulates you magickally. Maybe some whirling occult symbols, or a blend of colours which represent different qualities; for example, blue for peace, red for passion, yellow for ingenuity, green for patience. Perhaps you could use it as a magickal mental trigger; for example, every time it comes onto the screen, touch the screen with the index finger of your right hand and recite a 'power affirmation' like 'Every day my magick grows stronger' or 'Every day I achieve my magickal goals'. You'll be able to find masses of free screen savers on the Web with a rummage through a search engine like Yahoo or Alta Vista, so download a few promising ones and see which suit your particular magickal purpose. One particularly good screen saver for this sort of purpose is called 'Electric!' which lets you insert semi-subliminal messages to yourself into a great range of mesmerising patterns. At the time of

writing, this free saver can be downloaded from: http://www.
geocities.com/Paris/LeftBank/1140/electric.html

Another useful piece of computer magic is to create a spell
file which you can reactivate any time you've got the computer
on.

How to Create a Spell File

You will need:

❊ Different coloured text;
❊ The ability to cut and paste graphics or shapes and other
imagery.

Cast Circle so that your computer is within it. Boot up your
computer and open a new file, using whatever word process-
ing program you use (for example, Microsoft Word or
Wordpad). In a colour that relates to your desire (check out
Colours in the 'This Goes with This ...' chapter), type in capitals
and bold text a single word to describe your aim; for example:
SUCCESS (you would type this in royal blue).

Now, directly underneath, type the word again minus the
vowels, and then directly under that type the original word
again minus the consonants, and then centre the text. SUC-
CESS would look like this:

SUCCESS

SCCSS

UE

You have created an inverted triangle sigil through which energy can be transmitted via the base point to implement your desire. Underneath you then need to place a graphic image that represents your desire, for example, a drawing of a wallet. If you can't insert a graphic image just type, in italics, a brief description of what that image represents, for example, 'success in my work so that I am financially secure'.

Now, type in this incantation in bold type, capitals and underlined and, if you can, in the colour yellow:

I DRAW TO ME MY HEART'S DESIRE,
THROUGH BITS AND BYTES, SPARKS AND WIRES,
MY AIM IS TRUE, MY POWER GREAT,
BY TECHNOLOGY IS THIS MAGICK MADE.

Save the file and name it with the vowel letters at the base of the triangle – in this case, UE.doc. When you want to charge up the spell, open the file and save it – every time you save it you are restating your intent.

✦ *Note: The file shouldn't be altered for twenty-one days after setting it up. (You are facilitating an altered mental state, and twenty-one days is how long you need to get used to the fact that you will achieve your desire. Experts in human psychology agree that it takes twenty-one days to break old habits and establish new ones.) After this time you can go in, add extra graphics or comments, then close it again. It's good to save the file at least once a day, and the more you do it, the more impetus you put behind the spell.* ✦

When surfing the Internet the amount of information can be overwhelming – some of it is great and some of it is a load of

257

rubbish. Sometimes it can take hours to sift through fifty web sites to hit your mark. Here is a spell to help you cut through the dross and get the knowledge you want:

Eve's 'Give me the Apple' Spell

In this spell you will be invoking the essence of Eve, the temptress and knowledge-seeker whom the Judeo-Christian myth portrays as the downfall of Man. She was, in fact, a benevolent and switched-on sister, who, prior to being debased by later accretions of myth, was an incarnation of the original Pagan Mother of All. The Serpent was her companion and, in matriarchal lore, the greatest Keeper of Wisdom. In the patriarchal retelling of her myth, her desire for knowledge and her desire to share it with Adam was denigrated, but in this spell it is going to be celebrated.

Do this spell on Saturday which is ruled by the planet Saturn, and the best time for spells for knowledge.

You will need:

※ 11 pieces of dried apple in a sealable plastic bag;
※ 3 large leaves (fig leaves are perfect!);
※ 1 piece of snake skin (go to a pet shop which sells snakes and ask for a piece of one of the old skins);
※ 1 red texta;
※ 1 piece of clear quartz crystal;
※ 7 drops of benzoin oil;
※ 1 white cloth bag.

★ *Note: This spell is more powerful if you can do it skyclad.* ★

Cast Circle, and holding the snake skin in your right hand and bag of dried apple in your left, take three deep breaths and meditate on the eternal wisdom that is every human's birthright but that so many of us are denied.

In your mind's eye see a Serpent, which embodies all the knowledge in the world, coiled around a large red apple, which represents humanity. Now see Eve, magnificent, naked and proud, pick up the Serpent, coil it around her waist and over her shoulder, and take the apple in both hands holding it towards you. Put the apple and snake skin down and on the three leaves write with the red texta, 'Desire', 'Knowledge', 'Results'. Stack these on top of one another in that order, so that 'Results' is on top.

Drip the seven drops of benzoin oil (for clarity and wisdom) on top of the leaves, then place the pile of leaves in your left palm and place your right hand under your left. Now touch the pile of leaves to your forehead, your left nipple, right shoulder, left shoulder, right nipple and then forehead (tracing the Witch's pentagram) then place them in front of you.

Place a tiny bit of snake skin on your tongue and eat a piece of dried apple. As you chew this, be conscious that you are informing the Universe that you are a Seeker of Knowledge. After you have swallowed say this enchantment: *'The Essence of Eve is now within me. I find the information I need easily and effortlessly. So Mote It Be.'*

Place the leaves, snake skin, crystal (to keep the spell charged) and bag of apple inside the white cloth bag, and keep it near your computer. You are now ready to surf the Net, after you have closed

Circle, of course! Every time you go to surf, place a tiny amount of the snake skin on your tongue and eat a piece of the apple. And if you really want to invoke that Eve energy, surf skyclad too!

❋ Keep crystals around your computer, especially clear quartz and amethyst, to encourage effective communication; and hematite near the keyboard will help ease repetitive strain aches.

❋ Keep a cactus next to your computer – it helps absorb and nullify the radioactive emissions from your computer. Cactus spines work to protect their immediate environment from negativity.

❋ Wear a medium to large shell around your neck (perhaps on a leather thong or silver chain) to deflect unhealthy radioactive emissions and any other energy bombardments from your computer.

❋ If you have a report to write or some work that requires mental concentration, hold a fluorite crystal between the palm of your hands (in a prayer position) and bring your hands to your forehead and then over the top of the keyboard three times as you recite, 'My mind is focused, my hands are able'. This will help you translate your ideas to typeface spontaneously and effectively.

❋ Take advantage of Pagan and Witchcraft chat lines and expand your experience of your Craft in the virtual world as much as the physical. As much as Witches are drawn to revering nature, technology is not going to go away. It is a reflection of ourselves, our creation and as such is sacred. We need to find new and evolved ways to interact with it and thus learn more about ourselves.

The Internet is a great place to make contact with other people and there are lots of ways of doing that. First, there are by now thousands of web sites about Wicca and other magical traditions out there. Admittedly, some put style above content and, while looking absolutely spectacular, won't tell you more about the Craft than you'd find in a newspaper article on the subject. Even so, they are often works of art in their own right and can just be enjoyed on that level. As time goes by, though, more and more sites are cropping up which are full of genuinely indispensable Craft history, spells, rituals and so on. Most sites have a guest book or an email contact for the person who designed the site, so don't forget to take advantage of how easy on-line interaction is and compliment people on pages you especially enjoyed. Tracey and Lauren are the girls who design and maintain my website, and I appreciate the feedback! Check out my site at www.fionahorne.com

Another popular form of net communication is IRC – Internet Relay Chat – which is a real-time method (well, depending on how well the servers are working!) of 'chatting' to people interested in the same subjects as you via typed text. The programs that enable you to use this are freely available on the Web (MIRC and PIRCH are two of the most widely used IRC programs) and are pretty easy to operate. Once you've worked out the software and logged onto a server, you'll generally have no trouble locating channels of conversation dedicated to Wicca and virtually any other topic you could ever want to talk about (and a whole lot you wouldn't join if you had a gun pointed at your head!). Be warned, though, IRC channels can be a little disorienting at first. Many are full of very friendly, helpful people you'll be really pleased to have met, but others are less welcoming. Unfortunately the great Celtic traditions of hospitality haven't been taken on board by all Craft IRC channels and some are so cliquey that you'll be lucky to get a word out of anyone (except maybe other newcomers).

To further confuse you, a lot of conversations on these channels take place one-on-one, which means that the general conversation in the room might seem virtually non-existent at times. The best way to think of IRC channels is like a bar or club – some are warm, friendly places where you feel instantly at home, whereas others make you want to walk straight back out again. You might need to do a little hunting around until you find your kind of place.

My friend Carmela, one of the most committed and disciplined Pagans that I have ever met, has this to say about IRC:

I spend a fair bit of time on the Net – I have my computer in my bedroom! As I am pretty much a solitary Witch, I like to sometimes get on-line and talk to other Witches and discuss ideas and chatlines on an IRC are great for this. I usually use University servers, as they often have interesting and informative conversations going on. Using an IRC is like going to a huge house where there are lots of little rooms and in every room there are different conversations going on. Usually conversations will involve two to four people typing questions and answers back and forth, and sometimes if you connect particularly with one person you can go off to another space to talk privately. Sometimes you have to sift through crap once this guy kept asking dumb questions like, 'Do you practise skyclad? Do you ride broomsticks?' But most of the time you can have really, good enlightening conversations.

It's important to remember that while the Net can be a very

effective place for meeting people, it's also a place where people take advantage of anonymity to play all sorts of generally just stupid, but occasionally dangerous, mind-games. There's a famous cartoon showing a little dog tapping away at a computer keyboard, thinking to himself: 'On the Net no one knows you're a dog'. Well, while you may not chance upon any computer literate canines out there, it's likely that you'll encounter other strange forms of wildlife periodically so always take care in giving out personal details or arranging private meetings with people you know only from the Net. You might like to do a protection spell before you log on to Witchy web work, like this one:

Wetsuit Spell

You will need:

❋ 1 black candle;
❋ 1 white candle;
❋ frankincense incense;
❋ A tourmaline wand (this crystal comes naturally shaped as a terminator, being clear, long and slender).

✦ *Note: tourmaline can be white, green, pink, black and multicoloured. But white, black or combined, and multi-coloured are the best for this spell. Tourmaline can channel electrical beams of light (look closely at the parallel, striated lines within) and full-on New Age crystal freaks think tourmaline is not an indigenous stone to this planet, but that it was placed here by higher life forms to help humans evolve into the Aquarian Age. Whether this is the case or not (and the sceptic in me thinks, 'Bloody Hell!'), it certainly can surround you with a protective shield and encourage pure and uninhibited communication, especially when working with electrical telecommunication equipment.* ★

Light the incense and candles, placing the white one to the left of the screen and the black one to the right. Standing in front of your computer, hold the tourmaline in your left hand and the incense in your right, circling it deosil (sunwise, which is clockwise in the Northern Hemisphere) over your work-space. Think about how your computer is an extension of yourself, transmitting your ideas, aspirations, dreams and even your personality and energy through a web of others' thoughts, energy and reality. When you are ready, intone three times as you circle the incense: *'Like a spider I weave the Web, at home, protected and in good stead.'*

Spiders are traditionally considered to be protective and a sign of good fortune so focus strongly on this as you chant.

When you have finished, place the tourmaline in front of the computer and keep the incense and candles burning for as long as you are on-line. Do this spell every time you plan to log on to connect up with other Witches or to find on-line magickal information.

SPIN THAT WHEEL!

THE WICCAN WHEEL OF THE YEAR

Being connected to the cycles of the earth is an integral part of being a Witch. The cycle of eight Sabbats, which are spaced equidistantly throughout the year, relate to the acknowledgement and celebration of agricultural and astronomical events; and also to the continuing cycle of life, death and rebirth. These eight Sabbats – Samhain, Yule, Imbolc/Candlemas, Ostara, Beltane, Litha, Lammas and Mabon – are also known as the 'Witches Wheel', an annual cycle, which Witches can use to integrate their consciousness with the world of Nature.

The eight festivals are roughly six weeks apart. Four of the festivals relate to the astronomical year and are the Lesser Sabbats: these are the Spring and Autumn Equinoxes (also known as Ostera and Mabon), the Summer Solstice (also known as Litha) and the Winter Solstice (also known as Yule). The other four, the Greater Sabbats – Imbolc, Beltane, Lammas and Samhain (popularized in main stream society in a commercial way as Hallowe'en), relate to agricultural events, like the planting and harvesting of crops. Different traditions give the Greater Sabbats slightly varying names but these are the ones I use.

The festivals have evolved from a time when all humans lived close to the land and saw answers to the greatest mysteries, those of life and death, in the turning of the seasons, the sowing and reaping of the harvests, the blossoming of flowers and withering of leaves that fell from trees. Witches use the wheel as a unifying tool as much as a way of keeping in touch with the cycles of nature.

Unfortunately, in these modern times we are mostly divorced from any personal relationship with the Earth. We buy our food pre-packaged at supermarkets, and when we shop at fruit and vegetable stores we only have a minor experience of seasonal food, since so many things are grown under controlled conditions, or imported from overseas. We have heating and air-conditioning and experience most of the seasonal changes only as new suggestions for what to wear from fashion magazines, or through extra power bills.

Observing the festivals, whether as full blown rituals outdoors communing with nature, convening with coveners to re-enact the Wheel of the Year Myth, or as solitary meditation sessions, keeps urban Witches in touch with that which is the core of our spirituality, the divinity of nature.

The Wheel, which is accompanied by a myth, is the deification of the Wheel of the Year (see diagram), where the Sun/God is born in winter and peaks in summer, and that the Goddess as Maiden, Mother and Crone exists at all times in all things and also provides a framework for people to relate to. Witches consider the Wheel of the Year Myth a Sacred Mystery, reliant upon individual interpretation to give it meaning.

It's important to remember that **celebrating the Sabbats and the Myth are a way to feel close and integrated with nature,** and a way to explore the totality of being – recognizing that as cycles of nature revolve in the world around us, so do our inner cycles. The Sabbats are great for unifying Witches, bringing groups together to celebrate a common theme, but they can also be a time for personal reflection, clarifying life experiences and philosophies, reaffirming life-paths taken and future directions.

The key words for understanding the Sabbats and the Myth of the Wheel are 'cycle' and 'integration'. The Sabbats are Celtic and Nordic in origin, having descended from the seasons as experienced in ancient Northern Europe (before global warming!), and relate specifically to the planting and harvesting of crops.

✦ *Note: Because the seasons are experienced differently in the Southern Hemisphere, I have included dates for both Hemispheres.* ✦

267

In this chapter I explore the cycle and offer ritual suggestions for celebrating each of the Sabbats, with an explanation of how the Myth serves to introduce each part of the Celtic Wheel. There are quite a few varying versions of the Wheel of the Year Myth, depending on which tradition a Witch works within. This isn't a problem because the main role the Myth plays is that of one of encouraging the ability to feel close, and relate to, the turning of the seasons, and of our lives. The Myth expressed here is my personal vision where the Goddess is immortal and the God lives, dies and is reborn throughout the year. The God's experiences relate to the sun and its effect on the land as it varies in strength throughout the seasons.

I have also included notes on each Sabbat that I have made in my Book of Shadows. They encapsulate the way I relate intuitively to each Sabbat and cover the key factors of each part of the Mystery as it has revealed itself to me. I also give descriptions of objects and imagery relevant to each Sabbat that I have used to decorate my altar and space. Celebrating the Sabbat with ritual is an important part of a Witch's life, and I am hoping that my notes will encourage you to create your own rituals. There are lots of different ways to honour the Sabbats, however, the most vital thing is that your rituals are meaningful to *you*, in whatever way and for whatever reasons you choose.

All the ideas below can be adapted as solitary or coven rituals.

Samhain

❋ Greater Sabbat
❋ Oct 31 (Northern Hemisphere); May 1 (Southern Hemisphere)

The beginning and end of the Witches' Year. The God descends to the Underworld and the Goddess becomes Crone, the Keeper of the Mysteries of Life and Death. The dead are remembered and honoured, and as the veils between the worlds are thinnest at this time their spirits can be contacted. On the land, any final food storage for Winter is done. During now and Yule, the Goddess journeys to the Underworld and joins with the Dark God.

Witches consider that at Samhain a window opens between this world and the one beyond the grave. It is a time when most Witches believe we can best communicate with the spirits of those who have departed this world and it is a day to honour our dead ancestors. It is now that all the frustrations and failures of the past year must be buried so that life can be born again at Yule.

A Samhain Ritual

Samhain Incense

Grind together two teaspoons of dried patchouli leaves, one teaspoon of myrrh and add three drops of nutmeg oil.

269

Cover the altar with black cloth, perhaps with a silver edging. In addition to the usual altar set-up, place black and red candles on it and a bowl of red apples and pomegranates. Pomegranates are the sacred fruit of the Underworld which Persephone ate during her time there – the seeds will help you commune with the dead. Cut the apples so that the pentagram arrangement of the seeds is displayed and slice the pomegranates in half. Display photos of those people you have loved and admired and who have passed on, and place a vase of red flowers, perhaps chrysanthemums or roses, to represent the rebirth of life that comes after death. Have a cauldron with a fire burning in it (you can also just use a single black candle) and a piece of black paper and black pen ready.

Prepare by bathing (using the purification scrub from the *Spell Boundaries* chapter) and drinking a cup of mugwort and honey tea (to assist with psychic powers). Dress in black or work skyclad and cover your head with a black veil as a sign of respect to the dead

Open Circle as normal (use the Samhain incense) and, raising your arms in the air, invoke: *'I dedicate this night to Hecate, Goddess of the Underworld, great, wise Crone, Grand Mother of All. Witch Queen of the Night, bless the souls of my loved departed ones and my own.'*

Now eat one half of a pomegranate and say: *'Dark Lord of the Underworld, open the gates of your shadowy realm.'*

As you say this, sense the veils between the worlds being drawn back and say: *'All you who have gone before me, I honour you and give you my respect. Tonight is a time for us again to share in friendship and love. Join me in my sacred circle.'*

Eat the other half of the pomegranate and visualize those who have chosen to come sitting with you companionably. If you are in a group, you might like to share stories celebrating the lives of those departed. When you feel their presence firmly established in the Circle, talk to them, tell them your latest news, eat a few more of the seeds to continue the link and maybe tell them things that you wanted to but didn't have a chance  to before they died. Get everything off your chest, laugh, cry, be silent and listen to them.

When it is time, thank your loved ones and bid them farewell until next Samhain. Eat one of the apples to affirm there is always life after death.

Meditate on your own life now and reflect on the experiences and wisdom you have acquired. Acknowledge that life is too short to get stuck in a rut and that for rebirth and renewal of ideas and inspiration there must also be death. Write down on your black paper anything you need to let go of and throw it into the cauldron (or hold to the candle flame) and say: *'Hecate, Goddess of Magick and Keeper of the Secrets of Life and Death, accept my failings and my fears. May they be transformed into wisdom and inspiration in the Cauldron of your Eternal Fire.'*

Eat another half a piece of apple and throw half into the cauldron as an offering. Close Circle as normal, thanking Hecate and the Dark Lord for their assistance and blessings.

✦ *Note: When I perform the 'communicating with the spirits' part of the ritual, generally what I experience are very intense memories of my departed loved ones rather than outright communication with spirits. Sometimes my memories become so clear that it is like we are sitting*

271

next to each other – in my mind I hear their voices and I even think I smell them! But I don't always consider that I am contacting their spirits: more often it is, instead, a profound experience of appreciation of their lives and the time we spent together on the planet. ✦

Mystery of the Wheel: Samhain

❋ In myth the God descends to the Underworld and the Goddess becomes Crone, the Keeper of the Mysteries of Life and Death.

❋ The veils between the worlds are at their thinnest and so the souls of those departed can peer through and permeate the screen to commune with those in this world

❋ A time of divination and prophecy, a time to gaze into the Cauldron of Wisdom

❋ A time of introspection and withdrawal to ponder eternal life over and under physical death

❋ A time to let go of failure and sadness, to bury fear and prepare for renewal and good fortune

❋ A festival of honouring the dead, those humans who have bravely passed through the veils into the nurturing unknown of the Underworld

Imagery to use:

❋ Apples, cut to expose the pentacle arrangement of seeds, representing occult life, the dark moon, midnight, black and red candles, red chrysanthemums or dark red roses, dark crystals of divination, pomegranates, skulls and bones of the dead

Yule (Winter Solstice)

❈ Lesser Sabbat
❈ Dec 20–23 (Northern Hemisphere); June 20–23 (Southern Hemisphere)

The Longest Night. Sunrise marks the birth of the waxing year – from now the days grow longer and it is a time of feasting, celebration and making plans for the coming Spring. In the Myth the Goddess gives birth to the Male Child of Promise and the Dark God is reborn as the infant Sun God. A Yule log is burnt and the ashes are kept to be put into ointments and potions for healing as they have life-giving powers. Part of the log is also kept to rekindle next year's Yule log.

A Yule Ritual

Yule Incense

Grind together two tablespoons each of pinewood shavings and frankincense, half a teaspoon of cinnamon powder, three drops of cedar oil and two of ginger.

Even if you are a solitary Witch, try to have a bit of a celebratory gathering tonight. Invite some friends over and, even if they're not Witches, explain how this longest night is essentially a time of rebirth, because at sunrise the days will get longer as we head for Spring. Burn a Yule log in the fireplace or outside, setting it alight at dusk. The Yule log should be

Deja Vu

*About Reincarnation and
Past Life Experiences*

Most modern Witches believe in reincarnation. As Witches
turn The Wheel of the Year and celebrate the Sabbats we
explore the cyclical nature of existence and we learn to
love and acknowledge death and what lies beyond as
much as we love and acknowledge life.

As a Pagan and Witch I accept the concept of
reincarnation based on the way I see life come and go
and return in the world of nature around me, that is, as
part of an organic process. I like Einstein's observation;
'Energy can never be destroyed, it can only change form.'
I take this to mean that the energy that powers me up
has got to go somewhere when this body is over it!
However, the most popular theory of reincarnation, that
over several lifetimes we evolve from lesser creatures of
faults to greater creatures of perfection based on what
we do on Earth that's good and bad, I find a bit
simplistic. I came up with a saying a few years ago,
'When I gave up being a perfectionist my life suddenly
seemed perfect.' So the concepts of 'good' and 'perfect'
seem too subjective and elitist to base the validity and
standard of someone's or something's existence on. To
me every plant, tree, animal, vegetable, mineral and
every human, has a unique and integral role to play in
the evolution of life.

So I don't believe in reincarnation as a ladder to spiritual perfection, and I find the memories of present-day people living exotic lives as Pharaohs in Egypt and shamans in South America a bit bizarre. However, it makes sense to me that everything that has gone before exists within us and that we live on in the genes we pass on to our children. Perhaps consciousness is contained in our genes and that is how one could carry the memories of someone who has lived before.

I really do believe you (as in who you are right now) only gets one shot and so I'm determined to make the most of it. I try to conduct myself in an environmentally responsible way, I try to do positive and constructive things, I try to help others, not because someone's keeping tabs on a spiritual scorecard, but because I am grateful to be here. Life is an amazing gift.

There is plenty of room for new theories on – life/death/what comes next? And speculating is fascinating, fun and sometimes terrifying. Over the years I have spoken with many Witches and occultists and the one thing we all agree on is that to understand death you have to understand life – that is live it to the fullest. There are two guaranteed things that every human on the planet will succeed at – birth and death.

I don't know exactly what happens when you die, although I know something does – energy is being shunted around the Universe all the time. I'm comfortable with that. I don't need to know what happens when I die to make this life worth living.

275

pine or oak and is symbolic of the rebirth of the God in the fire of the Goddess's womb. Exchange gifts of goodwill and drink plenty of mead and mulled wines and enjoy hearty foods casseroles and caraway seed rolls, lots of spicy cakes, nuts and dried fruits.

If you are celebrating alone or with like-minded souls, set up an altar decorated with pine cones, rosemary sprigs and holly. Display fruits like oranges and lemons that are colourful and tangy and awaken the tongue as new life will awaken at sunrise. Put red, green and gold candles everywhere to burn all night.

Cast Circle and invoke the Goddess and God: *'Great Mother, tonight you give birth to the Child of Promise; tonight on the longest and darkest night we celebrate the fire of your Womb – the fire of Creation. The Sun God is born and everywhere rejoices. Hail and welcome ever-returning King and Eternal Queen.'*

Feast and celebrate, sit up all night sharing plans for the coming year and toast the Dawn, welcoming the Sun/Son.

After sunrise, gather some of the Yule log ashes and place them in little dark green silk bags which you've made espe-

cially for the occasion and give one to each person present as the ashes can be used for their healing and life restoring powers. Remember to save some for yourself!

Close Circle and save part of the Yule log, wrapping it in dark green cloth when it has cooled. Use the log to rekindle next year's fire. Now, go to bed!

Mystery of the Wheel: Yule

❋ In myth the Goddess gives birth to the Child of Promise in the longest night
❋ From the greatest darkness emerges the strongest spark
❋ Reaching down deep into the psyche, in the face of greatest adversity, results in tapping into true unconditional joy
❋ Yule is the time of the Great Feast when the last of the winter stores would be used up in joyful abandon and defiance of fear, resting secure in the knowledge that the Mother will always provide
❋ Gifts are exchanged and people share cheer and courage in the longest night. The Goddess rewards our optimism and trust with the birth of the sun
❋ Stay up through the night, lighting candles to 'welcome the sun in' at dawn
❋ Make plans for the coming year, as the Sun/son grows in strength, so dreams gain strength to manifest as reality

Imagery to use:

❋ Oranges and lemons – the tangy fruit awakens the tongue just as life awakes from the mother's womb. Holly; ivy; lots of green, growing vines; eucalyptus; rosemary sprigs and pine cones. Feasting – winter foods, root vegetable casseroles, nuts, dried fruits, lots of heavy spiced wine and mead. A burning Yule log, lots of red, green and gold candles

277

Imbolc/Candlemas

❋ Greater Sabbat
❋ Feb 2 (Northern Hemisphere); Aug 1 (Southern Hemisphere)

The end of darkness and a time of growth, the land is awakening and in the Myth the Goddess is now fertile again and the young God grows in strength. It is a time of purification – clean out the home, pay off debts and settle old scores, let go of what doesn't work anymore and get ready for new directions in life.

An Imbolc Ritual

Imbolc Incense

Grind together one teaspoon of dragon's blood powder,
one teaspoon of frankincense and five drops of musk oil.

Imbolc is a time of spring cleaning. Even though it's not quite Spring, it's time to get ready as we are well and truly moving out of Winter. Spend the day paying bills, cleaning out cupboards and sorting out your Winter and Summer clothes. Prepare for your ritual by bathing and wearing something simple and white or going skyclad with some snowdrop blossoms, or similar flower, in your hair.

Place a yellow cloth on your altar, and make a circle of seven white candles decorated with a wreath of snowdrop flowers. Also, have some white paper and a red pen ready.

Cast Circle and invoke the Goddess Brigid, the young

Goddess of fire and inspiration, and pay homage to the Young God: *'Fertile Brigid, blessed with fire, and Son God growing ever brighter, kindle in me a fire of love and sweet inspiration for the future. Lead me to the path I best tread so in this year my gifts are shared.'*

Now gaze into the circle of candles, meditating on your goals for the coming year and compose a poem about them. It doesn't matter if you're not a poet – Brigid is and she will show you how. Whether you're in a group or alone, read out your poem when it is completed and then lay it in the circle of candles for Brigid's blessing.

Close Circle and place your poem under your pillow. You will dream of ways to achieve your aims. Imbolc is all about feeling inspired – waking up from the hibernation of winter and looking to the future. Dreaming of ways to achieve your aims is Brigid's gift – the gift of inspiration.

279

Mystery of the Wheel: Imbolc

✱ A time of initiation into the Female Mysteries: the Virgin, in realizing who she is, knows she has the potential to be Mother and Crone. The understanding of the potential to be Mother comes with the onset of menstruation after the birth of the Child of Promise at Yule

✱ A time to ponder deeply the Feminine within all and to bless and inspire new projects

✵ The Celtic Goddess Brigid is sacred to the day. She is the Goddess of Fire, Inspiration and Poetry
✵ A time of cleansing – settle old scores, pay off old debts, clean out cupboards and drawers

Imagery:

✵ Lots of white candles, white flowers like snowdrops, representations of the Mother and Crone, but most emphasis on the Virgin: female things

Ostara (Spring Equinox)

✵ Lesser Sabbat
✵ Mar 20–23 (Northern Hemisphere); Sept 20–23 (Southern Hemisphere)

The Goddess as Maiden instructs the Young God of his burgeoning powers as new life springs from the earth. Again, in the myth fertility is recognized and celebrated and what was set in motion during Imbolc gains momentum.

An Ostara Ritual

Ostara Incense

Grind together one teaspoon of benzoin, one teaspoon of dragon's blood powder, two teaspoons of Dittany of Crete or sage and one of mint.

Ostara is a celebration of new life on the Earth and it's preferable to do this ritual outside in the daytime. Decorate the altar with a light green cloth, candles, daffodils and bowls of edible seeds – sunflower, sesame – whatever takes your fancy. Have eggs, colourful paints and brushes or textiles ready and get out all those  chocolate Easter eggs you saved from earlier in the year! This is the Witches' Easter – a time to rejoice in new life and a time to acknowledge the Sun God who is now a horny youth and fully armed with his creative power. Bathe and dress in pastel-coloured, Springtime clothing, or go skyclad, with ribbons tied in your hair.

Cast Circle and invoke the God:

Great Son and God who flourishes in the loving eye of the Goddess,
Who blooms in his power as the earth smiles at his feet:
Fill me with your wonder and desire;
Ignite in me passion, and eternal optimism;
As on this day I celebrate the life that pours forth in your
presence.

Eat a handful of the seeds and scatter some on the ground as a libation. Lay on the earth and feel life coursing through you; feel your body awaken fully to the regenerative powers around you and within your body and spirit. When you are ready, close Circle and go for a walk smelling newly blossoming flowers and delighting in all the fresh, green growing things.

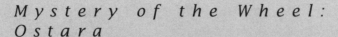

Mystery of the Wheel: Ostara

※ In myth, the young Sun God is armed with the knowledge of his creative power. He is initiated into the mysteries of his sexuality and his ability to become a father and a wise old man

※ Spring has arrived. Life is waking up everywhere: plants and animals are being born

※ Celebrate all that is great about being alive

※ Light and dark stand equal – a time of balance and harmony

※ The Male in all things is recognized and celebrated

※ At this time the Maiden and the Sun God become innocently aware of each other. 'Their eyes meet across the dance floor', but they will not dance together until Beltane

Imagery to use:

※ Seeds and eggs to represent new life, daffodils, lots of little suns, male things

Beltane

* Greater Sabbat
* May 1 (Northern Hemisphere); Oct 31 (Southern Hemisphere)

In the Myth the friendship of the Maiden and Young God becomes courtship and they join in the Great Rite (sexual union). It's a time of great festivity and celebration of life and fertility – with outdoor feasting and bonfires to light the proceedings, the Great Rite is enjoyed by lovers as a sacred part of this festival and many handfastings (a Witches' 'wedding' ceremony) are performed on this day. The land is well and truly ebullient with spring energy.

A Beltane Ritual

Beltane Incense

Grind together two teaspoons of sandalwood, a handful of dried rose petals, one teaspoon of galangal powder, one teaspoon of cinnamon and six drops of neroli oil.

This is the big one! It is traditionally a time of handfastings or renewal of vows and one of the best ways to celebrate is by making love. Get a group of like-minded friends together for a celebration. It is a time to celebrate the union of the Goddess and God, not only physically but spiritually. All lovers of any sexual preference should come together (literally!) and exult in the joy that lies at the core of being. If you are alone for your Beltane rituals, have a picnic in a beautiful park surrounded by blossoming flowers and read poetry or a love story.

For a group ritual, decorate the altar in rosy pink cloth, with vases of red and pink flowers, pots of violets and orange candles. Have lots of sparkling wine and don't forget oysters, spears of buttery asparagus, honeyed cream and bowls of strawberries, peaches, other succulent fruits plus any other aphrodisiac delights you may want to have on offer! If any of the women attending want to become pregnant on this night, make a special dish (to be eaten only by those women) of pasta, dressed with a pesto sauce of parsley, basil, ground hazelnuts, sunflower seeds and olive oil. (Of course they will still need to have sex at some point – there's only so much herbs and cooking can do!) Also, have some great music playing. It's most wonderful to have your ritual outside, with lots of little 'love nests' in appropriately private places. Sometimes a bunch of people cavorting in the bushes arouses unpleasant people's interest, so, if necessary, have your ritual in a home with lots of rooms, prepared and consecrated especially. Or be prepared for everyone to get all fiery and passionate and then close Circle quickly to let them get home and get down to it. It might sound strange to people who are dictated to by our oddly prudish, yet promiscuous, society, to have a party with all your Witchy friends so that you can all have sex together – but I don't mean necessarily *literally* together. I don't think a group grope is the only way to celebrate but the celebration should be a sensuous, flirty sort of event. It's most likely that couples will enjoy the Great Rite, but if there are people interested in threesomes and foursomes, it's up to you and what you're comfortable with getting involved in. (Remember safe sex is just as necessary during a Sabbat as at any other time.)

When sex is approached as a sacred and blessed act – not some-thing dirty or exploitative and shrouded in hypocrisy – it is the most beautiful thing in the world to be with your loved one (or desired, wise and lusty partner for the night) in the close company of others experiencing the same joy. Whether means being literally next to others or in separate rooms under the same roof is again entirely up to the people involved and what everyone is comfortable with. (As I said earlier, it's fine to close Circle and for everyone to go to their own spaces for the Great Rite too.) However, to experi-ence the Great Rite in a group environment can really break through the guilty hang-ups and 'sin'-based fallacies that so many of us are burdened with. To put this in perspective, I had a close girlfriend visiting me for a few days and her new lover came to stay one night. The three of us sat up talking until the early hours and it was too late to send anyone home. I let my friend and her lover sleep in my bed as the guest bed was a single, which I took. A little while later, after all the lights were out, I heard faint noises of them passionately making love. I didn't think, 'Urghh, yuk! In my bed!', I smiled and felt a deep, warm glow in my heart, knowing that their love was being consummated. I fell asleep feeling so happy to be a human whose birthright is to love and be loved.

For the ritual, cast Circle, invoking and honouring the Goddess and God:

285

Great Goddess of the Moon and God of the Sun,
Tonight we celebrate our divinity
As born from the eternal passion of your union
That stokes the fires of Creation
And blesses us all on this Great Night.

Then have a wonderful night!

✦ *Note: if you are too young to be having sex as part of your celebrations, recognize the beauty and sacredness of love and procreation. Everyone is born from a divine union, and our ability to procreate is one of the greatest, most amazing and holy mysteries – yet so often it is taken for granted. Have a huge party with all your friends and rejoice in being alive.* ✦

Remember, a Beltane ritual isn't a tacky orgy, it is a celebration of life, love and the Great Rite, and one of the holiest nights of the year.

Mystery of the Wheel: Beltane

❋ In myth, the Great Rite, the courtship and union of the Maiden and the Young God
❋ Sex is a sacred, creative fuel that can propel all desires and dreams to manifest in Life. All things are possible
❋ The time of the famous Maypole dance where people dance around a huge pole winding red and white ribbons
❋ The dance of sexual fire is symbolized through the

ribbons of the Maypole winding in a spiral, like the spirals of DNA

❋ Love, love, love!

❋ Fertility and copulation (not just heterosexuality). The fertility of spirit delights in the physical

Imagery to use:

❋ Celebration; abundance; bright colourful flowers in riotous shapes; Maypole ribbons: red and white – blood and sperm; strawberries and other luscious, red foods; phallic bananas; lace and beads – the connected patterns and chains of life; head garlands of woven willow branches and flowers

Litha (Summer Solstice)

❋ Lesser Sabbat

❋ June 20–23 (Northern Hemisphere); Dec 20-23 (Southern Hemisphere)

The longest day of the year, when the creative powers of the Goddess and God are at their peak. The Goddess is Mother and ripe as the baby conceived on Beltane grows within her, but from this day on the Sun God will weaken as the days grow shorter, and the Waning year commences.

A Litha Ritual

Litha Incense

Grind together two tablespoons of lavender, two of vervain and two of sandalwood, one handful of dried gardenia petals and three drops of frankincense oil.

The Summer Solstice is another time to get together with friends to celebrate the full bounty of the year. Have a picnic in the park or a party on the beach, under the noonday sun (with sunscreen and umbrellas, of course!). Have a feast of everything that is in season.

The point is to be out during the day and then have a ritual at home in the evening, because you are also acknowledging that from now – the longest day – the waning year has commenced and the slow descent to Winter has begun. The Sun God weakens, even as his new life grows in the womb of his partner, the Goddess.

Decorate your altar with gold cloth, gold candles, gardenias and poinsettias. Light a fire in your cauldron and throw in handfuls of lavender (or place a white candle in there) and have yellow paper and a black pen ready. Cast Circle and invoke the Goddess and God:

Great Horned God – Father, Lover and Son, in this moment I worship your divine creative essence more than I ever have before. As the Wheel turns, year by year I am constantly renewed by your eternal vigour and passion. I honour your wisdom and am blessed in your teachings; I understand the eternal cycles of Life.

Great Mother Goddess, all of nature vibrates now with the potent presence of your Life essence. In this time of your ripening I focus on all things I am undertaking. On this day I fuel them with your glory.

Meditate on any projects you are presently undertaking and acknowledge where they are working and where they are not. Write a list of what is great on one half of the paper and what needs to be improved on the other. Meditate on both and ask the God to take and purify that which isn't working and the Goddess to bless what is and propel it along to further fruition. Now throw the paper into the cauldron, give thanks and close Circle.

289

Mystery of the Wheel: Litha

❋ In the Myth, the seed planted in the womb of the Goddess at Beltane grows and she is full of the power and beauty of motherhood. The God will weaken as the days grow shorter

❋ The longest day – but a shadow must also fall as the sun now begins its descent towards winter

❋ Personal power peaks but everything is cyclical and as personal power peaks, so must it recede to peak again. Just as the sun rises, it must also set

❋ Spend time out in the sun absorbing its warmth and life giving powers to store for the waning half of the year

Imagery to use:

❋ Lots of sun and personal power imagery, images of full pregnancy, big oak branches, gardenias, poinsettias, cherries, plums, apricots, passion fruit

Lammas/Lughasadh

❋ Greater Sabbat
❋ Aug 1 (Northern Hemisphere); Feb 2 (Southern Hemisphere)

On the land the first harvest of grain begins and is turned into life – sustaining bread and brew. The Goddess sees with sadness that the strength of the Sun God is fading, but it lives on inside her as her child. The bounty of life is celebrated, with achievements and successful efforts acknowledged. Lugh, the Celtic Corn God, was traditionally sacrificed at this time to ensure a successful harvest the following year.

A Lammas RITUAL

Lammas Incense

Grind together three tablespoons of sandalwood, one tablespoon of hops and five drops of rose oil.

Lammas is a time of celebrating the harvest, not only on the land but in spiritual life, and is a time of joy and abundance.

The sun, while waning, still shines strong and the land glows with abundance. Lammas is the first but not the last harvest, and the lesson of Lammas is peace and patience in the face of uncertain outcomes.

In the morning, do this personal ritual to centre and focus yourself on the energies of this Sabbat. The aim is to recognize your achievements but also to focus on patience – knowing that some things need to go through a few cycles of life/death/rebirth for them to reach their culmination. The nature of life is multifaceted so, when something seems to be fading or over, it can be gaining steam in another dimension. Much like how, at this time, the Sun God is fading but he grows as the Goddess's child in her womb.

Place an orange cloth on the altar, with orange and dark yellow candles. Cast Circle and invoke the Goddess and God:

Lady and Lord of All,
witness and bless my rite of thanksgiving;
I rejoice in what is and what is not,
what is given and what is taken away;
as the tides of life ebb and flow,
I drift peaceful in the knowledge
that all things are as they should be.

Now simply meditate on things you have undertaken since last Lammas, perhaps goals you set which haven't been achieved or goals you did achieve but not in the way you thought you would. Be peacefully aware that all things eventually run their course, and detachment (sacrifice of the ego) is a big part of appreciating your achievements. When you are ready, open your eyes, close Circle, perhaps make some notes in your Book of Shadows.

In the afternoon, have a gathering with friends and feast on loaves of multi-grain breads, muffins and oatcakes baked especially for this occasion, with lots of fresh fruit, grapes, apples, berries, pears and vegetables, like corn, which are ripe for the season. Save some of the seeds from the fruits and vegetables to plant, ensuring successful renewal of crops. Also feel free to drink cider and ale with abandon!

Before the feast, give thanks for abundance by having everyone stand in a circle holding some bread and ale. Intone:

> *Goddess of the Moon and God of the Sun,*
> *as we enjoy this, the first harvest, we give thanks*
> *for your eternally renewing bounty and commit*
> *ourselves to preserving the fertility of the Earth.*

Have everyone crumble some of the bread and pour some of the ale onto the ground as an offering and say, 'Thanks be to Mother Earth.' Spend the afternoon sharing your experiences of the last year – lessons learnt and things fulfilled and unfulfilled – and learn from others' tales.

Mystery of the Wheel: Lammas

❋ In myth, the Goddess sees with sadness that the strength of the Sun God is fading, but it lives on inside her as her child
❋ The fruits of labour are celebrated and enjoyed – a time to look back and celebrate successes and achievements of the past year
❋ In cutting the corn the seed is gathered in, ensuring new life

Imagery to use:

❋ Corn and wheat, a large scythe, daisies for joy and success, grapes for opulence, loaves of beautiful breads to represent new creations formed from raw material and ideas and labour

293

Mabon (Autumn Equinox)

❋ Lesser Sabbat
❋ Sept 20–23 (Northern Hemisphere); March 20–23 (Southern Hemisphere)

Mabon is the second harvest as the rest of the grain is stored for Winter. Day and night are equal and the God prepares to leave his physical body and ready his spirit for its descent into the Underworld. The Goddess prepares herself to bid farewell to him, even as she feels him burning inside her. It is a time of introspection.

A Mabon RITUAL

Mabon Incense

Grind together two teaspoons of frankincense, one teaspoon of sandalwood and seven drops of cypress oil with two drops of patchouli oil.

Mabon acknowledges balance: the day is as long as the night. It is a time to study the harvests of your life, to look back over the year and acknowledge where the seeds of ideas and plans you had sown have now yielded results. It is a time to contemplate success and the returns for hard work done. It is also a time of letting go, of introspection and a time to ponder things of a spiritual nature and renew magickal commitments. Mabon is a time to honour the elderly and gain wisdom by connecting with the energy of the Crone and the Shadowed God who is preparing to descend to the Underworld.

Place a gold cloth on your altar with brown and orange candles. Decorate it with dried autumnal leaves, dried herbs like rosemary and borage, and vegetables like squash and sweet potato. Gather together documents, certificates, letters and cards of thanks, photographs and any other items (for example, a plant you have nurtured from seed in the previous year) that attest to your successful endeavours. In addition, write a list of everything you have proudly achieved in the past year on a piece of orange paper written in gold pen. In the centre, place images of the Crone and the Shadowed God, whether they are photos of elderly people whom you love and admire, and drawings or statues, and surround them with a garland of autumn leaves. Also have a piece of black or dark brown fabric and a large piece of red paper and a black pen.

Prepare by bathing and dressing in either black or dark red clothes or be skyclad. Cast Circle and call on the Goddess and God:

> *Goddess of the Night and God of the Shadows, witness and bless*
> *my rite of thanksgiving; in the face of your great wisdom I*
> *understand that for life to be given it has to be taken away.*
> *On this night I renew my commitment as a Witch to honour the*
> *earth and to understand her cycles of life/death and rebirth.*

At this point hold your hands over your bounty and say, *'I have sown, I have nurtured, I have achieved a good harvest.'* Spend some time feeling proud and fulfilled and when you are ready lay the black cloth over your bounty and say: *'On this night I let go of all goals and all efforts to contemplate the restful and renewing silence of the Underworld.'*

Then meditate on the velvety-black sphere of the Underworld. Allow all plans, expectations and sense of ego to fall and float away peacefully, safe in the arms of the Great Void. Do this for as long as you wish and when you are ready take three deep breaths.

295

Now focus on the Crone, who, in the autumn of her life, has experienced many harvests and knows that for new beginnings and life there must also be endings and death. Meditate on your Crone image, acknowledging the wisdom and experience of the person. If you are Crone (or Wise Old Man) yourself, contemplate your inner strength gained from your life experience. In patriarchal society, it is the Crone, the old woman, who is often vilified most, when in fact, of the three faces of the Goddess – Maiden/Mother/Crone – it is she who should be honoured most as the Keeper of the Secrets of Life and Death.

When you are in touch with Crone energy and are resonating with her deep, knowing presence, take the pen and write down future plans of a spiritual nature. When you have finished, hold the list in front of your Crone image and say:

Wise and honoured Crone, Grand Mother of All,
I ask you to acknowledge and bless my plans.
Guide me with your wisdom.

Hold your list and see what the Crone reveals to you. Write down any insights or revelations you may have. When you are ready, thank the Goddess and God and close Circle. Paste your notes in your Book of Shadows.

Mystery of the Wheel: Mabon

❋ In myth, the Shadowed God prepares to descend to the Underworld; the Goddess becomes Crone
❋ Day and night are equal but dark is on the ascendant
❋ Life's greatest mystery, Death, is faced and comprehended
❋ All great ideas cannot live forever in static perfection, they must ultimately break down to be perpetuated
❋ The second harvest is stored away for winter
❋ A time to reflect on what it is to be a Witch; a time of renewal of vows and of initiations

Imagery to use:

❋ Autumn leaves, storable food like nuts and dried fruits and herbs, books for study, a dark shawl to cover the head while contemplating Death

Esbats

In addition to the Sabbats, Witches regularly celebrate Esbats or Full Moon rituals.

The night of the Full Moon is when cosmic powers are peaking and it is the best time of the month to do magick of any kind. The ritual of 'Drawing Down the Moon' is performed at Esbats where the Priestess will channel Lunar Essence through her to embody the Moon Goddess. At this point the 'Charge of the Goddess' is recited. The following charge is from

About the Moon and Moon Worship

The Moon has always inspired awe in humans and has been worshipped by almost every human culture since we appeared on the planet. Occasionally the Moon was conceived of as male by ancient peoples, but it is mostly considered female because of its connections with water, the tides and fertility cycles. To Witches the Full Moon's perfect, round shape reflects our sacred Circle, and it has a meditative, hypnotizing effect when it floats in the sky, stimulating magickal experiences. Unlike the Sun, which can burn our eyes, the Moon is a highly visible celestial body that encourages contemplation.

The Moon has three major phases: waxing, full, and waning and Witches take these to represent the three faces of our triple Goddess: when the Moon is waxing she represents the Maiden – virginal and brave, known by such names as Diana, Brigid and Artemis.

When the Moon is full she represents the Mother – provider and nurturer, known by such names as Selene, Isis and Demeter. When the Moon is waning she represents the Crone, keeper of the secrets of life and death, known by such names as Hecate, Kali and Lilith. There are rituals to do for the three phases of the Moon and each phase also plays a role in influencing the success of certain types of spells, but it is usually the Full Moon that is celebrated regularly with formal ritual. The Dark of the Moon is often considered a 'day off' by some Witches, though many would consider it as one of the most potent times to do the dark work that requires the assistance of Hecate, like banishing, endings and clairvoyant work.

I am always instinctively aware of where the Moon is in her cycle, not in the least because I am born under the zodiacal sign of Cancer – and Cancerians are particularly sensitive to lunar influences. Human bodies are made up of at least 70% water and if the gravitational pull of the Moon can affect the tides of the ocean, it can definitely affect the tides of our bodies. During the month I feel my general sense of equilibrium shift and sway in conjunction with lunar phases, and being familiar with the effect of her waxing, waning, dark and full energies, I can work with them to enhance different endeavours. In the chapter 'This Goes With This ...' I have mentioned the best spells to do at each phase of the Moon.

Starhawk's book, *The Spiral Dance* (adapted from the original version by Doreen Valiente).

I who am the beauty of the green earth and the white Moon among the stars and the mysteries of the waters ... I call upon your soul to arise and come unto me. For I am the soul of nature that gives life to the Universe. From Me all things proceed and unto Me all things must return. Let My worship be in the heart that rejoices, for behold – all acts of love and pleasure are My rituals. Let there be beauty and strength, power and compassion, honour and humility, mirth and reverence within you. And you who seek to know Me, know that your seeking and yearning will avail you not, unless you know the Mystery: for if that which you seek, you find not within

*yourself, you will never find it without. For behold, I have been
with you from the beginning and I am that which is attained at the
end of all desire.*

The different phases of the Moon – waxing, waning, dark and
full – can all be utilized to enhance magickal workings but the
Full Moon is always formally recognized and celebrated, either
with a fully-blown coven ritual, a small personal ritual or a
gaze into the night sky to absorb the Goddesses' potent presence.

Many of the books in *'The Library'* chapter feature suggested full Moon rituals, involving special incenses, candles and
invocations. Often, however, it may not be possible to do an
elaborate ritual, or you might not even feel like doing one, so I
have included from my Book of Shadows a Full Moon ritual
that I did one warm night to illustrate that there are many
ways to commune with the Divine Lunar Essence. **The important thing is to do your own thing!**

*I went out to the garden with a very good bottle of champagne
that I had been saving especially for this occasion, my first night
home in a long time that happily coincided with the Full Moon in
Cancer. I popped the cork as she rose over the ocean and poured
myself a glass and poured some on the ground as a libation to the
Goddess. I smelt the cool sea breeze that seemed sweetly scented
by the Moon's luminescence and I slowly sipped the golden bubbles.
I sat for ages gazing at the ghostly lit landscape of my tumbling
garden and the whitecaps of distant waves glistening in her
presence. As the Moon rose higher in the sky she shone down upon
me and blessed me without words and I rose to my feet and
danced, watching my dark silhouette perform in her spotlight.*

I felt her energy enter my head and churn in my stomach, rush to my heart and float to my head, mixing with my own. I gazed up at her and said, 'Blessed Be – my dark, light, beautiful Mother.'

I took off my clothes and felt her glow coat my skin as I wandered around on the glistening, crunching grass, smelling the pungent jasmine night blossoms. I climbed the orange tree and felt the dark, glossy green leaves that were reflecting the moonlight with a satiny sheen. I stood in the tree with the Moon's relentless diamond light burning into my forehead and I listened to the ocean heaving and shifting to her call, and I felt the waters of my own body rise up and yield unto her. As I stared she glowed and I cried and laughed and tilted my face to match hers.

DAYS OF
OUR LIVES

WITCHY DAYS THROUGHOUT THE YEAR

As well as the Eight Sabbats and Esbats (full moon rituals) there are many days of magickal significance during a Witch's year. Following is a selection and you may choose to acknowledge and celebrate some of these days as a regular part of your Craft practices. Part of this list is compiled with the assistance of the wonderful Milissa Deitz, editor of Australia's leading magazine on the occult.

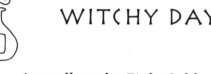

✦ Note: many of the days dedicated to Goddesses and Gods are dated according to agricultural events in the Northern Hemisphere and relate to the practices of the various cultures they originated from. ✦

January

1 January

Being the first day of a New Year, it is appropriate to honour the ancient Roman God, Janus (after whom this month is named). He is seen as having two faces which stare in opposite directions: one to the past and one to the future; so reflect on where you have come from and where you want to go. Burn some cinnamon and frankincense incense (preferably in a small cauldron or bowl), light a gold candle and write a list of New Year resolutions. When you have done this, throw the list into the bowl to catch fire (or use the candle) and as the smoke spirals up know that you are setting those resolutions in motion.

3 January

Sacred to Dionysus, Greek God of wine; feasting, pleasure and fertility.

6 January

On this day in 1988, the Circle Sanctuary of Mount Horeb, Wisconsin, USA became the first legally recognized Wiccan Church by local government officials in the world. It's a good day to re-affirm your commitment to the Craft. Spend some time brushing up on your magickal knowledge.

8 January

Sacred to Freya, Norse Goddess of love and fertility, and Felicitas, Roman Goddess of good fortune. It is also the anniversary of the death of Dion Fortune (1946), the brilliant occultist and author who, although not Wiccan, inspired a lot of current Wiccan philosophies and practices.

19 January

Sacred to Thor, Norse God of thunder and lightning.

23 January

Sacred to Hathor, Egyptian cow-headed Goddess.

February

2 February

Imbolc is one of the four Greater Sabbats and an agricultural festival, celebrating the awakening of the land after winter. It is seen as a celebration of the female mysteries and the coming of Spring. This day is sacred to the Celtic fire goddess Brigid.

6 February

Sacred to Aphrodite, Greek Goddess of love.

9 February

Sacred to Apollo, Greek God of the sun, music and prophecy.

10 February

Sacred to Anaitis, Persian Goddess of the Moon.

12 February

Light a candle for Gerald Gardner, founder of the Gardnerian tradition of Wicca, who died on this day in 1964. He was one of the most important figures in modern Witchcraft and author of the provocative *Witchcraft Today* which was written in 1954, only three years after the anti-Witchcraft laws of Britain were repealed.

14 February

St Valentine's Day. As much as this is a commercially exploited day, it's still a good time to do spells for love.

17 February

Sacred to Kali, Hindu Goddess of death and life.

22 February

Birth date of Sybil Leek (born 1923, died 1983). Famed Witch, astrologer and author of the best-selling *Diary of a Witch* and interesting *Complete Guide to Witchcraft*, both written in the 1970s, as well as books on astrology.

28 February

Sacred to the many forms of the Earth Goddess – Demeter, Ceres and Gaia. Show your respect by perhaps going to a park or beach and cleaning up any rubbish.

March

1 March

In 1887 the influential Western occult society, the Hermetic Order of the Golden Dawn, was founded. Members included the poet WB Yeats and occultists A.E. Waite (creator of the excellent Tarot deck) and Dion Fortune. At one time the infamous Aleister Crowley was also a member.

3 March

Because of its numerological significance, the third day of the third month is considered a good time for Witches to do spells of self-empowerment. Invoke the Triple Goddess of the Full/Waxing/Waning Moon and charge up your energies!

4 March

Sacred to Rhiannon, Celtic Mother Goddess. Play the wonderful song 'Rhiannon' performed by Fleetwood Mac and written and sung by the ultimate rock Witch (besides me, of course! ... I'm *kidding*!) Stevie Nicks. Also something very important is that on this date in 1968 in America the Church of All Worlds was formerly chartered, becoming the first federally recognized church of Neo-Paganism.

1 3   M a r c h

A lucky day for Witches – 13 is a particularly Witchy number, and March is the third month in the year. It's a numerologically charged time. Do any spells you've been putting off on this day as desired results are guaranteed.

1 8   M a r c h

Sacred to Sheila-na-gig (Pagan fertility Goddess). Give rock goddess PJ Harvey's song 'Sheila-Na-Gig' a spin today!

2 0 – 2 3   M a r c h

Ostara is one of the four Lesser Sabbats, and an astronomical festival – the Spring Equinox, where night and day stand equal. It is a time of initiation into male mysteries and celebration as Spring is under way and the land is waking up everywhere.

April

9   A p r i l

Sacred to the spirit of the Amazon. Invoke Artemis, the Greek Goddess of the Moon and Hunt, during ritual and ask her to empower you.

1 3   A p r i l

Sacred to Libertas, Roman Goddess of liberty.

2 2   A p r i l

Earth Day. A day to do something for Gaia, Mother Earth. Make a donation to an environmental conservation group, clean up rubbish and do a healing ritual for the Earth.

2 9   A p r i l

Pagan Tree Day. Plant a tree in honour of your favourite Pagan Goddess and/or God.

3 0   A p r i l

Anniversary of the death of Alex Sanders, founder of the Alexandrian Wiccan Tradition – he died in 1988. As much as he was a controversial figure who courted the limelight, many see him as an important player in the development of modern Wicca, so light a candle for him and say a prayer to the Lord and Lady.

May

1   M a y

Beltane is one of the four Greater Sabbats and an agricultural festival – one of the most festive! It is a time to celebrate the union of the Goddess and God, and procreation and life in general.

4 May

Faerie Day. Traditional Irish folklore says that faeries abound on this day and that you should leave an offering of tea and bread out for them so that they do not steal your children!

20 May

Sacred to Athena, Greek Goddess of wisdom and battle.

30 May

On this day in 1431 Joan of Arc was burnt at the stake for the crime of heresy, though some of the charges brought against her used the term 'Witchcraft'. She was a Christian and one who relied more on personal revelation than obedience to the Church, an important part of being a Witch. Do a ritual honouring of those who have died while being persecuted for their spiritual beliefs. Give thanks for your relative spiritual freedom.

June

1 June

Sacred to Carna, Roman Goddess of doors and locks. It has also been recorded that she is in charge of domestic life and exercise.

2 JUNE

Sacred to Ishtar, Babylonian Goddess of love, fertility and rebirth through battle.

1 2 June

Sacred to Zeus, Greek God of the Sky and Father of All.

1 3 June

Birthday of Gerald Gardner, founder of the Gardnerian tradition of Wicca.

2 0 – 2 3 June

Litha is one of the four Lesser Sabbats, and an astronomical festival – the Summer Solstice. It is the longest day of the year when the bounties and beauty of the Earth and Goddess in full blossom are celebrated.

2 4 June

My birthday! Everybody take the day off work and party on!

July

5 July

Sacred to Maat, Egyptian Goddess of wisdom and justice.

11 July

Sacred to the Greek God Kronos, Father of Time.

13 July

Sacred as the birthdate of Osiris, Egyptian God of fertility and harvests. Also birth date of John Dee (born 1527, died 1608), royal astrologer to Queen Elizabeth I and celebrated as an alchemist and wizard. I particularly wanted to include this information because I know a lovely English gentleman by the name of John Dee who is a direct descendant!

19 July

Sacred as the birth date of Isis, Egyptian Great Goddess.

27 July

Sacred to Hatshepsut, Egyptian Goddess of healing.

August

1 August

Lammas, one of the four Greater Sabbats, is an agricultural festival. Lammas means Loaf Mass, and the Celtic version of the festival name is Lughnasadh. It is generally a time of thanksgiving for a successful harvest and honouring the fertility of the Goddess and God.

8 AUGUST

Honour the Roman Goddess of love, Venus, on this day with passionate lovemaking!

13 August

Honour the Goddess Hecate by burning patchouli incense, lighting black candles and doing a ritual of divination at midnight (the midnight between 12 and 13 August).

15 August

Sacred to Vesta, Roman Goddess of the hearth and home.

17 August

Sacred to the Roman Goddess Diana, who embodies the spirit of the Amazon and is the Huntress and Moon Maiden.

2 3   A u g u s t

Sacred to Nemesis, Greek Goddess of fate.

September

7   S e p t e m b e r

Healers Day. A day to honour women and men who serve the community as healers.

8   S e p t e m b e r

In 1875 the Theosophical Society was founded by Madame HP Blavatsky, which still thrives today. It is an occultist group fusing Eastern and Western spiritual teachings with a strong emphasis on karma and reincarnation.

2 0 – 2 3   S e p t e m b e r

Mabon, one of the four Lesser Sabbats, is an astronomical festival – the Autumn Equinox in which night and day stand equal (the actual day of the Equinox varies from year to year). A time to meditate and reflect on what it is to be a Witch, and a time for renewing of magickal vows.

2 4   S e p t e m b e r

Sacred to Osiris, Egyptian God of death and rebirth.

October

9 October

Sacred to Felicitas, Roman Goddess of good fortune and luck.

12 October

Infamous occultist and magician Aleister Crowley was born in 1875.

15 October

Sacred to Mars, Roman God of battle.

18 October

A day to honour Cernunnos, the Pagan Horned God of fertility, wild animals, the forests and hunting.

31 October

Samhain is one of the four Greater Sabbats and an agricultural festival. On the land, it is the third and last harvest of the year (Lammas and Mabon being the first two) and a time to store the final food stores away for Winter. Samhain is the beginning of the Witch's year, a time of divination and prophecy and a time to honour the dead.

November

1 November

In Spain and Latin America, today is the Day of the Dead where offerings of food and flowers are made to loved departed ones.

11 November

Sacred to Bacchus, Greek God of wine, feasting and sensual pleasures.

14 November

Feast of the Musicians – a Druidic festival still celebrated by many Pagans where songs celebrating the Pagan lifestyle are written and sung.

27 November

Sacred to Sophia, Greek Goddess of inner truth and occult wisdom.

29 November

In Romania it is believed that on this day vampires rise after a year-long sleep to walk the Earth. Hang crosses and garlic on your windows and front doors (unless you like vampires, of course!).

December

1 December

The self-styled 'Great Beast' Aleister Crowley died on this day in 1947, alone and fairly miserable, so light a candle for him and read some of his work (perhaps *Magick in Theory and Practice*). Despite his promoted notoriety, he was a gifted magician, very influential in occult circles and very knowledgeable in a lot of areas.

3 December

Sacred to Rhea, Greek Goddess and Great Mother of Zeus and the Earth.

6 December

Birth date of Dion Fortune (1890), famous occultist and author whose work is very influential on the modern traditions of Witchcraft.

20 December

Sacred to Cerridwen, Celtic Triple Goddess of fertility/life/death, seen to take the form of a large white sow.

21–23 December

Yule, one of the four Lesser Sabbats, is an astronomical event – the Winter Solstice. The exact date varies each year. The longest night of the year and a time of celebrating the bountiful qualities of life in the depths of Winter. The Yule log is burnt (the ashes are kept for good luck) and gifts are exchanged.

31 December

New Year's Eve. Make a lot of noise at midnight to scare away any unpleasant times of the previous year and to welcome in good fortune for the coming year.

THE
WITCHES
ARE ALL RITE!

CELEBRATING THE LIFE OF A WITCH

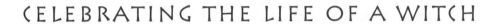

A Witch's life is marked by ritual; as we turn the Wheel of the Year in the world around us, so do our personal lives bear formal recognition of the passing of time and transitions of life. Rites of Initiation, of Maturation, of Bonding and of Passage are fertile and significant moments that are shared with others and become profound ways to enhance our Witchcraft.

The rites and rituals of a Witch's life can fill a book, and I would like to recommend one on the subject called *Pagan Rites of Passage* by Pauline Campanelli. Following, however, are insights into some of the important milestones that a Witch will experience.

Coming of Age

I remember my shift from girlhood to womanhood (the physical part of it) as confusing, scary and crushingly embarrassing. My mother gave me a little talk about the 'facts of life' and 'the monthlies' but I was not encouraged to celebrate my maturing – more to hide it away. I know she did what she thought was best, but I dreaded getting 'them' and when my first period came there wasn't a celebration, in fact I got in trouble. I was on a Girl Guide camp and during the assembly I couldn't stand up when we sang 'God Save the Queen' – my cramps were too bad and I wouldn't tell anyone what was wrong. I'll never forget how humiliated I felt as one of the Guide leaders ordered me out of the hall – and still I sat there!

For Witches though, the Rite of Passage (or Initiation) into adulthood is one of the most celebrated events in their lives. One ritual I like was recently described during a talk by Starhawk, author of *A Spiral Dance*. In this, a mother and daughter and other attending Witches go down to the beach together. The mother and daughter's wrists are tied together with red cord and together they run along the beach until the mother cannot run any further. Then they are cut apart and the daughter continues to run as far as she can alone. Finally, the group sit together and the older women tell the young woman stories of their own menstruation experiences, giving her insights into how to deal with and honour her monthly cycle.

Another Rite of Initiation into womanhood was included as part of a women's gathering I attended a few years ago. The girl was turning sixteen and starting to become sexually active. Her ritual meant she sat alone blindfolded in a cave for twelve hours. Every hour or so one of the older women would join her for a short time and tell her stories of their own experiences growing up, falling in love, and the sexual awakening of their bodies. The older women also took food and water to her, but for a long time the girl was left there alone to think. When she was finally brought out of the dark cave, she was led into a circle that we waiting Witches had created and she was asked questions by the older Witches as to what she had learned. When her answers were deemed satisfactory (and luckily they were or she would have been off to the cave again!) her blindfold was removed and she was washed and anointed with a special blend of oils (neroli and almond) by her mother and two older Witches. She was then given a special 'giftbox' that each Witch in the group had contributed something to – poems and messages, talismans and charms.

The group applauded her 'birthing' into womanhood and we spent the rest of the evening singing, dancing, celebrating and telling empowering stories about cool women that we knew and important herstorical events of women's liberation.

A Rite of Passage from boyhood to manhood is similar to a girl's, and usually takes place on or around a boy's thirteenth birthday. There is always a period of isolation, a challenge, and finally a welcome to the next stage of life's journey.

Every young person I have met who has experienced a

formal Rite of Passage has said that the experience was initially quite scary – especially the period of isolation – and all the attention when you are returned to the group and your blindfold is taken off is quite overwhelming. But overall, they say it's an experience they will never forget as it truly gives them a sense of appreciation and connection to their families, friends, other young adults and their growing selves. Rather than feel embarrassed or confused by their changing bodies and feelings inside, they feel excited and empowered.

Handfasting

Handfasting is the Witches' marriage. Traditionally it is 'for a year and a day or for however long love lasts'. To Witches, a handfasting gives earthly recognition to a spiritual union that takes place beyond body and form – it is a meeting of fate and destiny. In formally stating their love in this time and space the couple are blessed by the elements and spirit, and to each other declared Goddess and God.

Although there are an increasing amount of celebrants who can legally marry and handfast a couple often it is not officially recognized, so some people will be married at a registery office first and then have their handfasting ritual.

Because Witches choose to ebb and flow with the tides of life, we allow for a couple to be unhandfasted. Most often, however, a couple renew their vows after the initial 'year and a day' period.

Hawthorn is a Witch and High Priestess of a Sydney coven. Here she describes a handfasting ritual:

Well, normally it's written by the people who are going to be handfasted because the vows you make to each other should be really personal. It's usually performed in front of a group of friends – the coven. We recently did a handfasting at Beltane. Beltane is the yearly celebration of the handfasting of the Lady and Lord, so we made our prenuptial bride and groom to be the Lady and Lord and they were handfasted as part of the main Beltane ritual. They declared their promises that they had written to each other, then I bound their wrists together with a cord that they had made themselves and then they went off into the woods to do the Great Rite while they remained bound.

We had set up a love nest in the bush for them and we left them alone while the rest of us stayed and danced around the Maypole. They eventually came back, bright-eyed and rosy cheeked and they were pelted with handfuls of rice and potpourri as they ran around the Circle together, gathering up blessings of love and fertility. (It's better for them to go off in the woods first, then they can come back and feast and imbibe as much mead as they like and it doesn't matter if they are useless to each other later, because they've got that part over and done with!) Then they kissed and jumped over the broomstick. The broom represents the male and female together; it represents sex: the (male) handle being inserted into the (female) brush. It's a very old tradition that says a couple is married or trysted together.

323

Mother and Fatherhood

The procreation of life is seen by Witches as one of the most magickal experiences possible. I to and fro between feeling incredibly maternal one minute and 'I love kids – as long as they're someone else's' the next! However, I have enormous respect for those who embark along the challenging and difficult but ultimately supremely rewarding path of parenthood. All the more so because when one of my closet friends became a mother I got to share her experience of transition.

I have known Carmela for seven years now. We met through mutual friends and realized we had a lot in common, perhaps to the point of being 'soul-sisters'. For many years I watched Carmela successfully climb the corporate ladder of a large telecommunications company. In her private life I have watched her climb another ladder, one that she weaves herself, to the stars. Carmela is one of the most committed and disciplined Pagans that I have ever met.

Two years ago Carmela left her high-flying career in the city for a career as a mother and a life in the country. She has found her life partner in Alastair and conceived and given a natural home birth to baby, Galen. Here is her fascinating story:

Alastair follows a Pagan path as well, so we both agreed in terms of conceiving. We got together and we decided there was some kind of powerful force that was saying to us 'Wouldn't it be lovely to have a baby!' We didn't want to make a conscious decision so we just left it to the Universe. We just went on having sex and in two weeks I conceived.

I did a number of things to prepare my body as a Pagan during pregnancy. I really watched what I ate. I listened to my body too, 'cause even though I'm vegan I did have cravings for eggs and cheese. And yoga. My mother told me that my Grandma was digging up potatoes when she was almost due. I thought 'Well, that's the key, too.' Because I'd been sitting in my office, I hadn't had the lifestyle that goes with being fit and agile and physically ready to have a natural birth. So, I took that time off work, from when I was fourteen weeks pregnant, to prepare myself for a natural home birth. I knew it might be hard physically. I just did lots of gardening. A lot of people commented on how earthed and grounded I was when I was pregnant. I'm not sure if it's because I was away from work or because I was working in the garden. I was getting down on all fours with this huge belly and planting things, visualizing and having lovely thoughts about showing this to my child, sharing that with my child, and talking. I talked to my baby while I was out there. It was really nice.

I always observe the full moon. And during my pregnancy I did a ritual for being able to have a home birth. My mother had three caesareans. My sister two. So that's what I was up against because I really wanted a home birth. So on observing the full moon I just did simple things like writing words like 'Home birth, no pain, no drugs' on white candles and burning them. I just wanted protection from fear. I was worried that the fear was so big that it was going to drive me to the place that I was trying to avoid. I was petrified of ending up in a hospital having a caesarean.

Another thing I thought about while I was pregnant was all the women friends I have and how I could draw from their strengths, especially while I was in labour. A procedure I came across from another culture was where every member of the family gives you a bead so I thought I would make a necklace made up of trinkets

Wiccaning – A Child's Blessing Ritual

To represent the elements you will need:

Water: A bowl of sea water collected at sunrise;
Air: A feather;
Fire: A drip-less candle (beeswax is good); and
Earth: A bowl of rock salt with seven drops of
   frankincense oil added.

Have someone you are close to hold the child while you give the blessing. Still your mind and silently call on the Great Goddess and God of All to witness this blessing. Dip both hands in the sea-water and sprinkle it on the crown of the child's head, over the heart and over the feet saying:

(Name), you are blessed by the waters of our Mother Earth. Your mind, your body and the path you tread in life are sacred in the eyes of our Lady and Lord.

Take the feather and brush it across the child's forehead, heart and feet, saying:

(Name), you are blessed by the winds of the World. Your mind, your body and the path you tread in life are sacred in the eyes of our Lady and Lord.

Now hold the candle over the heart of the child and say:
(Name), you are blessed by the fires that are the core of our planet, your mind, your body and the path you tread in life are sacred in the eyes of our Lady and Lord.

Now take a handful of salt and crush it between your hands so that your fingers are coated in salt dust and oil, and, anointing the child's forehead (be careful not to get any in the little one's eyes!), heart and feet, say:

(Name), you are blessed by the fertile Earth. Your mind, your body and the path you tread in life are sacred in the eyes of our Lady and Lord.

When you are finished, hold the child in your arms, concentrate and declare, 'So Mote It Be' as you trace the pentagram on the child's forehead with the index finger of your right hand.

Feel free to elaborate on the above as it's simply a basic guideline.

from all my female friends for me to wear while I was in labour, so that I had all my female friends right there with me. Because my baby came two weeks early I didn't get all the beads in time, but I did get quite a few, probably more than half. When I started going into labour I made my little necklace of ten beads up and wore it that night. That was very special. Of course I've still got that. I've decided I'll give that to Galen.

I didn't put all the plans I had for the birth into practice and I guess I envisaged a bigger, grander ritual. I cast a circle. I wanted to have four elements on the altar. This really lovely friend of mine gave me a candle for Fire, a feather for Air, an amethyst crystal for Earth and she gave me a water bottle with one the those tops you can suck – 'cause when you're in labour you haven't got time to muck about. That was really lovely because I used that during the birth. That was on my altar. It was really bizarre, 'cause everything else looked really nice and really Witchy – and in the middle of it all is this sports drink bottle!

Apart from that I had my original altar set up with all my

Madonna and Child photos. She became an inspirational figure for me during my pregnancy: the Madonna, the ultimate Mother. Being raised a Catholic it was very challenging for me to embrace this image because of memories of church, the repression and fear – but I felt so drawn to it. I reasoned with myself that my attraction was to Mary as she was originally – Pagan, the Great Goddess – before Christian faith disempowered her to be a Virgin Mother.

When I was pregnant, Alastair and I came across this idea of Lotus Birth. You don't cut the cord – you leave it on the baby attached to the placenta until it falls off naturally, which all cords do. Most people cut off the placenta and get rid of it by burning it or burying it. We wanted to keep it attached out of reverence or respect for the baby, it being the baby's possession where it grew up for those months. That was a big post-birthing ritual for us. I made this beautiful bag, sort of shaped like a squash racquet to accommodate the cord and the placenta.

I also observed a forty-day stay-at-home ritual (which actually ended up being a thirty-six-day ritual because I had an appointment and I had to go out). This is done in some cultures where the newborn and mother don't go out and get waited on and looked after. Many cultures believe that it takes forty days for a shift in consciousness to occur (think of Bible stories – forty days and forty nights for Noah and the Ark, and forty days for Jesus in the wilderness). It also takes six weeks (approximately forty days) for a woman's body to heal. Alastair's family and our friends visited, brought food and cooked for us.

Alastair and I will review as we go along whether we raise Galen as a Pagan child. My ideas of Paganism are essentially respect and ritual – and they're the kinds of things I really want to instil in him. Respect for others, respect for living things. I want him to respect that there's magick everywhere in everyday life. I don't *want him to have a mundane life or treat things with irreverence and take things for granted.*

Recently Alastair wanted to take Galen to the beach, so we went to a lovely little spot. It was really instinctive. We had a vague thought about what was going to happen, but when it did we were both moved to tears. We baptized Galen! Alastair said, 'It has to be a rockpool' and we commented on how special it was that all the elements were there, the ocean/Water, sand and rock/Earth, the wind/Air and the sun/Fire. We were surrounded by the elements and it was really powerful even though it was so simple. All we did was dip Galen in the rockpool and asked for a blessing from the forces of nature to look after our baby. It was incredibly touching.

As a mother now I feel that my whole life is a brand new adventure! I feel charged by the energy of Alastair and I as we come together as parents and the growing energy of our baby and the energy of our lives woven together. I have never felt more passionate about life and love. As a Pagan and Witch I feel completely fulfilled.

The Final Passage

The only Witches funeral I have been to saw us taking part in a traditional Christian ceremony (to acknowledge the spiritual beliefs of the majority of the person's family) and then we Witches gathered together three days later. The ritual was one of celebration and respect, rather than grieving. Of course there was sadness and tears, but we were uniting to celebrate the transition of our friend to the next realm or stage of their soul's evolution.

The Circle was decorated with photos, red flowers and candles. We shared our departed friend's favourite foods, told happy stories of their life and raised our glasses in honour of them: 'Merry Meet, Merry Part and Merry Meet Again!'

One of the younger Witches had brought a Ouija board to try to contact the spirit of the dead one. However, at this kind of gathering this is not appropriate. The dead need time to 'settle in' to the next part of their journey. Most Witches will wait until the first Samhain after the death before attempting communication.

Once on my website I received a sad email from a girl whose young friend had died in a terrible seaplane accident. Tragically her friend was not recovered from the water and the person's loved ones were struggling to cope with not only the loss of such a dearly loved person, but the fact there could be no traditional funeral or farewell.

I suggested the following ritual as a way to help ease everyone's suffering and allow a sense of closure and completion.

Honouring Ritual

Those taking part in this ritual need to make a natural offering – a beautiful stone, flower, feather – something that reminds them of the person who has passed away.

Everyone must dress in red and at dawn go together to the edge of the ocean (in this case, close to where the person was lost). Light a fire on the beach and one person can say the following:

The light of this flame is the light of our love,
Together we gather to send you this love,

To guide your way to peace and rest,
Into the arms of the Great Mother (or you can say 'God' if you
prefer).

As everyone repeats it, each throws a small handful of sandal-wood (or perhaps cedar) wood chips onto the fire.

Then each person can say something about why they love this person and when they are finished, they throw their offering into the ocean (a feather or light object may need to be weighed down) saying:

I love you, _____ (name) rest in peace.

When everyone has done this, all hold hands and meditate for a moment on release. Focus on letting his spirit move on to its next journey as you move on with your lives, until you all meet once again in the next world.

The person leading the ritual then says:

Gone from this land but not our hearts,
Merry Meet and Merry Part,
Until we Merry Meet Again.

Then everyone throws sand onto the fire to put it out and walks away without looking back.

This ritual helps give a sense of closure. It also allows the departed one's spirit freedom – not to be uncomfortably trapped by people still wanting them here.

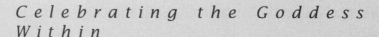
Celebrating the Goddess Within

Wemoon was the first women-only gathering I'd ever attended and it had a profoundly empowering effect on me. Here is an extract from an article that was published in a leading occult magazine in 1997.

WEMOON – Celebrating the Goddess Within' – I scanned the brochure, intrigued. Come Sisters, and join with us in the Community of Wimmin ... Sister Time is a sacred time, a time of heightened awareness, a time not to be wasted in the regular world, doing ordinary tasks, distracted by small talk or men. Well, this sounded right up my alley! I made the necessary enquiries and found we 'Sisters' would be gathering at a well-equipped bush camp on the far outskirts of Sydney.

... Within half an hour of arriving at Wemoon, I was walking down a bush track with forty other women chanting, 'I am a strong woman. I am a story woman, I am a healer, my soul will never die.' I balked at first, feeling self-conscious, and it took me a few goes to raise my voice above a whisper, but there was something very uplifting in these simple yet evocative words.

We arrived at a clearing covered in straw and ringed by tall gum trees. In one corner was a large gnarled stump which had been set up as an altar. We had been told to bring a statue or item which represented the Goddess to us and we were now instructed to place these around the altar as we filed in to form a large circle. We all held hands and Hawthorn – a High Priestess and initiator and co-ordinator of Wemoon – cast and consecrated the Circle, declaring it a sacred space, then she encouraged us to dance and run around the perimeter to raise power. Everyone joined in enthusiastically, until laughing and breathless we sat as one woman walked around playing guitar and singing a song, 'You are my Warrior Woman'. Now many of you are probably thinking 'Urghh – this all sounds like nauseating, "fluffy" New Age stuff!' I would've once too! But in the context of a women's only gathering, away from society's 'shoulds and shouldn'ts, appropriates and inappropriates', it all seemed very natural and spontaneous. When we were encouraged by the singer to turn to each other and say 'You are my Warrior Woman' with a hug and a kiss, quite a few of us shed tears and remained hugging for a while as a feeling of unconditional love swept around the circle.

Now we were to become 'Dancing White Women'. Four women left the circle as the rest of us were guided in song: 'Spirit of the trees has come to me in the form of a beautiful dancing white woman, and her eyes fill me with peace and the dance fills me with peace'. The tune was slow and meditative and the mood of our multi-cultural group was calm and reflective as the four returned, naked but for white paint, and carrying large bowls of water, a slab of white clay and a box containing long strips of white lace. These they placed at the centre as Hawthorn walked towards them removing her belt and dress. In easy camaraderie we all followed her lead, stripping quickly.

Tearing chunks off the slab of clay, we clustered together and after dunking our hands in the water we rubbed the slippery clay all over each other. Arms, breasts, belly ... I had six soft hands stroking my skin as I stood there with the sun on my upturned face.

The clay dried white, tight and smooth and surrounded by my ghostly companions I felt I'd stepped into another reality. Some had bound their breasts and hips with lace and others had tied it only in their hair. We looked strange and exotic and again we joined hands and danced a 'spiral dance', weaving in and out of each other's arms until, close together, a kiss was passed from one woman to the next. We all agreed it was then time for food and as the 'hunter/gatherers' went back to the hall for supplies a row of 'white women' sat outside the circle smoking cigarettes and talking softly. I was impressed with the ease at which we'd all embraced this situation. Forty women of differing backgrounds and yet we were a close tribe as we sat under the trees and ate fruit, cheese and bread together. We moved around freely and uninhibited, naked but for our paint, our lace, our sunglasses, hats, thongs, sandshoes, jewellery, tattoos and the flowers in our hair.

After clearing lunch there was a 'Virgin Consciousness Ritual'. Now this was not to re-establish some long forgotten idea of 'sexless purity'. Instead the cries that echoed off the surrounding cliffs were, 'Virgin, needing no other! Virgin, complete unto herself!' Hawthorn looked deep into our eyes and souls as she declared, 'Virgin, but not celibate!' That afternoon we were told the story of an evolving spiritual and biological woman – herstory – the greatest story never told, myth and reality blending until they were one and the same. We gathered around our altar and eagerly shared stories in the last part of the ritual. Childbirth, abortions, hysterectomies, menstruation – it was empowering discussing womanly cycles and experiences. I did not feel we were defining and confining our existence according to what our bodies could do. Instead, we were celebrating our biological importance, our strength and our resilience, adding these to the long list of unique capabilities and liberating achievements of women in modern society.

The next morning there was a rune workshop and an intensely moving Re-consecration Ritual before the Circle was closed. Arriving back at home I felt I was looking at things from a new perspective. In the following days I experienced a profound sense of peace and empowerment which months later had only slightly dissipated with the onslaught of everyday stresses. My experience at Wemoon encouraged me to no longer feel I need to compete with men or strive to be accepted on their terms. Instead I celebrate the fact that my attributes and achievements are unique, speaking for themselves.

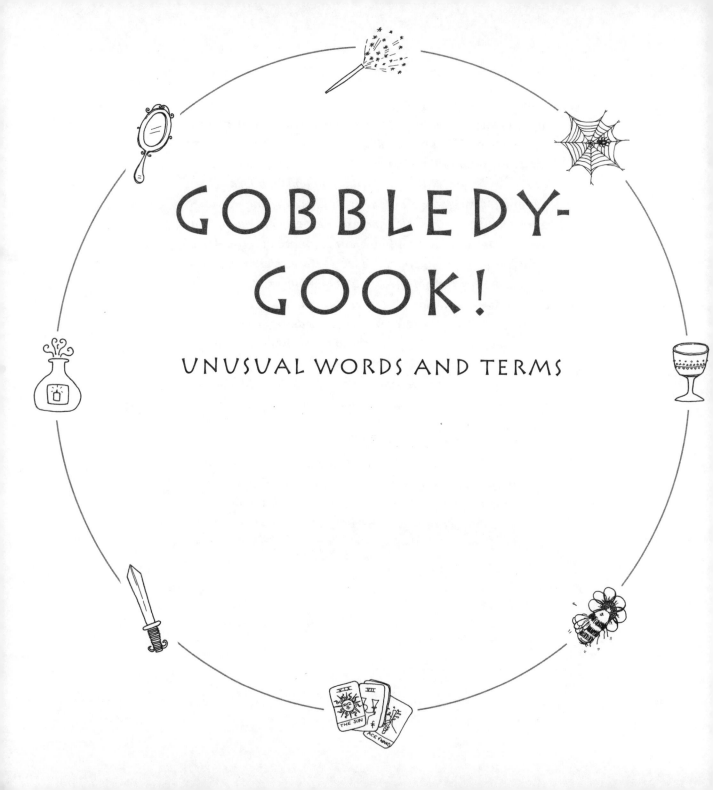

GOBBLEDY-GOOK!

UNUSUAL WORDS AND TERMS

Alexandrian Wicca: A popular tradition of Witchcraft developed in the 1960s by an Englishman, Alex Sanders.

Amulet: An object either natural or human-made which has powers believed to protect a person from general harm and trouble, and to bestow good fortune.

Athame: (Usually pronounced 'Ah-*thay*-mee' and '*Ath*-ah-may'.) The Witches' knife with traditionally a double-edged blade and black handle. Used for casting Circles and channelling energy. *Not* used for cutting up chickens and small children!

AURA: The 'unseen body' that surrounds the physical body and is made up of layers of energy.

Blessed Be: Traditional Witches' farewell and blessing.

Body Bits: Parts of the body to be used in spells – hair, nails, spit, skin, etc.

Boline: The white-handled knife used in ritual and magickal work for practical purposes like cutting herbs and engraving.

Book of Shadows: A Witch's personal book of spells, rituals, magickal lore and lessons learnt. It is traditional upon being initiated into a coven to copy by hand the coven's Book of Shadows before adding personal notes.

CHAKRA: An energy centre located in the physical and first energy layer of the aura. There are seven major chakras.

Charge: To imbue something with energy, usually by raising power and intentionally directing it into the object or perhaps, an event.

Charm: An object created to protect or bestow good fortune in various concerns. Also a spoken spell or incantation and often used instead of the words 'amulet' and 'talisman'.

Circle: A sacred sphere of energy created by a ritual called 'Casting Circle' and within which magickal work is done.

Cone of Power: Psychic power raised by an individual or coven that manifests as a cone-shaped energy field within Circle and which is used as a means of 'propulsion' to bring a spell to fruition.

Coven: A group of Witches which meets regularly to do spells and rituals. The traditional number of people is thirteen, but any number is fine – often smaller groups are better than larger ones as they are a bit easier to control!

Deosil: (Sometimes pronounced 'Jessil'.) 'Sunwise', or the direction in which the sun appears to move across the sky, which in the Northern Hemisphere is clockwise, and in the Southern Hemisphere, anti-clockwise. The direction in which a Witch will move when casting Circle or conjuring up energy.

Esbat: A coven meeting held at each Full Moon, or other appropriate times, for spellworking and socialising.

Gardnerian Wicca: An influential tradition of Witchcraft developed by Dr Gerald Gardner in the 1940s.

Grimoire: A book specifically of magickal techniques and spells.

Handfasting: A Witches' 'wedding' ceremony.

Libation: Wine or other beverage that is poured on the Earth as a ceremonial expression of gratitude to the Goddess and God.

Merry Meet/Merry Part/Merry Meet Again: Traditional witches' greeting and farewell.

Pagan: General term for a person who follows Wicca and other polytheistic religions based on Nature worship. All Wiccans are Pagans but not all Pagans are Wiccan.

Pathworking: Meditations and visualisations – sometimes guided, sometimes spontaneous – the object of which is to reach ever deeper levels of the psyche and even other realities and worlds.

Pentacle: A circular piece of brass (or other metal), wood or clay upon which the five pointed 'pentagram' is engraved. On a Witch's altar it represents the element of Earth.

Pentagram: A five-pointed figure of a star and the classic 'Witch symbol'. It is used magickally for blessings, as an invoking and banishing symbol when casting Circle, and it can be represented in jewellery and worn to bestow protection. Some Satanist and death metal music fanatics invert the star and say it is the 'sign of the Devil'. For Witches in some Wiccan traditions the inverted pentagram is a sign of second degree initiation.

Poppet: A doll made to represent a person or animal and used in spells and rituals.

Portal: A doorway or gateway to another realm.

Priestess/Priest: Name for an adept practitioner of Witchcraft – usually initiated into a coven. But everyone can be Priestess and Priest; the title should not be conferred because of hierarchy but because of magickal experience and knowledge.

QABALAH. The ancient Hebrew system of esoteric thought that organises itself around The Tree of Life. The Qabalah has had a huge influence on western occult practices. A good book to read on the Qabalah is Dion Fortune's *The Mystical Qabalah*.

Sabbats: The eight sacred festivals of the Wiccan tradition that relate to the turning of the seasons.

Scrying: The art of divination (opening the psychic centres of the self, e.g. the third eye – to gain insight into the past, present and future events and ideas), using for example, crystal balls, black water and magick mirrors.

Sigil: A seal or sign drawn or engraved on paper (or an object) and incorporated into some spells to confer magickal energy.

Skyclad: 'Clad only by the sky' – in other words, naked.

'So Mote it Be': Witches' enchantment spoken at the completion of a spell or blessing. Used in much the same way as the Christian, 'Amen'.

Talisman: An object that is 'charged' to have magickal powers and to perform a specific function as determined by the person creating it. Often it will be symbols and sigils carved in metal discs or drawn on parchment.

Warlock: No such thing except in Hollywood. A male Witch is just called a Witch.

Widdershins: 'Against the sun' or in the Northern Hemisphere, anti-clockwise and the Southern Hemisphere, clockwise. The direction in which a Witch will move when closing Circle or banishing energy.

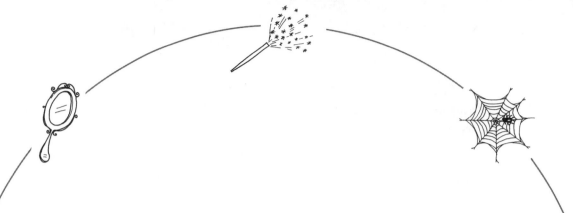

THE LIBRARY

FOR THE BOOKWITCH!

Following are listed some of the books in my personal Library of the occult.
I have a huge collection, but the ones I have included here are some of
my favourites and many had a big influence on me in my early
'Bookwitch' days. I have tried to list only those books that are
still in print, but I have included some particularly good
oldies that would be worth trying to track down in
public libraries and second-hand
bookstores.

Also, a lot of my books were bought many years ago, so the publication date might imply that the book is out of date. Not so. Every book I've listed here is helpful and relevant and in fact many of the titles have been recently reprinted.

Applied Magick and Aspects of Occultism, by Dion Fortune, Harper Collins, 1987. I bought this second-hand but I know it's still in print. Dion Fortune is one of the most important figures in 20th Century occultism. She not only writes extremely knowledgeably about the theory of magick and occult life, but her works of fiction are excellent too. This book covers topics like, 'The Three Kinds of Reality', 'A Magical Body' and 'The Psychology of Ritual', as well as lots to do with exploring psychic ability.

The Autobiography of a Witch, by Lois Bourne, Corgi Books, 1986. A fantastically down-to-earth story of a middle aged, no-nonsense, very psychic, English Witch. (The book is also known as *A Witch Among Us*.)

The Book of Lies, by Aleister Crowley, Samuel Weiser Inc., 1913, 1991. I enjoy this collection of paradoxical writings with notes by Crowley to help decipher his nonsense! Crowley is a provocative occult writer and this book leaves itself open to individual interpretation.

Book of Shadows, Phyllis Curott, Bantam Australia, 1999. This is a wonderful story of a woman's journey along the path of the Craft. She's a lawyer, a powerful Witch and my friend! An excellent and inspiring book.

The Book of Spells, by Nicola de Pulford, Random House, 1998. This is such a cute book – a black cover and bound with a silver ribbon. It even has a 'sealed section' of three 'emergency spells' (for example, to do with 'Thwarting a Rival Lover'). There are over forty spells – they're all really well concocted, and all in full colour! There's also a good basic overview of magickal practices. Highly recommended for anyone who's run out of spell ideas.

Buckland's Complete Book of Witchcraft, by Raymond Buckland, Llewellyn, 1990. An educational workbook on Wicca, that briefly covers each major topic a Witch needs to know about. Handy self-tests included.

The Complete Book of Incense, Oils and Brews, by Scott Cunningham, Llewellyn, 1990. An excellent and comprehensive magickal recipe book for incenses, tinctures, ointments, powders, soaps, charms …

Cunningham's Encyclopedia of Magical Herbs, by Scott Cunningham, Llewellyn, 1990. Indispensible guide to hundreds of different herbs' and plants' magickal uses.

Drawing Down the Moon, by Margot Adler, Beacon Press, 1979. One of the best and most comprehensive studies of Neo-Paganism. Highly recommended.

Eight Sabbats For Witches, by Janet and Stewart Farrar, Hale, 1981. One of the best guides to Gardnerian Witchcraft, focusing on the eight major Festivals of the Year.

Food of the Gods, by Terence McKenna, 1992. A brilliant investigative study into historical shamanic drug use in East and West societies. Like all of Terence's work this is a motivating and inspiring book.

Goddesses in Everywoman, by Jean Shinoda Bolen, M.D. Perennial, 1985. A thought-provoking study of a collection of archetypal Goddesses and their relation to modern day behavioural traits and patterns. Highly recommended.

The History of Witchcraft, by Montague Summers, Senate, 1994. Nasty piece of bigoted work written in 1925 that lets you know who the enemy is.

Hocus Pocus – Titania's Book of Spells, by Titania Hardie, Quadrille Publishing, 1996. I've a special, soft spot for this beautiful, purple velvet bound book – my Dad bought it for my birthday last year! It was thoughtful and insightful of him to buy it for me – for a non-Witch he made an excellent choice! This is a fantastic slab of spells covering varied needs: spells for attracting love, strengthening relationships, protecting family and loved ones, keeping family life happy and well-balanced, for familiars and pets, and for health and beauty, plus more! I emphasise in this book the importance of creating your own spells, but once you get the hang of that, books like this are blissfully fun!

The Holy Book of Women's Mysteries, by Zsuzsanna Budapest, Wingbow Press, 1989. Truly wonderful book on feminist Witchcraft covering just about everything you need to know. Brilliant and moving.

Kali – The Black Goddess of Dakshineswar, by Elizabeth Harding, Nicholas Hays Inc, 1993. The Hindu Goddess, Kali is a favourite archetype of mine. This book is written by a woman who travelled to India to worship Kali at her main temple in Dakshineswar. Fascinating.

The Learned Arts of Witches & Wizards, by Anton and Mina Adams, Landsdowne, 1998. A very well-researched and readable history of magical traditions through the ages, beautifully designed and illustrated. While dealing mainly with historical issues, the book also has useful sections on modern Wicca and some practical magickal exercises for beginners. A good book to give friends and family who are wondering what you're getting into!

Magick in Theory and Practice, by Aleister Crowley, Dover Publications, 1992. This was written when he was really on a high magickal track. Recommended.

Paganism Today, by Graham Harvey and Charlotte Hardman, Thorsons, 1996. Fairly recent collection of works on Paganism edited by two lecturers of religious studies at an English University. Excellent.

The Pearly Gates of Cyberspace, Margaret Wertheim, Doubleday, 1999. Wertheim introduces the idea of the Internet being the gateway for the soul. It's brilliant and thought-provoking, as she ties in the evolution of the Universe, us, religion and cyberspace.

Power of the Witch, by Laurie Cabot with Tom Cowan, New Age, 1989. Excellent work on how to practise Wicca with a fantastic chapter linking Witchcraft to quantum physics.

The Satanic Witch, by Anton Szander LaVey, Feral House, 1989. Written in 1970 this is quite a hilarious book on how to be a Satanic Witch. My favourite bit is when he suggests women 'let themselves dribble enough to get a small wet spot on the back of their skirts'. Apparently this will make us more able to seduce a man which, according to Loopy LaVey, is the sole aim of being a Witch. Bloody stupid.

Secrets of a Witch's Coven, by Morwyn, Whitford Press, 1988. Wonderful guide to Wicca. Highly recommended.

The Spiral Dance, by Starhawk, Harper San Francisco, 1979, 1989. Every Witch must own this book. Absolutely brilliant and beautifully written guide to Wicca.

What Witches Do, by Stewart Farrar, Sphere, 1973. Stewart is a direct follower of one of Alex Sander's original covens. Very informative on traditional Alexandrian Wicca, with cool black and white photos of Witchy rituals featuring Alex and Maxine Sanders. This classic is still in print today.

The Witch in History, by Diane Purkiss, Routledge, 1996. Extremely well researched and scholarly book on the figure of the Witch throughout history. Even though she ultimately construes the Witch is only a fantasy figure, it still makes for enlightening reading.

The Witches' Tarot, by Ellen Cannon Reed, Llewellyn, 1996. The Tarot deck and the cards are brilliantly researched and intuitively interpreted – plus Ellen is a great girl and now we're email buddies!

Witchcraft and Paganism Today, by Anthony Kemp, Brockhampton Press, 1995. A good overview of modern Wicca.

Witchcraft and Sorcery, edited by Max Marwick, Penguin, 1990. Various studies dated from the 2nd century AD to 1980 by brilliant thinkers on Witchcraft throughout the ages. The final section in the book is impressive in the way it relates Witchcraft to science.

Witchcraft, The Sixth Sense and Us, by Justine Glass, Neville Spearman Books, 1965. This hard to find, wonderful book was one of the first commercially released books on Witchcraft. Highly recommended for its classic photos of early 1960's Witches as well as its well written and informative contents.

Witchcraft Today, by Gerald Gardner, Magickal Childe Publishing, 1991. This book was first published in 1954 after the anti-Witchcraft laws were repealed in England. It contains Gerald's (founder of Gardnerian Wicca) findings and opinions on Witchcraft. Some of it is brilliant, other bits laughable – but it's an essential read. His other significant book is 'The Meaning of Witchcraft' originally published in 1959 and available from Magickal Childe.

The Witchcraft in Western Europe, by Dr Margaret A. Murray, London, Oxford University Press, 1921. This is considered a classic on the herstory of ancient Witchcraft, but some dispute its accuracy. However, it still makes for thought-provoking reading.

The Woman's Dictionary of Symbols and Sacred Objects, by Barbara Walker, Harper and Rowe, 1988.

A mostly well researched and impressively presented guide to symbols and objects from ancient history to now.

The Woman's Encyclopedia of Myths and Secrets, by Barbara Walker, Harper and Rowe, 1983. Good mythic historical reference book. It was awarded 'Book of the Year' in 1986 by the London *Times* Educational Supplement.

Before I leave the Library I'd like to recommend a few books, which, while not being specifically written about Witchcraft, will certainly appeal to Witches:

The Clan of the Cave Bear, Hodder and Stoughton, 1980.

The Valley of the Horses, Hodder and Stoughton, 1982.

The Mammoth Hunters, Hodder and Stoughton, 1985.

The Plains of Passage, Hodder and Stoughton, 1990.

Written by Jean M. Auel, the above series focuses on the life of a Stone Age girl, Ayla, who bridges the evolution of the 'Clan' (Neanderthals) and the 'Others' (Homosapiens). The books are amazingly researched (however history is interpreted with artistic license) and packed with knowledge about the healing powers of herbs, how to live on the land and Stone Age concepts of spirituality. They are comprehensive and creative lessons in anthropology, sociology and even feminism. They brilliantly capture the mood and images of a time when humans lived harmoniously with the land, the seasons and the animals.

WEAVING THE WEB

COOL INTERNET SITES FOR WITCHES

Witches and computers make magick together! The plethora of Pagan sites on the Web is testament to this. Here I've listed a brief selection of my favourites – and don't be afraid to get onto the Search Engines and see where they take you!

THE OFFICIAL FIONA HORNE WEBSITE

www.fionahorne.com

Ha! Had to put this one first! Of course it's great – Tracey Shaw and Lauren O'Keefe have done a brilliant job creating and maintaining this one. We conceptualised it together and I regularly give them info for updates, so everything you see on it is endorsed by me (except possibly a few of the guestbook comments!). There are heaps of articles and photos, including my infamous *Playboy* shoot, which, incidentally, was conceptualised and produced by me with an all-woman team. I also wrote the article to accompany the photos. Enjoy!

WITCHVOX

www.witchvox.net/links/webusa-w.html

This site holds a huge collection of Wicca, Witch and Pagan links and sites for you to browse and select to your personal taste. Network and craft with fellow Pagan groups and online forums. Find out about worldwide festival events and order supplies direct from specialized merchants.

SHADOWPLAY

www.shadowplayzine.com

For those who missed the internationally circulated *Shadowplay Magazine* in its first incarnation, the editors, Liam Cyfrin (who is a special guest contributor in this book), Rhea and Raven, have started up a recycling plant on the Web. Here's where you can find highlights of the mag's ten-year career and new material. The site is in its early days at the time of writing but it'll be one to watch.

PHYLLIS CUROTT'S OFFICIAL SITE

www.bookofshadows.net

Phyllis is the author of the bestselling *Book of Shadows* (Bantam Australia 1999 and she has a wonderful site full of Witchy wisdom and updates on her legal work to do with Craft issues. She is not only a successful lawyer but also one of the most influential Witches in the world today. Highly recommended!

THE WITCHES LEAGUE FOR PUBLIC AWARENESS

www.CelticCrow.com

Fantastic site maintained by the lovely Dylan Massan who responds to all emails and queries and runs a very magickal and informative site. Another one highly recommended!

WENDY RULE'S WEBPAGE

www.wendyrule.com

Wendy is a friend of mine who is one of the most inspiring Witches and performers I know. Through her website you can experience her amazing music and insights into the Craft.

AVATAR SEARCH – THE SEARCH ENGINE OF THE OCCULT

www.avatarsearch.com

This is an award-winning search engine and will really help you explore the most hidden occult corners on the Net. It has a monthly 'Top 20 Cool Links' feature that can point you in new directions you may not have considered.

The Yahoo Search Engine also makes navigating the Witchy side of the Net easy and stress-free. Go to Yahoo – www.yahoo.com – and click on *Society and Culture*, then click on *Religion*, then *Organisations,* then *Wicca* and/or *Pagan.* You will have onscreen a really good, concise selection.

✦ *Note: On many sites there are links to chatlines where you can join others to discuss Witchy things. These can be a great help to the development of your Craft if you are somewhat isolated from other Witches and Pagans in the physical realm.* ✦

If you don't have a personal computer with access to the Net, take advantage of the Internet Cafes that are springing up everywhere. For a small outlay you can cast a Witchy Net and for a few dollars more print out the results to take home. The Internet really is an incredible tool that you can use to enhance your magickal knowledge and powers.

Happy Web weaving!

CRAFTY
CONTACTS

WHERE TO GET WITCHY SUPPLIES

UK

Caduceus Jewellery, 624 Lea Bridge Road, London E10 6AP, England; tel: 020 8539 3569. Bewitching designs in hand-crafted silver, with gold made to order. Celtic designs, Torcs, Gem rings, pendants and bangles, Viking and Runic designs, Egyptian designs, Pagan Goddess and god designs. Headdresses, pentagrams, crystals, hand-blended incense, herbs. Handmade athames, boliines and swords. Made by witches for witches, and all magical traditions.

Cloakes and Robes made to order. Various styles and fabrics. Top quality – reasonable prices. 194 Stapleton Hall Road, London N4 4QL, England, or call Susan on 020 8341 1614.

Green Witch is the label for all my herbs, tinctures, handmade remedies, cosmetics and magickal candles and incences. 59–61 High Street, Aberdour, Fife FY3 0SJ, Scotland; tel/fax: 01383 860106; Website: www.greenwitch.co.uk

Thor's Hammer Wood Crafts, Glasgow. Occult emporium with luck charms, wands, wall plaques and magickal carvings. P.L. Morrison, Thor's Hammer Wood Crafts, 140 Glenalmond Street, Sandyhills, Glasgow G32 7TQ, Scotland.

Cauldron available from Mike Howard, Caemorgan Cottage, Caemorgan Road, Cardigan, Dyfed SA43 1QU, Wales is an informative journal of the Old Religion and one of the oldest Craft magazines. *Cauldron* is especially useful for those interested in solo or coven Traditional Witchcraft.

Marian Green, BCM-SCL QUEST, London WC1N 3XX, England is a magician in the Western Ways who runs courses in Natural Magick and produces *Quest* magazine. *Quest* has an annual conference.

Pagan Federation, BM Box 7097, London WC1N 3XX, England is the main Pagan body in Europe. There is a magazine *Pagan Dawn,* which lists groups, courses, conferences, contact networks, social meetings, etc, in Britain and other parts of Europe, covering all Pagan paths including Wicca. Also PF Scotland, PO Box, Edinburgh EH17 7PW, Scotland. The PF's web site – http://www.paganfed.demon.co.uk – gives information and lists events.

Invisible College, PO Box 42, Bath BA1 1ZN, England teaches all aspects of Western Mystery Tradition (of which the Craft is a part) including ritual arts, the Grail Mysteries, folk healing and much more. Teaching is provided through short courses.

Teenage Pagan, Minor Arcana, PO Box 615, Norwich, Norfolk NR1 4QQ, England. www.members.tripod.com/~Minor

NORTH AMERICA

Branwen's Cauldron of Light, 603 Seagaze Dr. #141, Oceanside, CA 92054, USA. Herbal products of oils, incenses, herb blends and magickal powders. Scrying balls, statues, beads and magickal seals personalized to each customer's needs.

Alpha Book Center, 1928 E. McDowell, Phoenix, AZ 85006, USA; tel: 602 237 3213. Books, crystals, cloaks, robes, oils, music, incense, candles to purchase.

The Arcanaeum: The Ultimate Source of the Arcane 5813 Lee Highway, Suite 11, Chattanooga, TN 37421, USA; tel: 423 893 8111. A comfortable, scholarly store where discussions, classes and lively debate abound.

Spice Island Speciality Shop, 5100 N Broadway, Knoxville, Tennessee, USA; tel: 865 689 9799. Middle Eastern clothing, amber jewellery, rare herbs, bath salts and incense.

Merlin's Attic, 2487 Old Philadelphia Pike, Lancaster, PA 17602, USA; tel: 717 295 5754. Items from local artists, which feature spell kits, gargoyles, faires, candles and pentacles.

Circle, PO Box 219, Mount Horeb, WI 53572, USA is a shamanic Wiccan Church. It organizes Pagan events, fosters contacts and networking, and publishes *Circle Network News*.

Covenant of the Goddess, PO Box 1226, Berkeley, CA 94704, USA is a federation of Wiccan covens that publishes a newsletter and holds an annual gathering.

Hidden Path, Windwalker, Box 934, Kenosha, WI 53141, USA. Offers advice on contacting Gardnerian Wicca.

Hecate's Loom, Box 5206, Station B, Victoria, BC, V8R 6N4, Canada, is one of the largest and oldest Pagan publications in Canada.

Wiccan Church of Canada, 109 Vaughan Road, Toronto, M6C 2L9, Canada is a network of Wiccan groups in the Odyssian tradition.